Honest, Open, Willing...

My Journey From Despair To Hope

Third Edition

By Steven R. Adelman

Front Cover Illustration

My wife and I were in the living room one night (April 29, 2012) with our 7 year old daughter, Jessie, who loves to draw, paint, and be creative. I jokingly asked her to draw me a picture of darkness and fear leading up to light and happiness. She drew the front cover illustration in about 10 minutes and then excitedly explained the many symbolic meanings.

Jessie pretty much said how the 'bottom' part was 'dark' blue with scary lightning, dark stormy clouds, and cold temperature looking up at the blue clear sky looking at the world with bright sunshine and warmer 84 degree temperature. At least to me, this was much more than just a beautiful picture she drew. All I could do for a few minutes is swell up with love, joy, and pride as I stared at my daughter's interpretation of......HOPE!

Third Edition – December 2012

Dedications

My Mom and Dad never gave me away or threw me off a bridge as a kid. I can never express how much their understanding, patience, tolerance, support, and love have always meant and will forever mean to me.

The members of my 'H.O.W. (Honest Open Willing) Posts' group on Facebook have been there supporting my entire life journey each day. Many friends and family have lived through some, most, or my entire life journey. Every one of my fellow anonymous group members need to be strongly thanked but I can't since they need to remain anonymous.

And to my wife, son, and daughter who give me the strength and continued determination each day to continue growing from a kid to an adult. Thank you and I love you!

Every single one of these people has been a huge part of who I am today and always will be! My friends, my family, and my Higher Power (whom I call God), are all very important to me. Each day I try to realize how blessed and grateful it is to have them in my life.

Preface

This book was originally going to be called 'H.O.W. Honest Open Willing Posts' which was a non-fiction but anonymous story about someone who posts on a social network in a closed group with about 260 understanding friends, family, school mates, and anonymous fellowship members. They start to relate in one way or another as each day he eventually tells of every brutal thing he did and was done to him going from birth all the way through his early 40s.

This includes feeling awkward, not fitting in, low self-esteem, bullying, mental illness, arson, theft, vandalism, special education, depression, marijuana addiction, alcoholism, drug abuse, sexual promiscuities, suicide, encounters with the law, accidents, illnesses, 9/11, and more. All of it leads down an even more vicious, destructive cycle while experiencing despair, loss of meaning, fear, and insanity. There is only one of two ways this could ultimately end but it does end with recovery, the 12 steps, and a brighter future with hope after 4 plus years.

No one would know exactly who it is but that it is 100% true. The only problem is that hundreds of people would have known right away and everyone else rather soon, that it was me.

First a brief background summary and explanation:

A lot of the initial notes for this book were already in my 4th Step 'fearless and searching moral inventory' and soon told to my Alcoholics Anonymous sponsor as my 5th Step. These notes only had a few words or a sentence about each thing in my life so I could then speak more from the heart. There were several pages of just these notes which were made on my computer in Microsoft Word so they could be edited many times before they were printed out onto paper when finished. After reading them all to my sponsor, he asked that I rip up those many pages into little pieces and throw them away because now all that is behind me and it was time to move on.

There was a huge sense of relief to have told him everything. I cannot express how it felt to hear him tell me that many of these things were done by others, many of these things were not wrong at all, and that the rest of these things are understandable for one reason or another. The worst reason was still a simple and acceptable one......I was extremely sick and twisted. Reality between the world and me was not the same. Several things were not my fault, should not have affected me as they did, or were not even about me at all. Now I had a lot more reality back and could work from there.

It was not easy having a 'clean slate' and needed to work on my 'defects of character' and 'shortcomings' in order to then make my 'direct amends to such people' (that I harmed). My program was maintained with constant 'personal inventory', 'promptly admitted it' when I was wrong to those affected, and continued to use 'prayer and meditation to improve' my spirituality for power and guidance. Then came the Twelfth Step 'carrying this message' to other alcoholics and 'practice these principles in all my affairs.' These are things taught to me, in the readings, and learned from meetings and these teachings and literature. There was another road block after about four years of recovery and working all these Twelve Steps each day......me.

My embarrassment decreased as my humility increased. Sharing at meetings, speaking commitments, chairing meetings, carrying the message to others in detox, MICA (Mentally Ill, Chemically Addicted) units, and other places let me know that the past is not something to close the door on. The same relief which was felt after I did my 4th and 5th Step was felt more and more as my honesty, openness, and willingness increased.

There is usually a group discussion after the speaker talks about their 'experience, strength, and hope' at a meeting. Others shared about their identification and personal experience whenever I was asked to tell my brief story for that meeting. Many came up to me afterward a little quieter saying how they were glad to know that they were not 'weird', 'different', 'unique', 'evil', 'broken', 'defective', or alone.

That was a huge reason that I thought this road block (or brick wall) would be gotten past by doing a massive 4th/5th Step with all my Facebook friends. This would be at least everything shared to my sponsor back in 2009. Those printed out pages were ripped up and destroyed because I considered that the end of my official 5th Step. This was never deleted or wiped off my computer because they could not be deleted of wiped out of my head. The guilt, blame, regret, resentments, and other things from that original file was forgiven or ceased to affect me nearly as much anymore! Many things were added as they were remembered, investigated, or told to me. That first file of my 4th Step was constantly updated until I felt ready to begin on January 1, 2012.

The H.O.W. (Honest Open Willing) Posts were first started on New Year's Day 2012. Originally they were posted each day to all of my Facebook friends. There was no filter who among my Facebook friends and family could read them. The inaugural first post was very short. This went on each day until #6 Honest Open Willing 2012 Post on January 6, 2012 discussed an accidental fire that I started in my house. That one event seemed to have triggered a lot of different things that set off a chain reaction in my life. Then there was some input provided to me from some of my Facebook family and friends who did not understand or accept what I was doing.

A new group was created on Facebook called 'H.O.W. (Honest Open Willing) Posts'. Now only members of this closed group were able to see these continued daily postings until it caught up with my current life. They were encouraged to add other interested people to the group and even share their own H.O.W. Posts. It was simply requested that people staying in the group keep everything discussed private and not told publicly.

Many people asked the reason for my daily 'Honest Open Willing Posts'. The past is something not to regret nor forget. These posts get out my previous shame so I can move on without any dark secrets or even dimly lit ones. If anyone can relate and know they are not alone or even learn what to possibly expect with their kids then thank God my past had some helpful purpose to others."

Here I continued with #7 Honest Open Willing 2012 Post on January 7, 2012. Each post was never written more than a day or two in advance. There were days that it was written that same day and a few times where I was on such a momentum that a few pages were written and had to be divided up. These posts started to get longer and longer as I was able to remember them in more details. Soon they were all much more than a few sentences or paragraphs.

From January 1, 2012 until April 20, 2012 there was one Honest Open Willing 2012 Post every single day for a total of 111 (because it was a leap year). All of them strung together show my entire life explaining in great detail where I was, how I recovered, and every single thing that happened in between. Writing this book is my way of expressing gratitude and carrying the message to others who feel alone and without hope.

Prologue

The following were two additional posts that I made in the beginning specifically for the members of the 'H.O.W. (Honest Open Willing) Posts' closed group on Facebook. All of the people added from my 'friends list' where specifically chosen because each one had a quality, trait, or identification which I thought would allow them to relate and also possibly share with me and the others.

"My daily posts are basically a linear timeline telling of the bad things that 'I felt happened to me' and that I did in the past while my reality was warped. I do not regret these things because they made me who I am today. These are not shared to just tell everyone about my life because I am either egocentric or eccentric. These I share to openly get the wreckage of my past out of my head and to hopefully have even one person relate. Then they might get out of their own head and feel less pain. This happens to me whenever other people talk about their similar experiences."

"One can usually see the beauty and reality in others that they sometimes cannot see themselves. My words are easy to say and mean, but are hard to personally always accept myself. The best things I see with this group are when other people share and express themselves here. That is one of the hardest things to do and I really am proud and admire those that have things that need to be out there. This is probably the best place to do that because (as hoped and expressed repeatedly) what is said in this room, stays in this room.

When you post to other supportive, understanding people then you are sharing those insecurities, self-thought defects, mistakes, and worries about the future without feeling alone and scared. Besides these feelings and experiences please feel free to also post any of your strengths and hopes! That gives me and others hope that there is good with the bad and that there is not always just bad."

Table of Contents

Disclaimer

Most of the following 'Honest Open Willing 2012 Posts were written each day. The content and feelings were more important to express than the grammatical and professional aspects. I have elected to keep these daily posts in their initial form to try and preserve the genuineness of the original process as best as possible. Minor edits were made with the help of a few friends to ensure clarity of my sentiments.

Here is how it began......

It is time to start my 2012 New Year's resolution of being more brutally honest, totally open, and entirely willing in my Facebook posts each day. That's H.O.W. I will roll this year.
January 1

#1 (Day 1) Honest Open Willing 2012 Post

In 1968, my brother was happy that his mommy's fourth child was going to be a boy so that he would have a brother to play racing cars with. Then when I was born he looked at me and said "I wanted a brother not a baby!" Forty-three years later I must say that I would be more than excited to play racing cars whenever he wants!
January 1

#2 (Day 2) Honest Open Willing 2012 Post

My mommy got sick when I was about 1-1/2 years old and was in the hospital for a little while. Supposedly I was very upset that she had 'abandoned' me. When she did come home, I was always checking to make sure she was there but kept a distance. Eventually, I did approach her again......to change my diaper.
January 2

#3 (Day 3) Honest Open Willing 2012 Post

Somewhere around the age of three, my dad would go to work and my siblings to school Monday to Friday. This left just me and my mom. The amount of clinging to her was quite a bit excessive and overwhelming. Just to get a short break she sent me to a playgroup one day a week until 3 pm. They told me mom to start picking me up at 1 pm instead because I was such a terror.
January 3

#4 (Day 4) Honest Open Willing 2012 Post

I got into trouble in nursery school while I was playing with a spinning top toy. Another kid was trying to take it away so I whacked 'em on the head with it. Never again was I allowed to play with spinning top toys......even to this day.
January 4

#5 (Day 5) Honest Open Willing 2012 Post

At a Lollipop School Pre-Kindergarten holiday party we had a piñata that

when burst open had lots of candies scatter everywhere. A few months later I found one behind a bookcase and was told not to eat it cause it was old and dirty......yep......I ate it a few minutes later......
January 5

#6 (Day 6) Honest Open Willing 2012 Post
(Here is the first of many biggies but as a disclaimer......I was only FIVE years old!) In 1973, I started a fire in my parents' bedroom with a pack of matches while they and my siblings were downstairs watching TV and NOT in the room! I really thought that lighting all of the bed comforter strings would be like the fuses on the Fourth of July fireworks and make the bed go up to the moon. It did not. Everyone in town knew I did it even though it was not with ill intent and this tarnished my not yet established reputation.
January 6

(These daily posts were then only published in the H.O.W. Group that only those members were able to see after input from some other Facebook family and friends.)

#7 (Day 7) Honest Open Willing 2012 Post
After the 'accidental' house fire I started at age 5, the whole family had to live at a hotel in Paramus for a few weeks while the house was being restored from smoke, fire, and a lot of water damage. My dad was furious at the cost and inconvenience. My mom was freaked out about what was wrong with me and why I would want to do this. While my sisters and brother were unbelievably pissed off because almost all of their possessions such as posters, clothing, and 8-Tracks were destroyed.
January 7

#8 (Day 8) Honest Open Willing 2012 Post
Still in 1973 (still at age 5), my family did move back into our Hillsdale NJ house after much restoration, painting, and new carpeting. About one week later I was in my bedroom and threw paint to my siblings who were watching TV in my parents' bedroom. The paint spilled out onto the new carpet. My sister called for my dad from downstairs and when he came upstairs and saw this he got very angry. He opened my 2nd story bedroom window and held me halfway out threatening to drop me to

make his life better without aggravation. My mom was hysterically screaming for him to pull me back inside and he did. That started my warped perception of being deathly afraid of him whenever I did anything bad. It lasted a very long time but we spoke openly of this just several years ago and the closure allowed us to be closer than I ever thought possible.
January 8

#9 (Day 9) Honest Open Willing 2012 Post
Besides the fire in my parents' bedroom and then the paint on their rug, the events of the next 12 months from August 1973 to September 1974 were quite interesting.

My first puppy, a Siberian Husky named Natasha, was so smart that she knew how to climb up and unlatch the backyard fence but not smart enough to know that running onto Kinderkamack Road would get her killed. My dad was in the hospital for several weeks having his Gall Bladder removed and then came home to recover for about a month. I began therapy with a 'special' doctor who diagnosed me as Hyperactive and prescribed Ritalin for 5 years until that stopped being effective.

The school board let me skip Kindergarten and start 1st Grade at George.G. White School in Hillsdale a year early because I was thought to be intellectually smart enough and maybe bored in Pre-K. Emotionally I was NOT ready! All the kids in the school knew me as the Pyro kid who lit his parents' bed on fire a year earlier because he thought it would go to the moon. They also knew I was Jewish and asked where my horns were and why did I kill Jesus. Boy did I feel alone starting back then.
January 9

#10 (Day 10) Honest Open Willing 2012 Post
Besides at school, I felt out of place and uncomfortable everywhere else. This even included the Cub Scouts and my immediate Mr. Roger's type neighborhood of Hillsdale NJ between the ages of 6 and 9 from 1974 to 1977.

You would think that an organization like the Cub Scouts would teach the boys to be fair, accepting, and courteous to everyone besides parents and old ladies crossing the street. It seemed to me that they were sneakier and stealthier like Ninjas with even more teasing and violence in these smaller groups than at school.

While at my neighbor's house across the street, I tried to push their cat out the 2nd floor window to see if cats do land on their feet when they fall. I was caught and asked not to return even though it was not to be mean......just scientific.

Two neighborhood sisters wanted to see me unclothed in the woods next to their house. I did this because I thought they would like me better. My oldest sister was yelling and looking for me because dinner was ready. Here I come running half-dressed out of woods having to then explain this to my parents.
January 10

#11 (Day 11) Honest Open Willing 2012 Post
November 1977 (9 years old) - Hebrew School made us go to Friday Night Services at Temple Beth Shalom each week. The Rabbi would ask all the young kids getting Bar & Bat Mitzvah'd in the next few years to come up to the stage for the blessing of the wine and take a small sip afterward. I was always the first one to run up eagerly waiting for the 'Amen' to take a big gulp before anyone else. After the service was over, there was a Challah, baked desserts, and mini wine cups again filled with Manischewitz. Downing 3 to 8 (or more) shots was easy and I loved the feeling out of self.
January 11

#12 (Day 12) Honest Open Willing 2012 Post
Another all-around fun year continued in 1978 still before turning even 10 years old ...... In spring, I started to take Karate lessons but was causing disruptions, got beat up in the dressing room, and stopped as a white belt ...... Early that summer, I went to Town & Country Day Camp and one day the rest of the kids went into my lunch while I was changing from swim time. They each ate parts of my lunch and the one kid that I punched & gave a black eye was the one that took my Cracker Jacks which I always looked forward to the prize! ...... Late summer, started to do extra mischief by using an extra key given in trust to my parents to enter and slightly vandalize our next door neighbor's house. My parents did not know what to do with my many wonderful different aspects.
January 12

#13 (Day 13) Honest Open Willing 2012 Post
As a kid in school, I was teased, made fun of, bullied, and beat up in

hallways, stairwells, bathrooms, etc. There were also a lot of times my antics were considered impulsive, wrong to do, and distracted the other kids in class. By September of 1978, the Hillsdale NJ school board decided what was best for me …… to start the 5th grade at another Hillsdale school but in Special Ed.
January 13

#14 (Day 14) Honest Open Willing 2012 Post
Starting Special Ed in the 5th grade did have a marvelous privilege. My chauffeured, private transportation between home and school was in a 'Special' green mini-bus. The 'Normal' kids at school affectionately called it a 'Tart Cart'. One morning I entered the 'Special' green mini-bus with a slight rip in the back of my pants. As I walked down the aisle, two other 'Special' kids each took a hold of the rip and tore it entirely open. My mom had to come to school to give me new pants.
January 14

#15 (Day 15) Honest Open Willing 2012 Post
Still at age 10, I was like most kids being sneaky and curious. There were lots of things hidden throughout the house which belonged to my parents that I should not have found. My father's downstairs office had a wooden chest in a secret spot which had a combination lock. This was the combination lock that I used a year earlier for camp. He never changed the combination! Inside the wooden chest were several pornographic movies, adult magazines and books. Of course I read and looked at the periodicals and watched the movies which included Debbie Does Dallas, Deep Throat, Devil In Miss Jones and other …… classics. There was another set of items in that wooden chest …… a handgun and bullets. I handled the gun and looked at the bullets but never loaded the gun or fired it. I am now very nervous that my kids will snoop around and find my naughty things (a few dozen Playboy magazines kept throughout the years for the articles) but I do not own any guns or weapons.
January 15

#16 (Day 16) Honest Open Willing 2012 Post
The Hillsdale Child Study Team had switched me from George G. White School to Meadowbrook Middle School (another school in Hillsdale) for 5th and 6th grade to escape the problems from my old school and to also attend Special Ed. This school only went up to 6th grade. With the rest

of my class, we all went back to George G. White for 7th and 8th grade in September 1980. A direct comment made by either the Child Study Team or my mom was the "ROOF FELL IN!" All the kids at George G. White remembered me and became friends quickly with the kids from Meadowbrook. They all shared stories and together made my life there horrible and unbearable. It was the worst year of school so far regarding insults, bullying, threats, punching, shoving, tripping, and more fun things. This is when I first started to think about killing myself.
January 16

#17 (Day 17) Honest Open Willing 2012 Post

January 1981 - Feeling greatly depressed in 7th grade, I started acting out, doing bad things to possibly compensate. One time I got suspended from school for just fooling around in Science class. We were all dissecting frogs (which were already dead). I took one in my hand and was flying it around the room yelling "SUPERFROG!" That was not good because of the embalming fluid or something getting everywhere. I thought it was funny and that people would like me.
January 17

#18 (Day 18) Honest Open Willing 2012 Post

Trying to get back at one girl who made fun of me in 7th grade, I wrote a made up 'sexual letter'. This was supposed to be a letter that she wrote to another girl about what she and a boy 'did' over the weekend. I had left this fake letter in the hallway outside her class for someone to find. It was hoped people would think she wrote it, dropped it by accident, and then she would be the one made fun of. However, another teacher had seen me put the letter there and now everyone in the school knew it was me that did this. Some of the boys kinda thought it was funny. This was NOT funny and thought to be VERY disturbing to the school board and my parents.
January 18

#19 (Day 19) Honest Open Willing 2012 Post

At age 12 while back at George G. White School in Hillsdale for the 7th grade, things were getting worse and worse. Constant fear, panic, dread, and depression were increasing each day from the time I left my house in the morning until I ran home after the 3 pm bell and made it home safe. In between at school, I felt like I was the weirdest kid that

deserved to be teased and did not know how to act or respond to the bullies. They chased me, hit me, and if they found me when in the boys' room......forget it. Yet I would act out and yell afterward and run away only to be chased and possibly hurt again. My social skills, disruptions in the classrooms, and emotion outbursts convinced my parents and the child study team to keep me in Special Ed for 8th grade but in a different school a few towns over in Paramus. No one would know me there and after 8th grade Special Ed and much integration with the normal kids in East Brook Middle School, I would attend Paramus High School the following year. This seemed like a great idea. A new start and all would be great and normal......
January 19

#20 (Day 20) Honest Open Willing 2012 Post

Before I started my 'new life' (again) in a new school where no one knew me and I would......fit in (this time) was the summer of 1981. I had gone to a 'special' sleep away camp in Thompson PA two years earlier and now again after unsuccessfully attending a normal day camp the year in between. The name of the camp was Rock Creek Farm which is no longer there. It was filled with Special Ed teachers, behavior specialists, and counselors from all over the world especially the UK and Germany. They were there to 'help' the campers with their many different problems, peer relations, and social skills. Some campers had various degrees of Autism, some had Down Syndrome, some had learning or social disabilities, and some had more severe behavioral problems. I have very vivid, haunting memories of this interesting mix of 6 to 18 year old boys and girls and the way we were all treated.
January 20

#21 (Day 21) Honest Open Willing 2012 Post

The methods of teaching were rather unorthodox at least to today's standards. We all had different bunks and they did keep the boys and girls separated as best as possible by age and handicap. They were all treated the same that if we did not listen or misbehaved would not get desert, be embarrassed in ways like needing to stand up in the corner in front of anyone, sometimes spanked, and even violently pulled or hurt. One night I was in the top bunk and was talking. The owner came in and pulled me down to the floor telling me to sleep there until he said otherwise.

I was and still am OCD. My trunk locker was very neatly, anally retentively organized. One day when we returned to the bunk, the trunk locker was there upside down with everything out in a mess. I freaked out crying and put everything back. That trick by the staff did not at all work. Many other stories and things stayed in my mind but the experience there each summer made me as good as someone scared and fearful of having to go back could be......until that wore off.
January 21

#22 (Day 22) Honest Open Willing 2012 Post
On Saturday, November 28, 1981 was my Jewish Bar Mitzvah (not that there were too many non-Jewish ones). I learned my Haftorah (Torah reading) and Saturday morning Hebrew prayers to recite and say in front of everyone while at Rock Creek Farm that summer before. Each day after lunch, I had to go alone to the music shack with my prayer book and listen to my Rabbi's voice on a tape. Then I went to East Brook Middle School in Paramus in September and had few friends there and anywhere else. It was an effort to get kids to come to my Bar Mitzvah. Luckily, my parents were friends with other parents that brought their kids. I also was able to drag a handful of other acquaintances and a few school mates that wanted to go to a party. Also, I had some cousins around my age that were brought there by their parents.

We all had fun and it ended up to be a good time. My dad made a speech saying that I was like a caterpillar entering a cocoon. Now as a Jewish man, I would come out this beautiful, wonderful butterfly. I thought this would be true now in my life (again). I stopped going to Temple (and partaking of the Manischewitz Kiddush Cup) because I was no longer forced to go. Still had Hebrew school for a year and then rarely went to Temple.
January 22

#23 (Day 23) Honest Open Willing 2012 Post
No longer was I forced to go to Temple on Friday nights after my November 1981 Bar Mitzvah. The only high point of going was the Manichevitz wine that the Rabbi allowed the kids between 9 and 13 years of age (practicing for their Bar/Bat Mitzvah) to partake after the blessing over the wine. There were also little shots of Manichevitz after the service to keep me with that warm feeling a little longer.

Now without Manichevitz, I started to help myself to my dad's liquor cabinet. He drank Harvey's Bristol Cream so I tried it too. I tried different liquors to see if I like the taste and to experiment and see what each type would make me feel. Suddenly, there were many times I got a stomach ache or stomach flu and my mom and dad had no idea it was alcohol ache and alcohol flu.
January 23

#24 (Day 24) Honest Open Willing 2012 Post

During the remainder of the 8th grade school year at East Brook Middle School, I was still getting teased and beaten up just like at the schools in my own town. A lot of this was because I was extremely immature and did not know how to handle myself in social situations. To vent out my continued feeling of 'being weird', I started to do more 'exciting' acts at home which included vandalism, stealing, and being a 'Peeping Tom'.

The first thing I remembered doing 'bad' after my Bar Mitzvah was pushing a shopping cart from the Hillsdale Shop Rite into the street. Why I decided to do this is something I cannot even fathom now. This could have done a lot of damage to cars and innocent people's lives! A police car saw me just as this was done and I saw that they saw me. Immediately, I threw down my bike, ran and hid under a car like a criminal. They found me under the car and brought me home to my mom & dad who punished me severely.
January 24

#25 (Day 25) Honest Open Willing 2012 Post

Another wonderful habit acquired through low self-esteem and trying to get that natural high was shoplifting. The stuff was never really anything I needed to have or did not have the money to purchase. I never understood why I did this when the gain was little and the chance of being caught and getting into trouble was so high. One time I went into a convenience store and shoved a Mad Magazine up my shirt yet took a Cracked Magazine to the counter and paid for that. When I was leaving the store, the Mad Magazine slipped down onto the floor. The clerk saw it and I quickly picked it up and said 'Oh Yea, I wanted to get this too' but it was too late and my mom was called to get me.

One other time was when I ripped open packs of Eveready Batteries to take out game pieces for a sweep stake contest they were having. All

the batteries were left in each package but I still got caught and my dad had to come to Shop Rite to get me and had to purchase the packs of batteries. Luckily, none of these times were the police called in. Maybe they should have been. Then I may not have continued until I was 18 years old and grabbed a 10 cent mini Reese's Peanut Butter Cup after already paying $14 for merchandise at a 7-11. An undercover police office grabbed my arm when leaving and asked what I had in my pocket. When I lied and was arrogant, he put me in a jail cell at the police station for a few hours. Then I needed to go to the town court a month later to plead guilty and pay a huge fine.
January 25

#26 (Day 26) Honest Open Willing 2012 Post
Upon finding my father's adult collection of films, videos, books, and magazines earlier brought about another excitement into my 13 year old life...... My sister was going to have a friend sleep over and her friends were now in their late teens and developed. When I knew this in advance, something clicked inside my head. I put a few holes in the wall between our bedrooms and in the bathroom door to sneak peeks at her friend and hopefully other friends later on. The holes in the bathroom door were not adequate enough to see her friend going into the shower that night. I was determined to be a 'Peeping Steve' and went out the back door, quickly climbed onto the porch roof, and spied into the bathroom window to catch her getting out of the shower. She saw me through the streamed window and screamed. I then even quicker climbed off the porch and raced back inside the house passing my dad who put 2 and 2 together knowing it was me. Of course I was not going to tell me dad that I liked looking at naked women as much as him.

A few months later, I put on a wig and padded my chest. Then I walked into the Westwood Racquetball Club women's locker room past several occupants. A few minutes later I was chased out by a woman yelling "Wait you're a guy!" I ran out, threw the wig in the dumpster, got on my bike, and got the heck out of there. Over the next year or two I made sure not to go there if invited to play racquetball with a friend in case I was recognized. The excitement about nude women, adult movies, and sex continued from 13 well into my adulthood.
January 26

#27 (Day 27) Honest Open Willing 2012 Post
I had already been mentioning that there were times in the first 13

years of my life that my actions were that of a vandal, pyro, pervert, thief, and more. At the same time, I was feeling like a victim, defect, rotten, and evil. My feelings after my Bar Mitzvah were that God made me born this way, God hates me, or that there is no God. These traits were a part of me so why even try to stop? This change in my reality were compensating for low self-worth, depression, anger, and low self-esteem which started a really bad pattern and cycle in my life. Other events remembered during this time are horrible. Here we go for a few that year between age 13 and 14......

I released the emergency brake on a parked car. Unlike the shopping cart incident, this was on a very remote street where there were no other cars or people. The car looked abandoned, very cheap, old looking, and was manual drive with a stick shift. This in my mind made all this totally fine. It rolled slowly a few dozen feet down the street into bushes and trees and gently stopped. There was no damage to the car or any property but it still filled me with the adrenaline rush of excitement. This same feeling happened when a few small fires were started in those and different woods. Everyone in the world knew and labeled me as a 'pyro' so why not fit the title role?

Money was stolen from my mom's pocketbook. On one occasion, I entered a house while selling candy and took $20 from their table. I did then put that $20 into a charity box at my Temple even though there were times I stole from the Temple too. I threw logs and stones into one friends' pool along with a second friend because these two friends had together destroyed an igloo built on my property earlier that winter. I let loose outside a huge bouquet of balloons from the kids' table at a friend's Bat Mitzvah making her cry and ruining her wonderful memories of that day for a long time.

Every single thing that I had done before, during, and after for many years are things I majorly regretted. This was especially true when I buried them down deep inside and then remembered all of them at once several years ago which filled me with over whelming guilt. Now I do know that I was not evil and have not done these or other horrible things for several years until I was ready to be H.O.W. What I do to amend is take this day forward without beating myself up. Now these experiences are being used in a positive way helping others who did these things or know people that do. However......this was only the

beginning of the 'harmless' things......
January 27

#28 (Day 28) Honest Open Willing 2012 Post

In May 1982, at 13-1/2 years old, I was still very socially and emotionally immature. Bergen County Special Services decided that I was not ready to enter Paramus High School with my 8th grade class at East Brook Middle School. Instead, it was planned that I go to Fieldstone Middle School in Montvale and repeat the 8th grade. Then I would go to Pascack Hills High School the following year.

A few weeks later that same month was when I said inappropriate things to another boy and his younger sister in my town. Nothing was planned to be malicious, I was just curious and wanted to play a game of ask and tell. Their mom was listening, attacked me with a rake, and then called the police. Even though no one thought I was trying to be molesting at my age, the parents wanted to press charges.

In the Bergen County Courthouse was where I went to Juvenile Court for the 1st time. I plea bargained by admitting to guilt of a lower degree crime. This got me one year probation for trying to corrupt a minor. If I stayed out of trouble for those 12 months, then this would not even go onto my permanent record. All I had to do was start fresh at a new school (in the same grade again), with new kids, and be good. That lasted 11 months......
January 28

#29 (Day 29) Honest Open Willing 2012 Post

While on my one year probation from Bergen County, I graduated on June 24, 1982 from East Brook Middle School as an 8th Grader. The Bergen County School board thought it was best that I not tell my classmates of my going to another school for 8th grade (again) instead of going with them as Freshmen to Paramus High School.

That summer of 1982, I attended the Paramus YM-YWHA (Young Women-Young Men Hebrew Association) Teen Travel Camp. These were day trips and activities with a couple of overnight trips. Again......I stood out as the weird one or there was a target on my head or there were those demons inside of me trying to get attention and/or stay in the role and manner accustomed to playing. It was not awful, but I still felt rather lonely. At the end of the summer we were going to Atlantic City even though none of us campers were nearly old enough to gamble (good thing for that in my regard)! We stayed at a school or YW-YMHA or somewhere in Margate NJ in a gym. Everyone had their bags on the stage behind the curtain and at some point I stole some money from several other campers. They thought it was me but could not prove it.

On the Boardwalk I was a spendthrift which looked even more suspicious. I felt like a big shot and that I got away with this. Later that night we returned to the gym. The counselors presented all of us with an end of the summer award show. The last 'winner' was Steve who wins the award of 'He won an award......but it was missing (or stolen)'! Then many of the other campers ripped off my pants with the counselors allowing this! I ran out of the gym with my pants torn and all hanging off one ankle with everyone (counselors and campers) laughing.

Then that September 1982 I attended 8th Grade (Again) in a Neurologically Impaired (Special Ed) class to advance socially at Field Stone Middle School, Montvale NJ with Emotionally Disturbed (ED) Status. The school board planned for me to graduate in June and move on to Pascack Hills High School that next September 1983. All I had to do was behave, not get into trouble, get along with my classmates, get good grades in new 8th grade classes like French, Algebra I, and (my favorite) Computers. Things were not as bad as 7th grade in Hillsdale or 8th grade (Part I) in Paramus but I still felt alone, made fun of, and was the least liked. I did become active in my Hebrew youth group BBYO (B'nai B'rith Youth Organization) with my older brother and sister.

My parents arranged for me to start having counseling sessions with a 'cool' young adult man. We would meet at his place to talk for about 30 minutes, go out to grab some dinner, and then head over to the local YM-YWHA (Young Men – Young Women Hebrew Association). This was once a week on the nights when there were youth teen activities and he was the supervisor. Seeing my interactions with the other kids, and giving me advice the next week, was supposed to help my Peer Relations.

On February 2, 1983 it was official that I was hereby authorized to Attend PHHS in September 1983 as a Freshman! Things appeared to be rather good except in March 1983 when I misused a computer & obtained classified info. Then I was banned from computers for the rest

of the year which was my #1 love at that school. At least in the beginning of May all the plans for getting to the High School and being released from Special Ed were in motion. I had about 2 months left of school and only one month left of my one year probation. Then (as my dad used to put it and was always waiting) the other shoe dropped......
January 29

#30 (Day 30) Honest Open Willing 2012 Post

Things were going 'decent' in 8th grade (part 2) at Fieldstone Middle School of Montvale NJ. There still was teasing especially from one girl who made a major fool of me several times including once yelling, in a sexy voice really loud, "Hi Steve your soooo sexy." This was right before doing a high jump in gym class and the distraction made me run into the high jump bar making everyone laugh. To get back at her I left many inappropriate phone messages on her home phone answering machine from May 7-12, 1983.

This lead to my 2nd Court incident about 11 months after my first one with only about one month to go before my probation was over. The police from that town came to my house in Hillsdale, rang the doorbell, and when I answered the door they asked 'Are you Steve?' I responded "Yes, what is this about?" They replied "We think you know what it is about. Please get your parents." My mom went to the police station with me and was given the phone transcripts and information about what I did. They also told me that the school did not want me to come back since one call was made from the pay phone there during school hours. May 18, 1983 was officially the last day of attendance (being expelled) at Fieldstone after being suspended.

The next day at a Bergen County Special Services meeting my parents were told that the "Prognosis of youngster very poor. Conduct Disorder, under socialized, Aggressive." I began home tutoring to finish the 8th grade and was very lucky getting probation again for a year. There was an extra warning this time that a third strike would mean going to a Juvenile Detention Center.

No one knew where I would be going next year to start High School. There were a number of 'special' schools in Bergen County that my parents and the school board thought would actually do me more harm than good. Finally they decided to send me (on a trial probationary basis)

to a special program called the 'Nova Program' within a 'normal' school in Oakland NJ which was Indian Hills High School.
January 30

#31 (Day 31) Honest Open Willing 2012 Post

On July 31, 1983, my oldest sister got married and had her wedding reception at Colonial Manor in Old Tappan NJ. Many of my sister's older male friends thought it was funny to give me many different alcoholic drinks. Even though my "Jewish Temple Wine Experiences" began at age 9, I was now over 14 and thought I could handle my liquor. It was not more than an hour or two into the reception before I got really drunk (not just tipsy) for the first time in my life. Everything was spinning and I was extremely sick in the Men's bathroom throwing up the rest of the event. What a great present to give my sister on her big special wedding day......

It was the summer of 1983 before I started to attend Indian Hills High School in Oakland NJ as a Freshman. My parents still had some hope for me and sent me to a 'normal' day camp in NY called Gateway Tours. We did regular camp activities like swimming, archery, kick ball, and arts & crafts. The cool thing is a few days each week we would go to the movies, bowling, rafting, or places like Action Park or Great Adventure.

We did go on an overnight trip to a dude ranch with horses, guns, poop, and other cool dude stuff. The four other boys in my room and I decided to sneak over to one of the girls' room later that night. We were NOT allowed out of our rooms but that did not stop us. We got excited that one of the girls invited us over even though most of us would not know what to do with girls back then even if they were naked with an instruction book. We snuck out, tiptoed across the dude ranch grounds, and went around to the window behind their room.

The window was like 6 feet up and about 2 feet tall and 4 feet wide. Only 2 (and 1/2) of us four were in when one of the girls freaked out and we had to leave and sneak back to our room. We thought all was clear and when we entered the room, the two head counselors were sitting there waiting for us! Our parents were called and we had to stay in the room the next day before going home. The punishment (from the camp) was that we were not allowed to go the following day down to Seaside Heights NJ which really stunk!
January 31

#32 (Day 32) Honest Open Willing 2012 Post

Before, during, and after this dude ranch trip I had switched from being teased to making fun of others to (finally) make myself look and feel superior. I especially tormented a kid at this camp who was also 15 by making up songs and pointing out funny things. Never ever did I get violent, threaten him, or did he seem to get upset. Just kinda treated him like it was a Celebrity Roast and others were already on the 'band wagon'.

At the end of the summer he finally had enough and did not want to go to the final trip because of mostly me. This end of the summer trip was a bus ride down and back to Florida for like 6 days. I was told that if he did not go then I could not go. I called him at his house to apologize and convinced him to go while taping the entire phone conversation. This was played on the bus while heading down to Florida. It was supposed to be funny but instead was mean. To this day, I regret doing that, other things including calling him 'Spaz', and wish I could find him to sincerely apologize.

However, this was the beginning of making good male and female friends who I am so lucky to still have in my life today! One of these female friends was dating another friend of mine while at camp. A few weeks after the summer ended so did their relationship. I had thought the way he treated her was wrong and we started to speak more on the phone.

She invited me to a party at her friend's house where there were several people including many from camp. We later went for a walk, and held hands. The following Saturday was our first date seeing a James Bond movie in Westwood. Another couple went with us to the Nanuet Mall the next day. Waiting for the bus was where we had our first kiss and when she became my very first girlfriend.
February 1

#33 (Day 33) Honest Open Willing 2012 Post

In October 1983, I was a 15 year old Freshman and had already been going to New York City several times without my parents knowing. One night was another routine escape from my house in Hillsdale NJ to NYC, NY. I dropped down quietly from my 2nd floor bedroom window and took the bus one block away to Port Authority. I was having too much fun that night and missed the last bus home.

There was no other choice but to stay in the Port Authority lower terminal until a bus left the next morning. I took a nap. An hour or so later I was awoken and robbed in front of many people who just watched while a razor was held to my throat, my pants pocket was cut, and my wallet was taken. I ran upstairs to tell the police who gave me a note to give the bus driver to take me home without charge. Then I took the wrong bus and had to walk 2 miles & sneak back into my house and bedroom before my parents awoke a few minutes later.

Now I learned my lesson not to take the bus into New York City so late at night. A short time later I went back into NYC but not by bus. Again I dropped down quietly from my bedroom window and this time took the car while underage. Even though I did not have a driver's license or even a driver's permit I was now 16. On my way home from NYC I was stopped by the NYPD & given two tickets. One was for going through a red light and the other for not having my driver's license which I said was left home.

People said I should just ignore the tickets. However, my mom later found out about these when I got summons in the mail to my house! She then called me at my dad's office to confront me. When my mom specifically asked me if I took my dad's Oldsmobile on a certain Friday night and got traffic tickets at a certain time in a certain location then I knew not to lie. I said 'Yes mom'. She then told me to give the phone to my dad......
February 2

#34 (Day 34) Honest Open Willing 2012 Post
There were times when I was younger that I would sell candy bars for school or youth groups but charge more money than was supposed to. I also used to go around town from house to house collecting money for 'charities' and kept all of the money. Money was another thing that made me happy and got me out of myself because then I could buy or do things that made me feel less depressed.

In February 1985 I was a Sophomore at Indian Hills High School in Oakland NJ. There was a candy bar sale going on and many people had their box of candy bars and money with them at school. My last class of the day was gym. I snuck into the boys' gym locker 10 minutes earlier than I should have and stole money from different boy's lockers. When the kids were entering the locker room to change a few minutes before the end bell, I ran out the main door to get back to my homeroom with the money in my pockets. The gym teacher saw me and asked if that was the gym shorts and shirt I was wearing home. I said yes and he quickly scolded me for wearing the same clothes in gym and school.

Then I ran down to the other end of school and one floor down to get my knapsack and get on the 'Special' van back home. Just as I was shoving the money in my knapsack the gym teacher was running up to the door behind me huffing and puffing telling me not to move. The kids in the locker room must have quickly noticed money was missing and the gym teacher immediately figured out it was me. The school suspended me for a few days and I knew life would be very bad when I came back.

My parents were away down in New Orleans for a work convention while I was suspended and the morning that I was allowed to come back to school. My grandma was at the house watching my brother, sister, and myself. I carried out a different plan rather than going to school. I called the school and the bus company pretending to be my mom saying Steve is not coming into school today. Then I left the house and went to the corner to catch a bus. That bus took me the next town over to my bank where I took out all of my money which was only about $600. Then I took the bus into NYC and got a room at the Times Square Hotel. I had one last day and night of fun and excitement.

Later that night, I went back to my room and took an entire big bottle of sleeping pills to end my life. It did not work because the next day at Noon, they were banging on the hotel room door telling me it was time to check out. I threw up in the hotel toilet, took the bus back home, & my parents had to fly home early from New Orleans. When I did get back to school there was a lot of negative attention towards me especially from the boys I stole money from. It was easier and they were much cooler about it when I lied telling them it was for drugs. That was not the first nor the last time I thought about or tried to take my life.
February 3

#35 (Day 35) Honest Open Willing 2012 Post
This suicide attempt with the entire bottle of sleeping pills in my New York City Time Square Hotel room was the last and most planned out of the three actual times I tried to kill myself. The first time was at age

13 when I had gotten into serious trouble with the Bergen County Courts for corrupting another minor. After taking half a bottle of Tylenol (about 15-20 pills), I only got sick with a bad stomach ache.

The second time was a year later, at age 14, when I again had gotten into serious trouble with the Bergen County Courts for verbally harassing and threatening my school mate over the phone. That 2nd time I waited until everyone home had left for the day and there would be several hours before they returned. One car was in the garage and the keys were hanging on a hook by the front door. The garage door was down, the door to the TV room was closed, and there were no garage windows. After starting the car and sitting on the driver's seat with the car window down, (again) all I got was very sick even after 20 to 30 minutes. So I turned off the motor, opened the garage door to vent out the Carbon Monoxide, and went back inside without anyone ever knowing.

This third suicide attempt in New York City made me think that it was not supposed to be because every time I tried to kill myself all that would happen is that I got very sick. At that point in 10th grade at Indian Hill High School, I decided to try and ride out my life......for then.

Shortly afterward, and for several years, things did seem to get a lot better! Outside of school I was becoming real friends with many other boys and girls, had girlfriends, went to dances, started to Breakdance, and were being invited to parties. In fact, things were so good that I started a mobile disc jockey service called DJ FLASH. (A funny thing is that the nickname 'FLASH' was tauntingly given to me a year earlier in High School for trying to impress everyone by running really fast around the bases in softball during gym.) Then I started to entertain at many different events for many different people and was told that I was really good! All of this plus adding the excitement of alcohol, pot, money, and starting to have sex really helped my self-esteem. Yep life was finally starting to go really, really well and I was so glad that my suicide attempts had all failed.
February 4

#36 (Day 36) Honest Open Willing 2012 Post

During the summer of 1985, I got a job as a junior counselor at a day camp which I think was in Morris County or somewhere about 30 minutes away. Each day I would take the train from Hillsdale to River Edge and then get picked up by one of the camp buses. One day I missed the train and the bus. My mom drove me to the camp but my group had already left for Sesame Street Place. Then there was going to be a talent show and camp sleep over. I practiced a Breakdance routine while waiting for my group to return with another junior counselor who played the piano.

Later that night, I performed my Breakdance routine and it was highly received! Afterward, one of the female junior counselors talked to me, walked with me by the lake alone, and then we started to kiss. My self-esteem was high! However, during a party a week later there was alcohol. She started dancing with one of the senior counselors that was my friend. They started kissing in front of me! My self-esteem was shot down.

A few days later, my group's senior counselor needed to take one of the campers somewhere and was going to be back in a few minutes. The other campers in the group were supposed to stand against one of the shed walls until the senior counselor came back. One of the campers was not listening and trying to be funny by constantly walking away. I put my hand against his chest to keep him against the wall. He started yelling that I was choking him and it looked like it from behind but I really was not and I know it and he knew it! The head counselor said she had no choice and eventually I was asked to leave the camp a few weeks early.

There was still a lot of the summer left and here I was without a job. One of the local ice cream restaurants gave me a job. During the next few weeks, I worked my way up from dish washer to one of the people who made the ice cream creations. Then I was given the responsibility of ringing up people at the cash register. Customers would get stuff and give me the money which was not officially rung up. I just opened the cash register, put the money in, and at the end of my shift take out the money not calculated to be in there.

There were two other things that I also did just like the other employees. One was to stick a finger into the different ice cream tubs to take a taste of that flavor ice cream and then stick a finger into another one and another one without washing our hands in between! This makes me a little weary whenever I eat out anywhere thinking this is a regular type of occurrence.

The other thing was that we all loved to suck out the nitrous oxide (N2O) from the (usually empty) whipped cream canisters. You hold your breath for as long as possible with the N2O in your mouth before you exhale. Then you get a rapid, cool type of high that lasts a few seconds and keeps you light headed for a minute or two until you take another hit off another cylinder. This got me to love doing 'Whip-Its' which was an unofficial illegal thing to do.

Some places sold a little screw off chamber where you put a compressed N2O capsule available in packs of 10, 25, or 50 wherever home whipped cream dispensers were sold. Then you screw tight the chamber and a pin bursts open the capsule filling a punching bag balloon you put over the one end with the pin hole. Then you remove the balloon and suck out all the N2O. This supposedly kills your brain cells but I never cared even after doing this over 1000 times. Then began my Junior Year at Indian Hills High School......
February 5

#37 (Day 37) Honest Open Willing 2012 Post
There were several pets in my life growing up. I remember and have memories of them from being a little 5 year old boy until about now in my posts. It is difficult to include them separately since they collectively affected me.

My oldest sister woke me up one Chanukah morning to say one of my hamsters named Sandy 2 escaped overnight. I was relieved when she said that because I thought something worse had happened. It did. The dog and the cat both got to him before it was too late! She was dead. Then I got another hamster named Mookie. Innocently, I was having fun gently tossing him onto the couch. He seemed to like it because I thought he was excited that he could fly. When I took a few more steps backward it required a little more force to land him on the couch. My strength was more than expected and he hit the wall with a splat! His body was broken and so was my heart. He was taken out of his misery and Mookie was buried in the flower garden on the side of the house. We never got another hamster again at our home.

Tanya was our beautiful, white, Samoyed dog that I loved so very much. She was my best friend for about 11 years since I was about 5 until I was almost 17 in 1985. We kept her in the back with a fence and would walk her on a lease. Occasionally, I would drop the lease and she would run slowly so I could catch her. She like the short freedom sprints. One day when I was about 15 and walking her, I did this again but she ran very fast a few blocks and onto a busy street called Kinderkamack Road. A car hit her but luckily only nipped her on the side and at a low speed while slowing down. I yelled "TANYA!" Her belly and nipples were bleeding and I was so sad because this was something I never ever wanted to happen. She then had hip and bladder problems for a few years. We had to eventually keep her in the front hall because she would pee overnight. It hurt her to get up as she got a little older.

She went to the vet many times to get shots and pills but it got to a point where my parents and the vet thought it was too cruel to let her go on. One day when my parents came home after a visit with Tanya to the vet, I saw my mom exiting on the passenger side crying with the leash in her hand and without my doggie. It was not told to me that Tanya may not be coming home so that I could say goodbye and again tell her how sorry I was for letting her off the lease, getting hit by the car, and giving her a few years of pain and early death. My inner anger went outward by saying to my parents "How would you like it if I put you to sleep when you get older and sick?" We never got another dog again at our home.

Later that same summer in July 1985, I was about to head out to catch the train so I could be picked up for my job (at that time) working as a day camp Junior Counselor. Right before I was heading out of the house and after everyone else had left for work, the phone rang. Someone said "Do you have a black cat named Midnight?" I said "Yes......why?" The reply back was "Well it says this on her collar tag and she just got hit by a car here on …. Kinderkamack Road." Immediately, I hung up the phone and ran the one block up to that street back and forth a block or two both directions looking for our Midnight. It was technically my sister's cat which we had for about 8 or 9 years and has always been an outside cat. Our cleaning woman had just come to the house like she did once a week for the last several years. She loved our animals and when I told her about the phone call, she said she thought she saw a dead cat on the road and we both got into her car and drove a block away. There was Midnight lying next to another orange striped cat that looked like Morris the Cat.

An old lady came out of that house and explained that the first cat got hit by a car which did not stop. Then my cat crossed the road without looking to see about her friend. That was when another car hit her. That driver was devastated and called me using the information on Midnight's collar tag from that lady's house. After 15 minutes she told the old lady she was sorry, had to go to work, and did leave her contact information. Our cleaning woman and I got back into her car and drove to the vet with Midnight. He immediately looked at her and said "She's dead...do you want me to take and cremate her?" I said no and we got back into the car to go home.

My brother said not to tell my sister until she comes home or she will be distraught all day. It was said that dead animals rot, smell, and could ... open up if it is too hot. So we put her next to the air conditioner's cold air vent until my sister came home. Then she took her to the vet to be cremated. We never got another cat again at our home.

Midnight and especially Tanya were two of my greatest loves of my life when no one else cared about me and when I had no friends. Midnight had a great personality and always jumped onto my lap giving comfort and love in return for being petted and loved back. This was the same about Tanya who always seemed to know when I felt lonely and depressed to come up and tell me she cared and loved me. Now I had no more pets that could do this and for me to love and care back.

Around this same time is when I turned 17 and started to have sexual relationships with women...a lot of women. They liked that I wanted to please them more than myself. That was a great feeling. Now I was addicted to love and sex as I was becoming addicted to nitrous oxide, alcohol, marijuana, and soon gambling, food, and other drugs and things. February 6

#38 (Day 38) Honest Open Willing 2012 Post

September 1985 was my Junior year at Indian Hills High School. It was also the month that I officially started my mobile disc jockey entertainment service called DJ FLASH. My 1st party was a BBYO (Jewish Youth Group) East Brunswick friend's Sweet 16. A friend of mine who was a DJ came with me to help and my brother had to drop us and the equipment off because neither of us were 17 (or had a real driver's license). There I met a cute girl who was constantly talking and flirted with me. I had some confidence and flirted back. Then we slow danced as she wore my hat and we kissed during the song. After the song was over, I went right up to the turntable from the front side and started the song over which everyone thought was funny. After the song, she had to leave an hour early because her mom was picking her up on the way home. That sucked! But at least I did get her phone number.

Two minutes later, she ran back saying she could stay to the end of the party if my brother could drop her off at home when he came back afterward. I volunteered on my brother's behalf and said 'yes'! We talked and danced some more and then I asked my friend to take over with the music so she and I can go for a walk.

She took me upstairs in this Elks Club where there was an empty, dark hall with a couch against the back wall. We sat there, made out some more and the next thing I know she was kissing my neck, unbuttoned my shirt, and … headed further south. This was a first and rather exciting thing to happen at my first DJ gig! Then after the party, she had to sit on my lap since everyone and everything in my brother's car made it very cramped. We dropped her off at home and kissed goodbye.

Two weeks later there was a BBYO dance in the same area. So I called her and we made plans to get together at that time (she did not want to go to the dance because she was not Jewish and did not feel comfortable going). I got on the bus which took all us Northern NJ Jewish kids in BBYO down to the New Brunswick Temple for the dance. Her and her mom picked me up and we went back to their house. We talked for a while and then went for another 'walk'.

This time, she took me behind a Racquetball club and put down a blanket. Again we fooled around but this time went all the way! 'Holy Crap Wow!' I thought. This was only the third time ever having sex and the first time without having to pay. We held hands and talked while heading back to her house.

I thought we were boyfriend and girlfriend by now. She said it was fun and that I was NOT her first or her last. In fact, it was the end of September and she said she was with two other guys in the last few weeks. Believe it or not, I felt cheap and was heartbroken. That was when I first thought that sex did not have to mean anything and had nothing to do with love and relationships. That was the beginning of many mutually enjoyable escapades. Again, I was so high and confident each time because everyone always had a lot of fun and was satisfied. No one ever got hurt except the people I was cheating on and myself in the long run......

February 7

#39 (Day 39) Honest Open Willing 2012 Post

Saturday, November 16, 1985 was my 17th birthday which meant I could finally get my real New Jersey driver's license. Of course....I had to wait two more days afterward for the NJ DMV to open Monday. That night was my first date with a girl that I met in a more religious Jewish youth group called USY. We had met a week or so earlier at a small social gathering at Temple Emanuel in Woodcliff Lake NJ. There was flirting, playing pool, and later her chasing me with two pool balls banging them together like she was going to smash my nuts (but in a playful way).

A day or two later, a mutual friend called me and asked me what I thought of her. My being naive had me ask "Why does she like me?" The response was "Duh!" I got her phone number and called her to see if she wanted to go out. She asked "Out on a date or go out with you like boyfriend and girlfriend?" I said "Why don't we go out on a date and take it from there." She was a very nice, smart, older, Jewish girl and her family was more religious and closer with each other than I viewed my family back then.

We went to the movie theater in Ridgewood NJ to see "Once Bitten" that starred a very new and young Jim Carrey. My brother had to drive me, pick her up, and drop us off, then the reverse since I still had no license. He did not charge me $1 each way like he did in the past when I dated non-Jewish girls. He was not trying to make money or get paid for the gas since my parents did that. My brother was just trying to encourage me to meet women of my own faith since he was trying to be a good Jewish boy. Meanwhile, a few years later he married a non-Jewish girl, had three children together, and then divorced. That really did not (and still does not) give me any happiness or feeling of what-goes-around-comes-around. It was definitely not pleasant for my brother and of course as with any kids having parents divorcing is never ever a good thing!

Later on, this girl and I did become boyfriend and girlfriend. We did get closer emotionally and physically and saw each other often. She went to my high school prom. Even when she went to college about three hours away, we would still see each other every few weeks. I was very much an insecure 'scum bag' because I was always jealous of her even though I did start seeing (fooling around and having sex with) many other women before, during, and after her four college years. We were together 'exclusively' from the end of 1985 until we got engaged in 1990 and then married on May 27, 1991 at the Richfield Regency in Verona NJ. A few dozen of my male friends attending the wedding were all taking bets how long the marriage would last with most of them saying under a year.

Never at any point was I honest, giving, or faithful to her in any way. Everything was selfish and self-centered on my part and she was never really my equal partner although I do feel that I truly did love her. There were many times and things during the next few months that I know hurt her mentally, emotionally, and maybe even spiritually while being married to me. I was never physical or used any violent force towards her but my final realization that she had been dating, engaged, and now married to 'someone like me' made me even more distant until I asked for a divorce. She wanted to work things out but I did not want to hold her hostage anymore in my stupid and messed up life. I told her that the entire time we had been together from my birthday on November 16, 1985 up to my last birthday just recently on November 16, 1991 that I was unfaithful.

Never did I name any names of the numerous women I was with but I did tell her there were several women that I paid for sexual favors. That was the final straw which got her to strongly agree on a divorce because we just were not (and could not) be happy together. We moved out to separate apartments by the end of that same year on December 31, 1991. We were legally divorced in the Bergen County courthouse by June and got a Jewish Gett in August so that she was no longer married in the eyes of Judaism and could re-marry again in the future.

The guilt and remorse inside my head over the next many years constantly ate away at me. I finally found her again on Facebook around 2008 after more than 16 years had passed since our last contact. It was over half a year since I had decided to become Honest Open and Willing with everyone including myself (this was with God's help and the assistance of those he brought into my life). I sent her a Facebook message to please agree to meet with me so I could talk to her. A few days later we met at a diner and I made my most humble, sincere, and honest amends to her.

She knew I was indeed sincere and accepted my apologizes saying that maybe she had a little bit to do with this too. Her claim was that we were both immature back then, possibly she did not see (or want to see) the truth about me, and perhaps thought I could change with time and her help. I told her that it was of no fault on her part whatsoever who I was and what I did. Then I thanked her immensely for understanding my full responsibility!

We have been Facebook friends since then and have seen each other on two other occasions having several common friends. We have been very civil and mutually nice to each other. She even said that what happened back then is what made us who we are now so there cannot really be any regrets. That gave me even more relief and less guilt. It was even better when we spoke on the phone on May 27, 2011 (which would have been our 20 year anniversary). That is when she admitted how much she did hate my guts after our marriage, wished I got hurt like I hurt her, and maybe even died.

Now she said her feelings are not at all like that and really wishes me the best for a bright future with my great second wife who deserves me like I deserve her. There is a lot more of my story between first meeting her, our wedding, nine months living together, our divorce, and the 16 years in between meeting her again. However, this needed to be shared all at once to be fair about how innocent, trusting, and loving she was to me then and how understanding, accepting, and forgiving she is now!
February 8

#40 (Day 40) Honest Open Willing 2012 Post

Starting from 1983, and increasing each year, it seemed like positive momentum was finally happening in my stupid life! There were still a lot of bad things happening to me and that I did. But there were less bad things and more good things happening to me and that I did. A lot of these have already been discussed in some previous posts. The below summarizes things old and new from 1983 until 1987. Things were still getting better from 1987 on but the below at least takes me out of high school and into the 'real world'.

The involvement with my Jewish Youth group (BBYO) increased and by Freshman year was elected the President of the Pascack Valley boys' chapter (AZA). Again I was starting with new classmates at a new 'normal' high school and my probation from the two different encounters with the Bergen County court system was over by the end of the school year. In school I still felt like I was an outsider with no real friends and got teased but not really beat up. After school was over for the day and I got home, no longer did I feel isolated, utterly alone, or like a loser.

The summer of 1984 was when I went to a weekly Monday to Friday travel camp called Baron Mini Tours. There I met a few other friends and was asked to stay in different groups of boys' hotel rooms when we were away making me feel social, accepted, and wanted. There was one time that a girl punched me in the crotch. Involuntarily, I hit her in the face giving her a black eye but that was the only really bad thing that summer.

My youth group often held dances throughout northern New Jersey and it was a lot of fun to attend them. I had started to learn how to Breakdance rather well by 1985. That was also when I was introduced to what would become my best friend more than anyone or anything for the longest time of my life, marijuana, by smoking a joint outside of one dance. Afterward, I felt very uninhibited, fearless, and funny. Then I got very aggravated at everyone for many reasons before I then felt depressed and cried. It was great!

The summer of 1985 was when I became a junior counselor at a day camp showing off my Breakdancing, meeting and kissing a female junior counselor, and then having her break my heart a week later at an outside counselor alcohol party by kissing another counselor. I was kicked out of that camp for 'being too aggressive' with a rowdy camper. Conversely, I became DJ Flash, made money, had real sex for the first time (and it continued), got my driver's license, and had a new steady girl friend from another Jewish youth group (USY) that was smart and had a good solid family. My confidence was high but my attitude and cockiness was also getting too high having all this plus so many friends and alcohol now at some parties along with occasional pot.

Then I did try to run for high school Senior class Vice President and lost supposedly by not too many votes. I got those many votes because I had said in my speech that "I cannot promise longer lunch hours or porn in the library but I can promise to listen to you." This was misheard on the speaker system as "(Blah blah blah blah) longer lunch hours (blah blah) porn in the library (blah blah blah blah) you."

In 1986 I was elected to be the Vice President of my Jewish Youth group (BBYO) for all of the Greater New Jersey boys' division (AZA). Our chapter Pascack Valley AZA finally got respect and won a huge spirit weekend competition that three years earlier our chapter was seen as a joke. My self-esteem & ego were extremely inflated. Drinking alcohol at almost every party and smoking pot most days during school lunch hours were both becoming more regular. During Easter break, I flew by myself the first time all the way to Los Angeles and stayed with the President of the Greater Los Angeles boys' division (AZA) of the same worldwide Jewish youth group (BBYO). There I did all the cool touristy things for about three days and then stayed with my uncle and aunt for two days before flying home.

A few weeks before Senior year was over, the Bergen County Special Services gave me an award for being the Valedictorian of all the Bergen County Special School programs in the entire .... Bergen County. Then shortly afterward, they declassified me from Emotional Disturbed to ... normal! This was after nine years being Emotional Disturbed and being in Special Ed classes and programs. I graduated as a 'normal' classmate with the rest of Indian Hills High School. My dad hugged me saying how proud he was when I received my diploma. He may have said he was proud and hugged me a few other times but this time I felt he meant it and I felt I deserved it. In fall of 1987 was when I started to attend the Oxford University Honors Program at Ramapo College in Mahwah. Things continued to get soooooooooo much better......until the very end of 1988.
February 9

#41 (Day 41) Honest Open Willing 2012 Post
By the beginning of 1987, I had already applied and was accepted to a few colleges before graduating from Indian Hills High School in June 1987. My official GPA was 4.27 which may sound incredible but for some reason our normal high school gave a 5.0 for 'A's in honors classes

instead of a 4.0 so it was easy to make things sound like you have an A+ average when it really was a B+ average. My SAT scores were 710 in math …. but only 450 in verbal. Like my life, things were never balanced. Luckily, it did help to be in extra-curricular activities like the high school choir and student council (representing the NOVA 'special' program) plus my five years of participation and leadership training in my Jewish Youth Group BBYO.

The decision where to go was made easy when I was actively approached by distinguished members of Ramapo College starting a new 'special' program called the Oxford Honors Program. This was not 'special' like Special Education used to be for me in grade school and high school. It was 'special' because the professor leading this program and some other professors working with this program were graduates and in very good standing with Oxford University of the UK. This joint program between Ramapo and Oxford allowed for 15 well rounded American students each year to start. It involved taking one advanced class each Semester involving British Studies and a one day a week gathering / discussion. All of us would be living and working close together like a 'think tank'.

After six semesters (three years), everyone who was still around would be accepted to study two different classes involving Western Studies that summer at Oxford University over in the UK! Upon completing those college credits, turning in a senior year paper, and then graduating with at least a 3.0 would get us automatically accepted into Oxford University to obtain our Master's Degree! Who cared if you got a Bachelor's Degree at Ramapo College of NJ when your Master's Degree would be from Oxford University of the UK!

Now life was going to be taking a really good turn for once into a direction that would put my life where it should be after 18 years of crap. It seemed like the worst was behind me and that finally now the world was my Oyster! However, the worst was NOT over and there was still A LOT more in front of me still yet to happen. After all, Oysters smell fishy and are not Kosher!
February 10

#42 (Day 42) Honest Open Willing 2012 Post
Freshman orientation weekend for students attending Ramapo College of New Jersey was towards the end of August 1987. I was nervous about

being the one who would again stand out as the weird one that was teased, made fun of, or even left alone being shunned by the other students. Ironically, everyone there was also nervous, overwhelmed, and pretty much alone too. This was not like grade school, middle school, and high school where people already knew each other and had cliques of kids making other kids feel inferior (like crap) to make themselves superior with their friends. Upon realizing this, I then did everything with a positive mindset. Now I was a friendly, social butterfly making friends quickly with a lot of kids! Later they all started to become friends with each other and formed smaller groups of friends which were not mean like cliques. In many ways, it seemed like I got a good first impression with all these kids before they made good first impressions with other kids. I traveled from room to room all over the Freshman dorm within the first few weeks of college.

It was cool to have so many different kinds of friends from all over NJ (and some other places) that were diversified. Some were from families that were either wealthy or middle class or even struggling to make ends meet. Some were from the country, urban, or rural regions and from many different cultures. It really was a sort of melting pot to me and the first time that I was living away from home like an adult and not a scared kid getting into trouble or getting picked on.

My second semester started in January 1988. Being that I was already 'DJ Flash' the mobile Disc Jockey for several years, it seemed like a good fit to join the college radio station WRPR 90.3 FM. At first I was given the really early Saturday morning shift since I was new to the college and to this 1000 Watt FM radio station which reached maybe a few miles away on a clear day. Eventually, I became more involved with productions and then became the Public Affairs Director. This gave me a chance to interview many different politicians like the Mayor of Mahwah NJ (and once an actual U.S. Congressmen). I got to meet and interview singers (the Cover Girls who had a few late 1980s hits like 'Show Me'), actors (Michael Swan from 'As The World Turns'), nude models (Penthouse Pet of 1988) and other people.

Things were going great until a girl admitted to me some ditzy, stupid things she had said and done since getting to college. I did have the red 'On The Air' light on but she still did not know we were live and she was being heard. The radio station executives gave me a warning since I did it on purpose but nothing illegal or against the FCC was done.

My third semester was about to start. I was working at the radio station over that 1988 summer and found a key outside the main doors of the Student Activities office wing that opened the radio station and newspaper office doors. When the third semester started, some other radio station people said I should hold onto it since I was a director and had early morning shifts. It ended up that the key opened many doors including the college Priest's office. Money was taken from the charity box and they blamed me because I had the key. No other rooms were illegally entered by me and I did not take the money. I was found guilty simply for having this key that I was not supposed to have.

The station had no choice but to take away my Public Affairs Director position and its privileges. Luckily, my radio shift was still mine and I was able to fill in for other DJs if they could not make their shift. This allowed me to be on the air 1 or 2 added times during the week. There was a format each day during the different shifts and you had to still play the same type of music for whomever you were filling in for.

In January 1989, during the beginning of the fourth semester, I was working the late night heavy metal shift for someone. It was cool to pretend I knew what I was playing and used a cool heavy metal 'Wolfman Jack' type radio voice. A cute sounding girl called the station and asked me to play some songs and we talked a bit that night. I asked her if she goes to school here. She said no and that she goes to the local High School. I asked her if she was graduating there this year and her reply of yes lead me to believe she was 17 or 18. We met that night when she snuck out of her house. She did look 18 and we fooled around a lot (3rd base so to speak) but did not go all the way.

The next day when I called her to ask where she would be going to college next year is when she admitted of only being a 15 year old high school Freshman! I was 20 but still wanted to meet her again that night to talk and waited down the block from her house in my car. After an hour, she did not arrive but the police did. They asked why I was here in my car and I told them to meet a girl (not saying who she was or her age) whose parent s did not like me because I was Jewish. The policemen said to go home and the next day a detective from the police department asked me to come into the station. This girl's dad saw her trying to leave that second night and she explained everything to her parents. They had taken her to the doctor to see if there was penetration or fluid (which there was not) but the detective told me her dad was still furious and wanted to press charges for corrupting a minor.

The detective told me how horrible it would be for me in jail and he felt bad. He wanted to help me by making a deal that he could convince the dad not to press charges if I did him a favor. All I had to do was become Confidential Informant (CI 34) for them and introduce an undercover cop to my drug connection at college. Otherwise, the underage girl's dad would press charges against me and I would go to jail getting raped, hurt, and possibly killed.
February 11

#43 (Day 43) Honest Open Willing 2012 Post
There was no other choice but to do what the Sgt. Detective of the police department asked. If I went to jail then I knew (or thought) that the prison guards would find me raped and beat up or dead somewhere. No way could 'someone like me' survive being incarcerated. My response to becoming Confidential Informant 34 (CI 34) for them in return for immunity of being prosecuted for corrupting a minor was "OK." They let me go back to the college and it was made clear that if I said anything to anyone about this then the deal was off and I would immediately be arrested and thrown in jail. A week later, they had me go back to the police station. There I met and things were arranged with the undercover person. He would be introduced the next day as my brother's friend to my good friend the pot dealer. Then I would go with him again a few days later so he can get a larger amount. From that point, he was going back himself to buy more and more stuff.

A good amount of marijuana was already being bought every few days and being indulging several times every single day. This never stopped as it would look suspicious. It had helped when my second year moved me from the Freshman dorm to the student apartment on the other side of the campus. Then the first day of that semester in September is when my new roommate moved into our four person, two bedroom apartment (with kitchen, eating area, and living / entertainment area)! He asked "Do you smoke pot?" and when I replied "YES!" pulled out a bong (oooops water pipe). That is when I learned and practiced the term "Wake & Bake." Working on the weekend as DJ Flash got me all the money I needed for pot or whatever since my parents were paying for college, the rent, food credits, and still given a weekly allowance.

Life went on as I was getting sicker and sicker with myself for reverting to partying instead of academics, doing bad (evil, sick) things again, and becoming pretty much a NARC. I tried to forget all this and continued pledging my fraternity to get out of myself. Even though I felt again like a dirt bag, it was fine because I was now a follower and was not responsible for my actions.

There were no fraternities or sororities at Ramapo College until the semester before. One member of an established fraternity had transferred from another college and started a chapter there becoming the first one. Now the second group was pledging including me. Most of them were a year younger and we did the usual, 'top secret' things plus learn the Greek Alphabet, know everything about each other, and getting woken up in the middle of the night. My liquor and pot intake had increased dramatically over the past few weeks. This was also done to try and forget how I had fallen in only one and a half years at college. What the F*ck....I might as well do more and more plus try some new drugs too.

We were having a get together in one of the campus apartments with some girls. Never had I done anything more than alcohol, whip-its (nitrous oxide - N2O), or marijuana. My pledge master gave me a handful of psychedelic mushrooms (or shrooms) for the first time and told me to eat them all at once which I did. It was important to continue being accepted (or at least something) and was already smashed from alcohol and stoned from pot. About 15 minutes later I saw one of my fellow pledge brothers (who was larger and better seasoned in partying than me) lying on the floor looking up at the ceiling while freaking out. That was when they told me that he took mushrooms earlier and my handful was much more! Then I myself freaked out and went back to my apartment to throw up as much as possible. My paranoia was intense as I sat on the couch trying to get through my 'trip'. A roommate and his friends were watching WWF (this was before the World Wildlife Fund enforced their copyright and made the WWF change its name to the WWE). I swear that Macho Man Randy Savage was reaching out to grab me while going "Yeeaaahhh brotherrr."

After this experience, I did mushrooms several other times but in much less amounts! One night, we started a freakin' awesome band and played all night. I was the drummer on the pots, pans, and containers. The next day when the trip was over, and we listened to the tapes, is when we realized that we really sucked. All this intense partying affected not just my grades but my other college activities including Radio Station, Oxford Club (which I got removed as President), and Student Council for the Oxford Honors Program. Now my need for excitement and getting into trouble was intensifying ... again. It was inevitable that before the end of February my world would become combustible......again!!!

February 12

#44 (Day 44) Honest Open Willing 2012 Post

The fantastic new world of finally being a successful young adult was crumbling. Here I thought my past self with all my bad judgments, faults, and horrors were behind me. It seemed that the better things got later in life became worse every single time when they eventually failed later in life. My brilliant success on top with everything at Ramapo College after one and a half years was just about gone. All I had was my fraternity pledge brothers and the fraternity itself. They seemed to be there for me and accept me 100% no matter what. One late night there was a pulled fire alarm at the freshman dorm Pine Hall while at a fraternity gathering in one of the rooms. Everyone had to evacuate the building immediately and go outside until all was deemed safe. This turned into a fun social party with the fraternity outside along with everyone else especially their female friends still scantily dressed for bed.

All of a sudden there started to be more frequently pulled fire alarms and then a few small fires in the different garbage can areas. All of these areas were behind heavy doors in fire proof cement rooms. No damage was done except the smoke would sound the smoke detectors and the fire alarm would go off by itself. No one had to pull a fire alarm and risk getting caught. There was less of a chance getting caught if someone threw a match in a garbage can while lighting a cigarette that caught on fire several minutes afterward then there was pulling a fire alarm. Alcohol, pot, mushrooms, and now being depressed and feeling like a failure made me really want to fit in. This got me back where I all started as an insecure, five year old looking for excitement ... being a 'pyromaniac'. I was 'good' at that and this seemed to be the 'in' thing.

This was now becoming a regular 'fun event' whenever there were small fires in the garbage rooms. The entire building would be evacuated for several hours. Many people had to go to the apartments on the other side of the campus to hang out or sleep while investigations were happening in Pine Hall the freshmen dorm. I had my apartment on the other side of the campus and so did a few of the fraternity brothers. All the brothers (pledging and full member) and many of the ladies would go back and party, hang out, watch movies, and have fun. We would all bond and my own selfishness prevented me from realizing someone could get hurt and that almost everyone was inconvenienced. I cannot even recall how many fires there were, when they were, any specifics, or even who else did some of these fires. All I can say is that I did a fair share of them but almost always in a garbage can in one of the fire proof garbage rooms.

The excitement and adrenaline started to take over and my purpose changed. I have no real remembrance why but a cardboard box outside a room was lit on fire on February 27, 1989. As I ran towards the stairs a guard yelled "Stop!" No one else at the college had a DJ Flash Complete Party Entertainer jacket so it was obvious who the running boy was. The Detective Sargent who was my 'Confidential Informant # 34' contact at the police department called me the next afternoon on the phone and asked if I knew about the recent fires. He was told that I was identified being in the building having that DJ Flash jacket and signing the guest book at the front desk. No one said it was me that did anything since there was no proof of anyone seeing me actually doing anything. All he was asking his 'Confidential Informant # 34' is if I had an idea who might have done it because it was worse this time. A handicapped kid tried to put out the box on fire, things almost spread, and he or others could have gotten hurt or killed! He really needed my help again. That is when I heard myself say "I lit that fire...."

He told me to come down now to the police station. If I did not then he would send a police car to arrest me. I went there and admitted to starting some of the fires. When asked why I admitted this I said because I was sorry. They still processed me and took me to get a lie detection test at the Bergen County court house in Hackensack that afternoon. This was where I had been at 13 and 14 years old to get sentenced to juvenile probation. Now I was 20. The lie detector told them that I did not light all the fires, probably did not know who exactly did the other ones, and this it was not to get back or hurt anyone.

The detective was very upset like I let him down which I did. His undercover officer was still active and very close to busting up my pot connection at the college. Only because he liked me and thought I really was messed up did he call the town judge that evening and asked that it would be accepted to use my AAA card as bail bond and be released on my own recognizance. This meant that no bail money was needed to be paid to the court and no bond had to be posted.

Afterward I was strip searched, finger printed and a mug shot was taken. The police said that the college didn't want me coming back until further notice. They had all my contact information anyway, said that I needed to get a lawyer immediately, and to report to Hackensack the next day on my own to register myself for court or something like that. In the meantime they asked where I would go, stay, and be so they could contact me. I said back to my parents in Hillsdale......and they said to make sure I stay there.

While I drove the 25-30 minutes ride home from Mahwah to Hillsdale there was nothing in my head. What would I say? I was so emotionally, physically, and spiritually exhausted that I just wanted to sleep. My bedroom is where I lived when not in college and I was always welcome to stay there. My parents did ask why I came home without any notice on a weekday evening. I said that I was in the area and wanted to sleep in my own bed. They accepted that for that moment. The phone rang there a short time later. My mom yelled up to me that there was a man on the phone from the Bergen Record newspaper. He wanted to know if I had any comments on my recent arrest for aggravated arson at Ramapo College!
February 13

#45 (Day 45) Honest Open Willing 2012 Post

The looks and unspoken feelings (or vibes) that I got from my parents will never be forgotten on that already horrible day. It was like I could feel the anger, rage, and embarrassment from my dad and the tears, worry, and sorrow from my mom as I picked up the phone and said "I have no comment." The reporter said "If you don't have any comment then I will just have to write what I was given." Again I said "Please I have no comment." Again he said "If you change your mind then here is my phone number otherwise I will write my article either way and you may want to give some input." I took the number and hung up the phone to now do more than get looks and unspoken feelings from my parents. Of course my dad said in shaky, angry tone "WHAT...DID...YOU...DO!" and my mom was crying.

All I could do was what I always did to get the pressure off of me and that was to vent and be over dramatically saying things about myself such as how stupid, dumb, a moron, not worth living, should run away, can't do anything right, what is wrong with me, outta kill myself, O my God why...and other things. My dad was still mad but could not be furious with my poor mom grabbing and hugging me saying it will be OK, they will protect me, they will get me some help, and not to worry because I am not a bad person just sick. All of a sudden ... I was 5 again. But I knew that I could not let them baby me or enable me like in the past. After all I am now 20 and should try to be a man. That is when I started to do some things for myself.

The next day I went to a county court office in Hackensack by myself to register for court like the police said I had to do. Next I went to the public defender's office and made out an application. Without using my parent's money or their lawyer, I was accepted to have a public defender work with me. He thought best to go get help at the Mid-Bergen Mental Health Center in Paramus. There too I went by myself and applied for financial help and again was put on a sliding scale according to my salary. Without a job yet, they let me pay $5 a session which was a good bargain. There were two different therapists that they wanted me to see. One was a substance / addiction counselor and the other more of a psychology counselor. After two sessions, the substance / addiction counselor said that I was not really a substance user with an addiction. She said to just continue with my psychology counselor which I did.

Then I got a job in customer service for a copier and fax dealer (in Mahwah) with sales, service, and contracts for customers throughout the Metropolitan area. Customers would call to complain saying their copiers or faxes were not working right. A work slip would be generated and then the slip was handed to the appropriate dispatcher for that area. Each dispatcher had 8 to 12 different service techs throughout their territory. It was their job to evenly divide the service calls by routing the technicians to the customers making best of where there were nearby. You could not send someone from New Brunswick to Princeton and then back to New Brunswick but some customers had priority 5, or even higher priority 1 status. After a few weeks, I had one of those jobs! It was long tedious hours with medium pay but the responsibility and fact that I had a job was good. Now I had to pay $10 per session at the Mid-Bergen Mental Health Center while awaiting my day in court. Having a public defender, getting mental health, having a solid job, and trying to remain a good boy was my goal.

Then my tonsil cells grew back along the inside of my throat. My tonsils were first removed when I was like 12 but these were just tonsil cells?!?! They had to laser zap them while I was under anesthesia at Pascack Valley Hospital in Westwood (where I was born). It tasted like burnt throat and was very sore for a few days but I was back at work two days later. Then I got a bad case of Bronchitis which meant going back to the hospital so a specialist can stick a long telescopic probe down my nose into my lungs. This required getting shots in the butt to dry me out and get me relaxed with codeine. Then he sprayed cocaine in my nose and every few inches again in my throat down to the lungs. I was not unconscious. Just so zoned out and groovy while they found out I was close to pneumonia. It was a great excuse to take disability leave at work for just the right amount of weeks so I got my pay and even the first two weeks' pay which you get after four weeks out.

Then I was able to get tickets for me and 5 of my friends to attend the Z100 6th Anniversary Ball at the Palladium in NYC. We went right up to stage just as Gloria Estefan came out. I was looking up at her tight pants trying not to look at her crotch while seeing what songs were next on the playlist by her feet. There were other performers and I felt cool being there. A week or two later, I won a pair of tickets to see Poison (1989's Poison) with Cinderella opening for them at Jones Beach. I called my cousin in Long Island to see if he wanted to go. He was as psyched as I to see them. Again, I felt cool going and being able to hang with my cousin there. All in all....I was becoming responsible, getting my own help, feeling like an adult, and still having a fun, cool, exciting blast!

I quit my job on Halloween 1989 because the human resources guy yelled at me and I said "That's It" because I did not need that stress. Then I worked for two months at a Jewelry store in the watch repair department. My job was to replace the many different batteries in many different watches. Also, I put on new watch bands or adjusted the ones already there by replacing or adding links. The owner needed someone to take his nieces and girlfriend's daughter to NYC for a New Kids On The Block concert. No one else wanted to go (including him or his brother) and he offered to pay for everything so I went for brownie points and a free concert. It was unique because Dino, Sweet Sensation (or something) and some other ... cool... acts performed too.

By the end of December 1989 it was time to go back to college. The University of Paramus (Bergen Community College) accepted me in January 1990 and took some Ramapo College credits. During that year, I attended a live talk show in New York where the Cosby Show was taped. Besides Bill Cosby seeing me, waving, and smiling... I met and got autographs from Lisa Bonet, Phylicia Rashād, and Malcolm-Jamal Warner. One time I went to NYC to an S&M club but was too weirded out with the women in leather bikinis whipping a man tied up without pants. The good thing is I was able to remove, hide in my coat, and take home some cool hand / leg restraints. Where they are now is a good guess......

In May 1990 is when I successfully finished my first semester back at college. However, it was not certain that I would be able to attend summer classes or even come back for another semester in the fall. That was about the time when I did finally receive my sentence from the Bergen County Court in Hackensack for my 2nd degree crime...... February 14

#46 (Day 46) Honest Open Willing 2012 Post

My arrest was at the very end of February 1989. There were probably a dozen times that my public defendant and I went to the Bergen County Courthouse in Hackensack together over the next fifteen or so months. During that time he was trying to get the Prosecutor's office to drop the charges from 2nd degree to 3rd degree. Then I would possibly be able to get Pre-Trial Intervention (PTI) since it was my first offense as an adult. This would mean that when my probation was over that it would be erased from my record as an adult. However, there was a woman that moved from the Essex County Prosecutors office to one of the supervisor positions at the Bergen County Prosecutors office that was very strict. She would not allow her Prosecutor handling my case to allow for Pre-Trial Intervention or to lower the crime to 3rd degree.

My public Defender was very experienced and incredible. I was so lucky to have gotten him. After all this time back and forth they all arrived at an agreement. If I pled guilty to this as a 2nd degree crime then the prosecutor would agree to allow the judge to hand out whatever punishment he decided without arguing for anything harsher. Finally at the end of spring 1990, about 15 months later, it was time for my sentencing.

That morning I got dressed up and went to the courthouse with my parents. My fiancée at the time and her parents met us there. My oldest sister and my next oldest sister also met us there. My lawyer told us that there were a few cases before mine and that we would need to wait. The judge allowed only one case in his court at a time so we all stayed in the hallway until he decided to take a one hour recess for lunch. All of us went out to a local diner for lunch ourselves. I wish I knew right away what would be happening to me and do not remember that being a very good meal. When we got back to the courthouse, the judge got us in shortly afterward. The Prosecutor went up to the table on the right and my lawyer and I went up to the table on the left before the judge. My parents and everyone else there to support me (for this pivotal moment) were seated in the back behind us. We all rose as the judge entered the room. Then it began.

My public defendant started. He said how I was not a bad person and that it would not serve justice for me to go to jail. This was my first offense, had gotten help, obtained a job, went back to school, and had the love and support of my family. The things he said really were amazing and his argument for a reduced punishment was almost magical and not deserving of me. Then after several minutes he sat down and the Prosecutor made his argument. It lasted about 15 seconds. He just said that I am not seen as a menace, has been cooperative, and that whatever the judge decides is fine with his office. Wow! Now the judge did his verbal deliberation for the next few minutes out loud.

Back and forth he said that I was not a hardened criminal......but I could have caused great harm......but I would not do well in jail......but what I did was wrong......but have a lot of support and good things going......but deserve to be taught a lesson that something like this is not taken lightly. My heart kept rising and falling at least 5 times that I would not go to jail, that I would go to jail, that I would not, would, would not, would, would not...... Then I stood as he made his decision. Five years' probation and that I had better be thankful for a great lawyer, family, and this lenient sentencing. OMG!

Still I could not embrace my family. They took me right away down the back stairs into the courthouse jail. That was scary as they then handcuffed me with a few other prisoners and put me in a van to go a few blocks down to the Bergen County Jail Annex for processing before release. The big prison gates opened and then closed behind us as we were then led out into the prison annex. Luckily, my holding cell was with three or four of the less scary criminals I guess like me. Right across was a larger cell that had maybe 20 scary prisoners like you see on TV and movies. An hour or two later, they got me out of my cell and took my fingerprints and mug shot again. Then I was processed for release and told me where to go within the next few days to report for probation. Then they let me walk out of the prison building door, down the yard walkway, and opened the big jail gates to let me leave.

My parents and fiancée were on the other side waiting for me. I hugged all of them, cried, and then we drove home. My prayers were immediately that I can move on with my life and please be good without doing anything else stupid ever again. Please. Please. Please God is what I was begging. It was not fair to my family who loves me. They don't deserve this crap I had been putting them through forever. Let me not give them anymore pain and anguish for the rest of their lives if not for me then for them.

Not being sentenced to jail allowed me to continue taking summer classes at Bergen Community College. That fall 1990 semester was filled with enough classes giving me enough credits to receive my Associate Degree by the end of the year in December 1990. My behavior was better. I was keeping myself on the right track. Now I was on five years' probation and had to. There was no room for anything illegal especially pot or any drugs.

In that upcoming May 1991 was my long-awaited wedding to my childhood girlfriend that was with me (and that I did not let go of) through thick and thin (or at least my thick and thin). Now it was time for me to grow up. If there were any doubts about my relationship with her that it was just my own cold feet and immaturity.

Little did I know I would soon be getting into more cheating escapades before and during my marriage? Little did I know that some of these would not just hurt my fiancée / wife but hurt several other people emotionally? Little did I know that my last fling vacation alone before marriage would introduce me to the greatest thing ever to come into my life?

February 15

#47 (Day 47) Honest Open Willing 2012 Post

It was a brand new year on January 1, 1991. Usually the day after December 31 is a new year but that's not the point. The point is that the past was behind me and everything would be different (...yeah...uh huh...again). I had just turned 22 years old in November and was about six months into my court sentence of five years' probation.

At the end of December 1990 is when I received my college diploma with an AA degree (Associate Arts...not Alcoholic Anonymous...that was not until 17 years later in 2008). Now in 1991 I needed to start seeing my probation officer weekly, get a job, and prepare for my May 27, 1991 wedding. This was going to be my first and always marriage and commitment to my childhood sweetheart that I kept with me over 5 years and would not, could not let go. There was always something inside me that knew she was mine but could never ever really feel in return that I was equally hers. Instead there was cheating, lying, stealing, and I always selfishly came first. My thoughts were that there should be no more pain, anguish, or embarrassment to my poor family, myself, or even to my fiancée now that I will be working and getting married soon. Whether I liked it or not, felt it or not, or wanted it or not, it was time for me to grow up. If there were any doubts about my relationship and pending marriage that it was just my own cold feet and immaturity.

My parents started to let me work at my dad's office in Emerson that year. This would only be temporary until I decided what I want to do (or what I want to be when I grew up some more). It was my father's company since 1973 when he bought out a gas analysis division of where he worked in NYC. My dad patented a unit called the TGM 555 which stood for Toxic Gas Monitor and the 555 was the street address in NYC where he had worked. We were living in Hillsdale at that time and he opened his first office the next town over in Westwood selling this gas analyzer and a few other portable and wall mounted gas monitors for industrial, governmental, and laboratory applications. My brother, sisters, and I had all worked there at different times when we were much younger. I started at age 13 in 1981 making copies, stapling papers, and sending out mailings. It was a boring, uninteresting job back then and I knew my future would not involve selling gas monitors when I got older.

Ten years later, I was back full circle. The real reason that my parents wanted me to start working with them (temporarily) again was to keep an eye on me but did not tell me that right away. My fiancée would also be working there as the receptionist / secretary. The days became weeks, the weeks became months and soon I was learning about the products and much more interesting things other than copies, staples, and mailing machines. I got to take calls and started to take an interest in these different sales, support, and more advanced mathematical, scientific, and business aspects.

Reporting to my probation officer in Hackensack was weekly at first. He needed to know I was still working, getting mental help, staying out of trouble, and had to take spot check drug tests by peeing in a cup while he watched in the bathroom. I always had problems peeing in front of people so this was torture. Finally he would let me go in, take off all my clothes, and hand them to him. He would see I had no hidden vials or bags of someone else's urine and gave me privacy for a minute. If I got into trouble with the law, got drunk, left the state without him knowing first, or tested positive for drugs then basically I screwed myself. It was not fun to screw myself so I thought why not screw women and at least have non-illegal fun until I got married. During this time, there were a few female friends that did not mind having fun with me until I got married. It was harmless because my fiancée did not know, my family did not know, and they knew there were no strings attached because I was getting married on May 27th.

There were some later problems and/or hurt feelings when other people found out about these women like where we did, when we did, and what was going on while we did these things. Of course, most of these things were because of my big mouth saying these things. Amends have been done since then and there is no regret of the past because many say they are happy where they are now. The joys of the present include their current lives and children. As far as I know...none of their children are mine. Gulp!

The honeymoon was set for my wife-to-be and I to go to an All Inclusive resort called Le Sport in St. Lucia after our May 27 wedding. We arranged this though a really cool guy who was out travel agent. Many friends thought I should go away for one last single vacation before (as they put it) I was dead. A friend had told me about a wild, adult, partying place in Negril, Jamaica called Hedonism II. That sounded like a great place to have some last fun before marriage. I called this same cool travel agent and he secretly arranged a May 10-13, 1991 trip package for just me to Hedonism II in Negril, Jamaica. Still DJ'ing, I had enough cash to pay for the trip without anyone knowing (except all my male friends).

My parents, siblings, and the woman I was going to be marrying two weeks after I returned thought I was going to Minneapolis, Minnesota to see a male friend. Instead, I drove to JFK Airport in NYC and took my flight down to Jamaica by myself while thinking how stupid some people believed my destination was instead up to Minneapolis, Minnesota (including my probation officer). Once I got down to the Montego Bay, Jamaica airport is where I met a few people from other flights to take the 90 minutes van drive to Hedonism II in Negril. One person that I met was living in New Brunswick NJ about 60 minutes away from where I was living in Bergenfield NJ. That person took a different flight from Newark Airport in NJ to go to Hedonism II also alone. Funny how you meet someone an hour drive away from where you live at home in a mutual place over 1500 miles away taking different flights from different cities to get there. This was a very cool, amazing person to meet......and fall in love with during those few days in paradise. However, the extremely sucky reality was that it was two weeks before you were getting married to someone else and could not cancel this late......
February 16

#48 (Day 48) Honest Open Willing 2012 Post
On May 13, 1991 was my flight back from Montego Bay, Jamaica to JFK Airport in NYC. This very cool, amazing person that I met down there also had her flight about an hour or so later on another airline to Newark Airport. The two of us boarded the bus from Hedonism II in Negril for the hour and a half ride to Montego Bay. We waited at the airport together and I had to take the escalator up to my gate when they called my flight. It was depressing and tearful as I waved goodbye to her. After just a few days together, I really had already started to fall in love with her.

Again, reality hit hard that it was two weeks before my marriage to my fiancée and that I needed to prepare for this new arrangement. Maybe I should have told this woman (who lived an hour away from me at home) that I was getting married on May 27th? Maybe it was Karma that I got a flat tire on Route 4 in Englewood while I was driving home from JFK Airport to my apartment in Bergenfield. This is where I moved into about six weeks earlier and where my soon-to-be wife and I would be staying after we got back from our honeymoon. She was old fashioned (and especially her parents) and did not live or stay there until then. It was MY first place to live away from my parents since the Ramapo College years. Maybe my fantasy world should have stopped from that point on?

My dad and I took a flight together less than one week after I got back from Jamaica (and my family thinking my sun tan was from four days in sunny Minneapolis, Minnesota). We flew off to the yearly American Industrial Hygiene Association Conference and Exposition. This year it was in Salt Lake City, Utah and every year our company has had a 10 x 10 foot booth in the exhibition hall with a few hundred other companies. Gas detection equipment was one of many different products, services, and publications that served the Industrial Hygiene markets. This was my first trade show and trip alone with my dad. I wanted to make him proud and I think he was proud having me attend and work the show with him.

When my dad was growing up in Queens NY, he went to Thomas Jefferson High School and was friends with a young man named Sidney Liebowitz. This young man changed his name to Steve Lawrence and became a famous actor and singer that married Eydie Gormé. My dad lost contact with him since 1955 but wanted to reunite with his childhood friend performing in Salt Lake City with his wife who was opening for the one and only Frank Sinatra. We had tickets together and were watching the concert. I went to the back stage area to ask Steve Lawrence's manager to give a message from my dad to Sidney Liebowitz. She barked at me "NO! His name is Steve Lawrence!" and she either did not give Steve Lawrence the message or he did not care about the message. Either way it made my dad depressed and down. This actually let me see a little more that he was human and it did make me feel a little closer to him.

Later that night we went back to the hotel. Each of us had our own rooms on different floors. I went out on the balcony and actually yelled "Salt Lake City you crazy town. Where's the party?" I got a reply "Down here!" A few floors down and maybe one or two rooms over were some girls on their balcony. They said to come down and were hanging out with some of their male and female friends. I thought "Why not?" and went down to their room and drank, smoked, and had a wild party with actual 'Black Sheep' Mormons (and one Christian Scientist). Some of them came back to my room later because one couple wanted...privacy.

We all crashed but in the middle of the night I heard one of the drunken guys stumbling around and then start to pee behind the curtains until I yelled "HEY!" Then he went into the bathroom and I had to run in there soon after because it did not sound like urine hitting a toilet. He was peeing in the bath tub. That was gross but I had showered earlier that night and was checking out of the hotel that morning (being that was the last day of the exhibition). The girls and I left him asleep in the room with a bucket of water spilled on his crotch because he really seemed like a callous, careless, dumb ass to all of us. Hopefully he left before the maid arrived or he would have had to explain why he was there in my room. Of course I had made sure all the girls and the boys were over 21 years old to make sure I was not partying with minors! My dad and I flew home that Wednesday night. I was getting married that upcoming Monday on Memorial Day.

Some friends were having a party at one house that Friday night (May 24, 1991). When I got there with another friend, there was a fake tombstone on the front porch with candles lit all around it. The tombstone said something like "Here Lies Steve....because on Monday he will be leavin'!" It was a sort of pre-wedding, surprise, bachelor party with both my male and female friends.

My brother threw me an actual Bachelor Party the following night (Saturday, May 25) which started at my parents' house in Hillsdale on their back deck with my family. Around 5 o'clock is when my male friends started to arrive. After I had at least 4 to 6 beers, they put an empty beer box on my head to hide the upcoming surprises, and got me in one of three cars that were caravanning from place to place. We kept drinking beer and we eventually arrived at Show World Center near 42nd Street in New York City near the Port Authority.

First we went to Nathans Hot Dogs to eat. There must have been some strange symbolic meaning to eating weenies before entertaining your weenies. I was given a hundred $1 bills and we all had as much fun as a lot of 22 to 25 year old boys could have at a peek show, live show, and adult center. Then we went home because my family was having another BBQ the next day at my parents' house for just my family and my fiancée's family. I had invited this wonderful woman that I met in Jamaica to drive up and see me in my Bergenfield apartment that Sunday late morning. She already knew that it would only be until mid-afternoon because I said I had to go to my parents for a family Memorial Day Weekend BBQ. I still did not tell her I was getting married the very next day. She drove home and I drove to my family Wedding Eve BBQ.

The next day was Memorial Day (Mon May 27, 1991) and we all started to arrive at the Ridgefield Regency down in Verona NJ. Our cocktail hour, wedding ceremony, and reception were all held there throughout the next 6 or 7 hours. It was a place that was Kosher enough for my fiancée's side of the family. We were all Jewish but they were a lot more Jewish than my side of the family. The ceremony had to wait for my dad's parents to get there from Queens. They were only 10 minutes late for the ceremony because of traffic and a Memorial Day parade there in Verona. They walked down the aisle together right after the two Rabbis and then my mom's parents. After that came the Bridesmaids, Maiden of Honor, Ushers, Best Man, Groom (me) with my parents, and then Bride with her parents. The hug and kiss from my mom and dad after they escorted me down the aisle and moved to the side was very emotional. All was good up to that point and the wedding was (as my friends have said later on) "A really fun party!" We all danced, laughed, and had a blast. This truly seemed like it was the beginning of a great life. This was until I came home from my honeymoon about two weeks later......
February 17

#49 (Day 49) Honest Open Willing 2012 Post
While away on my honeymoon, this woman that I met in Jamaica called my office to look for me. The person who answered the phone said I was away on my honeymoon with my wife. She was very understandably upset and sent a letter addressed to my then wife about her "Wonderful Husband" and what he has been doing up until the day before the

wedding. This was already the start of a strong realization that my marriage and new life was a bigger mistake than anticipated. It was not fair to anyone especially my wife. Plus it made me feel extra rotten how emotionally I had hurt both women including the one that I just met who was much more wonderful that I deserved anyway. My wife said she can forgive but it would take a very long time to forget. It almost felt even worse that on top of all this I would need to make things up and always seem to 'owe' my wife.

Things did not change and I continued to treat her bad mentally. Never did I want to go anywhere with her and I would go out by myself or with everyone else except her. This was my way to turn her away from me so she would be the one insisting to move out or want a divorce. She was way too nice and patient. Instead, she wanted to work things out and to wait until I changed into the nice man she thought I could and would become. No way was I going to be the bastard telling her to leave and that I wanted a divorce because I was too sick of myself.

On Tuesday, July 30, 1991 was the Z100's 8th Anniversary Party at the Palladium in NYC. I had convinced the public affairs department of Z100 to let me go as a VIP to take pictures, interview some local listener ticket winners, and write articles for the different North Jersey Newspapers. My best friend went with me to take notes and find some people who lived in different Bergen County towns so the different Newspapers would accept my articles with local residents being the focus. I did this the year before and it benefited the radio station, the newspapers, and definitely me more than anyone. My friend and I were allowed to be on a special balcony in the special VIP section above all the regular people. I did get another pair of tickets so another friend and my wife could attend with the regular people.

We were somehow special and all the other people in the VIP section and down on the main floor in the mob scene thought we were too. My ego was higher than just about ever before and I was so full of myself and my crap that I really started to believe my wife did not deserve me. Why should I feel like I am letting her down when maybe she is the one keeping me down? That feeling kept going while I continued to cheat and do whatever I wanted.

My DJ Flash career was going better than ever with an average of two parties a week and everyone telling me how great I was. It was Rosh

Hashanah night and I had to DJ a party because I could care less about this holiday that meant nothing to me and only meant something to those that had nothing better to do. At least I did agree to go to Temple in the morning for the first actual Day of Rosh Hashanah services. It meant a lot to her and to her family. After the party did I go home? No. My assistant and I went to Passaic to have fun and get some pot. He had been there before and told me where to go. Before I knew what happened next, we were not smoking pot but were smoking crack in a crack hotel with two crack 'ladies'. I had never ever smoked crack or did any hard drug before then. That was not the glamorous life but it felt good while I was smoking that plastic tasting crack and getting attention from the ladies who wanted to partake of that crack with me.

The next morning my stupid ass dragged itself back into my apartment as my wife was waiting for me to get ready for Temple. I just said that I had hung out with my assistant too long and had fun all night. I said to go to Temple with her family and went to sleep for a long time. That really hurt her feelings in many ways. It was probably about then that she started to doubt if I would change. Other nights I went out and did not come home until the next morning giving her no excuse. One night was another first for me of snorting two lines of cocaine with a hot woman that I had met while auditioning for DJ dancers. That was just another me me me time and there was no sex (this time) because although I was so wired and coked up, she just kept moving around and talking nonstop.

The final straw was when I went to my second work trade show in New Orleans and again got involved with another woman. This was a woman (or 22 year old girl) there at the show as an attendee with her college. She had been with the same guy for three years who was the one and only one that she was with. Thanks to alcohol, a great massage, and my evil persuasion, I was her second. She was very willing and the next day came by the booth to see me at the show.

However, my regret of still being a scumbag and corrupting another nice, innocent woman (being the second person she had ever slept with) in addition to knowing I was still being a scumbag to my wife is what made me finally come out and ask for a divorce shortly after I returned from New Orleans. She still wanted to work things out and was willing to wait as long as it took. That was when I told her a few vague, non-specific

'evil' things that I had been doing, and the number of women I had been having sex with. Never were any names given to her because I was already an asshole and should not hurt anyone else. That did the trick and she agreed we should both move out into different apartments by the end of the year. On January 1, 1992, I was already moved into my new apartment in Oradell NJ and she in her apartment elsewhere.
February 18

#50 (Day 50) Honest Open Willing 2012 Post
Before I moved out, there was one last thing that I needed to do. This was to apologize to the woman I met in Jamaica. It was never her fault to have met someone who was as big of a liar, cheater, and jerk like me. This had always been in my mind about how sorry I was for hurting her and that I hoped she was doing well and was happy now. I called her again the day after Christmas on December 26, 1991 which was a few days before I moved out into my own apartment. Of course, she was very skeptical about why I was contacting her again. I was really sincere when I told her I was sorry, was wrong, was confused, and never ever wanted to hurt her. It was just that I did not want to continue my life living a lie being married, was getting a divorce, and moving out.

She was told that I was planning on making a new start and really hoped all was good with her life. I admitted about not being mature and not handling things the right way but really had cared for her too much to know what was right to do then. In my opinion, she just needed to hear the truth from me for the first time......just like I needed to actually tell the truth for the first time in a long time.

I cannot express the extent of how wonderful I felt when she said that she understood why I did what I did. She actually asked if we should meet to talk and give things another shot but slowly and more cautiously. She said the same thing my wife had once said which was something like "I am willing to eventually forgive but do not think I can ever forget as easy." That was all I needed to know and wanted to give this love a try. This was like salvation and my wasted years turned into a new fresh beginning with a wonderful woman who I had already fallen in love with as an adult and really thought it would continue to be strong and real as an adult.

We have now been married over 18 years and I am so glad she gave me a second chance. My life would never had been the same if my wonderful,

tolerant, patient wife did not see in me what she sees in my today...the person I wanted to be. This was not because she or anyone insisted but because I wanted to be for her, for our two children, and myself. This life together since the start of 1992 marked a new beginning with several rough patches and sorrows. Things changed all for the positive over the years and up to today. She has been a huge part of our life together with more extreme joys than hardships. I feel like our happiness today is also filled with tons of hope and expectations for a long life and future together!
February 19

#51 (Day 51) Honest Open Willing 2012 Post
The New Year 1992 would begin with me out of my apartment in Bergenfield, my 7 year relationship (including 7 month marriage), and the burden of all my lies and guilt. Even New Year's Day began with me in a cooler apartment in Oradell, a wonderful new girlfriend, and yet another new life with better ways to think and act. I still had three and a half years remaining of my five years' probation and a divorce to plan and get through. But my full time job with my parents was working out well and I was still entertaining many different weddings and other events as DJ Flash.

Recently, I had gone to several bars and restaurants and tried my hand with Karaoke. Another entertainer who ran his own Karaoke business thought that I was great, funny, and needed someone to help him Karaoke M.C. at other restaurants, bars, and private parties when he was already booked himself. This all added up to great money and positive feelings. Both my self-esteem and my ego were getting major boosts from the attention and compliments. This was not going to my head (yet) because I had learned that the bottom falls out from under me when all seems good and I get cocky.

My relationship with my family was also a little less strained. I applied for my family to be contestants on the Family Feud. My mom, dad, brother, and second oldest sister went with me on Wednesday, February 19, 1992 to NYC when we were accepted to try out. This was a good bonding experience even though we were too argumentative, did not know a lot of answers, and were not as charismatic as they were seeking. At this stage, I was not doing anything bad or embarrassing to my family. All of us seemed happy, having good jobs, raising kids, and growing up.

The job at my dad's company literally and really took off into the sky. He was staying in the office a lot more often as I was the one flying all over the place for customer visits, expositions, and training sessions with sales groups. My dad trusted me to arrange my own flights, hotels, rental cars, schedules, and expenses. At 24, I was doing everything that a more responsible, older, business trained man would be doing. It was the company that I was representing even with companies we represented. Some of these companies were much bigger and more established than our company. A few were even from foreign places like Japan and England.

On Monday, April 27, 1992 was my Atlantic City bus trip from the Alexander's Parking Lot in Paramus to attend the Hazmat Expo '92 with dad. I thought it would be easier and save the company money by taking one of these 'senior citizen' bus exertions where they gave you food vouchers and rolls of quarters to gamble. You did not have to gamble that money or your own money but it was Atlantic City. My new girlfriend came down for a night to enjoy the hotel and that we can spend some time together. At one point, I was up $1900 at the Black Jack table before she arrived. When she and I went back to the Black Jack Table together is when I started to lose. She thought I should walk away (as the voice of reason) but I did not listen since I wanted an even $2000.

Slowly, the money profit was dwindling and we did go back to the room all the while blaming her negativity on my losing streak. I asked her to take the money now so I do not lose it when she went back to work the next day. She said just don't gamble it and had me hold it. All I had to do was keep it in my hotel drawer and I would still have over $1000 profit. My bus home was at 8 pm on Wednesday, April 29, 1992. I left with only $50 ahead. It seems like I was not able to control myself and stop gambling when I should have.
February 20

#52 (Day 52) Honest Open Willing 2012 Post
One of my very good friends was getting married in May 1992. His bachelor party was planned by me and some of the other ushers a few weeks earlier. Almost all of us there were drunk and kept going on and on for several minutes (thinking we were funny) saying things about a mutual female friend. When this got back to her there was no

forgiveness. I called a few weeks later after not hearing from her for a while. She told me how our stories made her life horrible and it was mine and all our faults. I was told to lose her number and never ever call her. Again, someone was hurt by things I did or said just like in the recent past. My friends told me it was not their or my fault and don't feel so bad. Things like this happen and it was not our intention of messing up someone's life. After all, we are just a bunch of guys having fun and were drunk.

This friend of mine got married and it was a beautiful ceremony and reception. There was a lot of alcohol and I had no choice but to drink my large share. It was my responsibility as his friend and as an usher to do so. I was such a good friend and such a great usher that when the reception was over and got back to the hotel that I did my large share of being sick. Being this drunk had me throwing up several times in what I thought was the bathroom. The next morning there was a lovely surprise. It was not the bathroom I was entering each time to throw up....it was the closet. My girlfriend's shoes were covered in this loveliness. We had a brunch that morning back at the house of my friend's relatives but did not have a great appetite. The story of that night before and my using the closet as a barf headquarters was really funny to everyone.

Our flight to London, England was later that night at 9 pm. My friend and his wife were having their second wedding over there with her family. Several of us were heading over to join in on the festivities of this second wedding. By then, I was a little less sick and made it through all of the airport lines and onto the plane. With much thanks, I was not sick during the really long flight. I could not image tossing my cookies in an airplane bathroom. Ewwwwww. We arrived into the UK and did all the touristy things like seeing Big Ben, Parliament, and visiting the London Hard Rock Café. The cost was lowered by being allowed to stay at a UK friend of my friend. The difference in culture was interesting to all us Yankees who were accustomed to all things American. Never did I think anyone in the world had less than 5 TV channels, still had a rotary phone (that took money) in their home, and had a bath without a shower curtain. Guess all this was really my own ignorance which showed because we also saw the Thames River and went to Madame Tussauds Wax Museum. I kept mispronouncing these and many other names over there. Thames is not pronounced Thames like James (with a T) but is pronounced Thames ('temz) like Gems (with a T). Also Tussauds is not pronounced Toss-odds but is pronounced Tussauds like the family themselves pronounce it ('tuːsoʊ). This really must have showed my ignorance especially with the locals.

Wednesday, May 27, 1992 would have been my one year wedding anniversary between my first wife and me. My girlfriend and I stayed at a very cute Bed & Breakfast country type establishment in Abington while hanging with a salesman from a UK company that my company back home represented. The next day I went with him to his company to learn their products better. Then he drove my girlfriend and me about an hour away to Oxford for a one night's stay at an expense, way-too-fancy hotel. That is about when I 'would have been' there one year in that town going to college working for my Master's Degree after the Ramapo College Oxford Honors Program.

On Friday, we took the bus from Oxford to Cheltenham which is where my friend's wife grew up and her mom was living. We stayed at another Bed & Breakfast where our hosts in London were staying for the wedding. We think they may have been swingers or maybe just very wild partiers and people. After my friends' 2nd wedding at a fancy castle like place, these two seemed like they wanted my girlfriend and I. Not wanting the two of us to necessarily do something in particular...just wanted us. He said to come on in their room and that if he doesn't get some sex soon he's gonna burst all in the same breath. The next day after the wedding was Sunday, May 31, 1992 when we flew out of London back to the USA.
February 21

#53 (Day 53) Honest Open Willing 2012 Post

My first wife and I went to the Bergen County courthouse in Hackensack the following month in June 1992. This was the same place where I had to go for my two juvenile problems and received both of my juvenile probations. This was also where my sentence to five years' probation was given to me about two years earlier. This visit was the quickest and least painful. Within an hour, my first wife and I were divorced. The conditions were that everything was already divided and agreed upon, that she could take back her maiden name, and that I would agree to get one more thing. This was to go with her (in the next month or two at the latest) and get a Jewish divorce called a Gett (pronounced

Get) so that she could 'get' married again at some point in the eyes of Judaism. On August 6, 1992 is when I met her in NYC at a special Rabbi's office to go through with this ceremony and have him prepare an official Jewish Gett. This was done and over with but she was rather unhappy that my current girlfriend had come with me and was waiting in the stairwell. Those two had never talked or seen each other in person. It was my girlfriend's birthday that exact day so we wanted to be together regardless.

My girlfriend and I had a big party at what was now 'our' place. There were a lot of people having a lot of fun with a lot of liquor. I do not remember doing it, but apparently started doing jumping jacks and my butt went through the apartment window. This was very entertaining to everyone except my girlfriend and later to me when I stopped throwing up on the bathroom rug. Shortly after the party is when I realized there was a problem. I did not think I had a drinking problem. All I had was a problem knowing when to stop for the night. Every time I would drink socially, would be until I passed out or puked. Most of my friends knew I had at least one or more types of problems. They started to always wonder what Steve would do today or tonight when there was alcohol?

Things started to (because I tried very hard to make sure they started to) calm down a bit before things got too out of hand (this soon). In August 1992 is when my girlfriend and I got our first cat Beow from a pet store in Paramus Park Mall instead of getting a ferret as originally planned. Now we had something cute, loving, alive, and was both of ours to love and share together. After all, we both agreed that we never ever would want to have kids. That was understood but we did like animals (better than children) and thought it would be good to start a family ... of cats. Even though we were not married (yet), animals can handle separation or divorce if that would ever happen even though we knew it would not. We really thought back then that our relationship was amazing, real, solid, and would last forever. We were right....it has!
February 22

#54 (Day 54) Honest Open Willing 2012 Post
Two friends had a big party on Saturday, October 3, 1992 in their apartment up in Suffern NY. A joint was pulled out of another friend's jacket to smoke and I thought "COOL!" However, one of their girlfriends saw this and immediately got their boyfriend. He said it would NOT be

cool to smoking pot at this party. I was still able to enjoy myself at this party with just alcohol even though I was getting used to always smoking marijuana especially at parties. Here I met some more of their other friends who were also fun, entertaining, and enjoyable to be around for more than one or two reasons.

On Sunday, November 1, 1992 my girlfriend and I flew down to Orlando Florida. That was the location for this year's NSC like the one last year in New Orleans where I had my last 'fling'. The exposition was that Monday to Wednesday. She got to meet her half-brother for the very first time in her life. It was not until recent that her father revealed about his first child from another woman to his kids. Thursday, November 5 until Sunday, November 8 was a Disney area vacation with all the touristy places to go and things to do. One night we went to Paradise Island. This is part of the Disney nightlife with many different children, family, and adult bars, dance clubs, and restaurants. I signed up to sing Karaoke with my favorite "The Lion Sleeps Tonight." Afterward I was told to report to the center stage at 7 pm. This was not a normal bar Karaoke singing. This was a contest on the main center stage in from of everyone!

There were a total of about 15 performers. Everything that I had learned and everything feeding my esteem and ego kicked in. I was funny, danced around, sang the song very well, and got the crowd going. This was not the same person as a few years ago or even the same person growing up awkward in school. They announced the third place winner....it was not me. They announced the second place winner....it was not me. Then they announced there was a tie for first place. The first place winner was one guy who sang 'My Girl' and the guy who sang 'The Lion Sleeps Tonight'! I performed in Disney in front of about 1000 people on center stage and won?!?! Wow! Then when we ran into people the next day or two at different theme parks I was recognized. They said I was great and asked if I really worked for Disney. Just what I did need in one way and what I did not really need in another way...more praise, compliments, and feeling like a big shot, celebrity, and greater than thou which I was NOT.

A few weeks later it was already December. Another friend was having a party at his parent's house while they were away. He had permission to have the party with his brothers so it was not like being a sneaky kid having a party at their parents' house while they were away. That was something I did a few times growing up when my parents went away. A couple of times I got caught having parties at my house and got into trouble and/or grounded. But this party was really cool and there was a really good friend of mine there....weed (pot, ganja, marijuana, shit Mary Jane, cannabis, and other wonderful nicknames). Several people were smoking and it was fine unlike the party I attended a few weeks back where pot was a no no. I got to smoke with my girlfriend, friends, his brother and even bought a little for home consumption. Yeah.... marijuana was now something that I got to keep and stock up on in my place. There were no parents and no one else that could catch me smoking pot there. It was safe to do, not a hard drug like heroin, kept me mellow, out of trouble, and caused a lot less problems like vomiting and destroying things. Everything was great, there were no worries, I was numbed when I wanted, and we even got our second cat Tigger from a Waldwick home. February 23

#55 (Day 55) Honest Open Willing 2012 Post

My brother was getting married so I drove down to Shrewsbury NJ with my girlfriend and ...wait....I drove down with my fiancée. Guess I should have mentioned that this wonderful woman I met down in Jamaica, who gave me and us a second chance, was now my fiancée. We knew that we wanted to get married and spend the rest of our lives together. She had been married once before and so had I. She told me not to get her an engagement ring but instead to save the money and that maybe we would get slightly fancier wedding bands. We usually had gone away every month or two using our Entertainment Card 50% off at participating hotels. There was a special Romantic Getaway Package which did not accept the Entertainment Card but was still a very beautiful sounding deal...at the Hasbrouck Heights Sheraton in Hasbrouck Heights NJ.

Everything was perfect with Champagne in the room, a fancy dinner in the restaurant at the top, and then in the morning I awoke first. She was not expecting me to put a diamond tennis bracelet on her wrist while she was still asleep. Lying back in the bed, while staring at her face, she awoke with a smile. She noticed the diamond tennis bracelet on her wrist and let out a surprise gasp just a few moments later. That was when I went down on the side of the bed on one knee and asked if she would official make me the happiest man alive and be my wife. Without hesitation she said "YES!" and a wedding in July of that year 2003 was planned. Now back to my brother's wedding......

So I drove down to The Shrewsbury Inn with my 'fiancée' where everyone else was staying the night before at a local hotel. This was Saturday, January 30, 1993 and the next day was going to indeed be a Super Sunday. His wedding that next day was Sunday, January 31, 1993....the day of the 1993 Super Bowl! My only real job as his Best Man was making a speech....and quickly plan and throw a last minute bachelor's party! He originally told me not to have one because he did not want one. His fiancée said he was just saying that. I felt like a schmuck for not assuming he was lying.

All the men went to a few strip clubs like he did for me when I got married the first time. It was not wild but was not lame. The next day he got married, I made my corny brother Best Man speech after 3 or 4 or 5 or 6 (or 7) glasses of Champagne, and had a great time dancing, laughing, and drinking some more. This event was not spoiled by me getting too drunk or making a fool of myself too much. See, I did have the will power and could control my over drinking for his special day.
February 24

#56 (Day 56) Honest Open Willing 2012 Post

Saturday, June 26, 1993 was the Ufruf at the Temple for my upcoming marriage. My fiancée was Protestant and not Jewish. My parents and everyone else still loved her and thought she and I would make a great husband and wife. Later that day was a men's' rafting trip / bachelor's party my brother had for me. It was not stripper or adult in theme. We did go rafting and then went back to one of my friend's house for food and drinks. They had me take a shot glass of beer every minute for 100 minutes. I believe I got to 70 something shots after 70 minutes before I passed out. That was when they put things on and around me to be funny as they took pictures. My brother told them to stop because it was going too far when they took out a chain saw! That was the very definition of bad judgment even without pulling the starting cord!

Jamaica is where we met, so Jamaica is where we went back to get married. Flying down on Thursday, July 1, 1993 again to Montego Bay but headed the other direction east to Ocho Rios for a few days and our wedding ceremony at Couples Resort. The next day (Friday, July 2, 1993) we went over to the resort's remote island across the water. This was the day and then the night before our wedding. We stayed on this remote island for way longer than expected and I had way too many Bay breezes than expected. Then we took the boat back where I ate way too many pre-dinner Hot Dogs than expected and finally went back to our room to be extremely sick for way longer than expected. But...I got better and we went off to our last dinner as just fiancé and fiancée. It was a romantic dinner and we got our picture taken together. We looked very good and I did not look sick or messed up but still do not quite remember anything that day from about 4 pm on. Thankfully, the Jamaican Medical marijuana helped me recover from the hangover. Marijuana from any country always helped me recover, get over, and feel better from anything.

That next morning, Saturday, July 3, 1993, we got married while being pleasantly relaxed, mellow, and stoned (hey it was Jamaica)! My 'wife' and I stayed there at Couples the next day July 4th (Independence Day) and went to Dunn's River Falls. Then on July 5th we traveled back west to Montego Bay for a one night stay at the lovely Holiday Inn Montego Bay. The following day we headed back south to our favorite place in all of Jamaica....Hedonism II in Negril! There we stayed for our honeymoon, partied, and got a lot of special attention when everyone found out that we had first met there about two years ago (because I had a big mouth...back then). We flew back home to our apartment in Oradell NJ USA on Sunday, July 11, 1993 together as husband and wife!

My parents (and her parents) really wanted to see us have another small USA ceremony although we were already officially married in Jamaica. My parents volunteered to let us have this second wedding in the backyard of their home in Hillsdale where I grew up. This was not just a second wedding, or a USA wedding, but was a Jewish wedding. Everything traditional was there including the Chuppah, breaking the glass, and of course a Rabbi. Near the end of the ritual was the drinking from the Kiddush cup filled with the same Manichevitz brand wine like when I first had Manichevitz wine in Temple at age 9. First my wife took a sip of the wine and then I had the wine...all of the wine (which the Rabbi remarked about and was funny).

This second ceremony and small reception brunch was actually very nice being with about 40 of our closest family and friends. A few relatives did not attend this 2nd wedding to my second wife because they thought we only had it to get presents and attention. This was NOT true and I wished those people had attended even without a card yet alone a

present or attention. Either way symbolically it was cool to be married in the eyes of Judaism, the United States of America, and Jamaica so...no problem mon!
February 25

#57 (Day 57) Honest Open Willing 2012 Post

Steve was again married and still being his alter ego (note the word 'ego') DJ Flash for about 6 to 10 parties each month. My reputation of being a very charismatic, entertaining, DJ/MC, with a lot of experience and tons of music was making me in high demands. People did not really need to see big ads in the North Jersey Newspapers. They were referred to me by their family and friends or were at a party with DJ Flash.

Slowly, I was traveling more and more across the USA for my dad's company selling portable and wall mounted gas monitors and sensors to the many different industrial markets. Most of the time, I was flying into different cities in different sales group's territory to train their sales people. Then those sales people would visit their respective customers, sell our products, and make a percentage of each sale for them and their company. In return, we made money less their percentage and the cost of goods. This was becoming more time consuming but was also starting to make both the company and myself more money. Padding my expense accounts from my trips gave me back a lot more money than I was spending on food, taxis, and other things.

It was difficult balancing DJ Flash and entertainment fun while being the young Mr. Sales Manager traveling as the big shot, partier, having fun across the country. They could not both keep going the direction that they were going for much longer. Even my dad said I needed to make a choice between my hobby / pastime and my career / future. For now, I was going to try my best and have everything since I was so cocky and full of myself being the center of the universe as a wonderful entertainer and also business protégé.

In 1987 and 1988, Z100 had let me win several sets of tickets to their 5th and 6th year anniversary ball celebrations in Roseland and then the Palladium. This was also because I would constantly call and plead for tickets. This way I was able to bring friends with me to these events to share (and impress them) in the fun and see the musicians and music groups performing each time. In 1990 and 1991, I had convinced Z100 that I was a free-lance reporter with the North Jersey Newspapers and wanted VIP passes for me and my photographer. Now I got to go to these events (respectively again at Roseland and then the Palladium) as a high-and-mighty VIP. Either I missed the next year or they had no 9th anniversary party?

The next Z100 anniversary Ball was held on Wednesday, July 28, 1993 in NYC's Madison Square Garden for their huge 10 year celebration. With two years of 'reporting' and writing newspaper articles with photos, I was allowed a special all access (almost) backstage VIP press pass for just myself. This included being allowed right in the stage photographer pit while almost all of the acts were performing. Usually they would send all of us 'photographers' there for half the time the acts were performing and had us come backstage in between. The excitement of seeing, nodding heads in the direction of, and taking close up pictures of Natalie Merchant (10,000 Maniacs), The Proclaimers (500 Miles), Duran Duran, and Bon Jovi was probably one of the coolest things I had ever done. Thank God my dad let me borrow his very fancy, expensive 35 mm camera with the big zoom lens or I would have been laughed out of the photographer clique that night.

Nothing else really horrible had happened in a very long time. At least there was nothing specifically that I did or was done to me in all of….1992 and 1993. In the beginning of 1994 is when my bipolar manic-depressive mood swings started to sway more erratically and more intensely in both directions. Maybe it was a conflict of Steve the DJ vs. Steve the Salesman? Maybe it was a conflict of Steve the Egomaniac vs. Steve with the Inferiority Complex? Maybe it was as I used to call it….a conflict of Steve with the Angel on one shoulder vs. Steve with the Devil on the other shoulder. Adding alcohol, an increasing amount of marijuana, and other mind altering drugs made things even worse. There was less and less of Dr. Jekyll and a lot more of Mr. Hyde after a while….a short while.
February 26

#58 (Day 58) Honest Open Willing 2012 Post
Some of my sales trips for work ended up being really cool. There were places that needed to have me visit where part of the time I can enjoy other things. Most of my visits involved getting to Newark Airport and

flying Continental Airlines (or another airline if I had to) to another city. There I would usually get a rental car and drive around until I dropped it back off at that airport or a different airport to then fly home. Occasionally there were sales trips more locally that I could drive to and from home in my company car. One memorable trip was training two different sales groups in the Rochester and Syracuse NY area. Thursday early afternoon was my last training session in Auburn NY. Instead of heading home and going to work Friday, I visited and stayed two nights with a close friend of mine who was attending Syracuse University. He was a few years younger and had been one of my DJ assistants for many, many parties while he lived at home. It was great being a 25 year old married guy hanging out at a "college house" with half a dozen "college roommates" in a "college town" with thousands of "college kids" all a handful or more years younger than me. My Peter Pan syndrome loved this!

There I saw (and was most impressed) with a secret "growing room" and got to meet a very hip entrepreneur who owned an iguana and sold different quantities of various qualities of my favorite herb. The most potent type got me so messed up that I walked out the room and fell unconscious on the side of my head onto the wooden floor in the hallway. It left a big, discolored bruise and got me the nickname "Face" for the next two days. This was the location and date of the one and only time that I tried the ....acid test. Yes, I took a sheet of acid and was told to continuously tell myself "I am in control...relax, I am in control...relax, I am in control...relax" for if not then I may just freak out. It was a lot more intense than tripping on hallucinogenic mushrooms but I held onto control while teaching another couple tripping how to juggle pool balls. By the end of the night they were really good!

Another tripper had gotten into a phone call fight with his girlfriend. He hung up the phone, ran out of the house, and drove off in his car. We were worried about him driving while on acid but luckily he came walking back in the door an hour or so later. Although he was unharmed, the next day it took one of his other roommates several hours driving with him to find where he had left his car. That one acid trip during that one business trip is something I really felt (or thought) stayed with me long term affecting my brain.

There were several times that I had been in New Orleans by myself and with others. This next time that I was down there is when I got so drunk that I broke a restaurant window from the outside while passing by with my bare hand. There must have been something that got me that angry but don't remember exactly what? I strongly denied that I broke the window when the owner (or manager) ran out to confront me even though there was blood on my hand. I just walked away. My arrogance and attitude with him and several other 'stupid', 'old', and 'idiotic' people was getting worse and getting me more and more in trouble.

Part of my problem was chronic back pain that I had for a while and was intensifying. After an X-ray, MRI, Bone Scan, and CAT scan they found nothing to determine my severe pain. They also found no problem with my cat (during the...umm... CAT scan). The doctor said for me to exercise and that it may go away if I lost weight. Until then I was prescribed Ambien to help me sleep at night without waking up every hour in agony. No one ever told me that I must not drink alcohol while taking Ambien and that it was an extremely bad combination doing both.
February 27

#59 (Day 59) Honest Open Willing 2012 Post
In August 1994 at a Pittsburgh PA hotel, was the first of what would eventually become several blackouts. The front desk had given me two vouchers for complimentary glasses of wine during their after work cocktail hours between 6 pm and 8 pm. Two other businessmen were not going to use their vouchers and volunteered then to me! This got me at least six glasses of free wine. Shortly afterward, I got some dinner and then went upstairs to my hotel room. There I called my wife, watched a little TV, and then took my nightly Ambien before passing out in bed.

The next morning I took the elevator back downstairs to the lobby to check out. Two women at the front desk where looking at me and each other while smiling and acting a little strange. Being slightly paranoid I asked what was going on with a smile of my own. They were surprised that I did not remember coming downstairs just after midnight wearing only my boxer shorts and just one sock.

At this point in my life is when I had decided to stop smoking (for the second time) and was wearing the Nicotine patch on my foot. Every time that I wore the patch on other parts of my body it would fall off. Now I was alternating putting it on each foot and each time in different spots so the same foot and same spot was not used again for about 8 days. I left that particular sock on my foot while sleeping so it stayed on overnight. Then I would take it off, shower, and put a new Nicotine patch on the other foot the next morning. This is why I was wearing just one sock in the middle of the night.

There I gave them a five dollar bill and asked for five singles to use the change machine that only took dollar bills. The quarters from the change machine were used to purchase some snacks at the vending machine and play a few games of Ms. Pac-Man before going back up to my room. This was kinda funny because I never ever did something exactly like this before. Maybe this was just a freaky one-time thing and it was sort of harmless. Thankfully I was wearing boxer shorts and not briefs (or less). However, this was not going to be a one-time thing and only this first time blackout was 'harmless'. Over the next three months there would be a few more blackouts with each one being more devastating than the one before.

My company (and my dad's) was growing bigger and bigger since I had joined in January 1991. The product line from a UK company that we acquired around the same time for all of North America may have also has a great deal to do with it than just me. You could not have told that to me back then because it was me who understood these products, me that traveled all around North America, me that trained all these sales groups, and it was me that was a humble part of the company. This UK based company was just coming out with a new line of advanced, wall mounted continuous gas monitors that could have up to 16 remote sensors connected and controlled. This was going to rapidly become a big money maker since it was a superior product at a competitive price with increasing demand in markets where the competition was limited. The best way to introduce this to all of our sales groups at once was a big combined sales training weekend here in the USA.

Four of our company's top level executives including my dad, myself, marketing manager and manager of technical services were flying out to Chicago the Friday before a WEF (Water Environmental Federation) Conference and Exposition that Monday. Those last two were going to stay out there in Chicago to work the company's booth at that trade show while my dad and I flew home to be in the office Monday morning. That Friday afternoon we would be met by four of this UK based company's top level executives including their sales director, sales manager, marketing director, and technical director. Our two companies rented out conference rooms for the weekend in one of the more affordable but decent hotels in downtown Chicago.

Chicago was deemed to be the most easily accessible cities to fly into from other USA and Canadian cities and with public transportation from the airport to downtown. All the sales groups needed to do was get to and from the hotel in Chicago. Their rooms and food would be provided from Friday, October 14, 1994 dinner until Sunday, October 16, 1994 lunch. Those expenses were also going to be split by the UK based company and our company.

There ended up being anywhere from one to four people representing each of the different sales groups from all across the country there. It was really cool to have everyone that I had been visiting all in one place for work (and play). The sales training was going extremely smooth, I felt very confident, and everything went even better than expected. All of the intense training was done by early evening Saturday. The next morning was just going to involve something like four different workgroup stations in separate corners of the bigger conference room. Each corner would involve an aspect of things we already went over where the sales people could go from one to another asking more questions to learn in greater detail.

That meant Saturday night was all about going out, drinking a lot, dancing, and being stupid as a large group. My guard was down and I let myself have a great time being the center of everything with all of 'my' salespeople. Everyone was continuously buying me drinks (of alcohol) and after a few hours had consumed way too much like I usually would do. February 28

#60 (Day 60) Honest Open Willing 2012 Post
Past experience told me to head back to the hotel while I could still stand and it was not the wee hours of the morning. Many of them were going to stay out even later than midnight and go to another night club. It was important to get through this entire weekend responsible and proud even though they were encouraging me to stay. Our hotel was a few blocks away so I walked back by myself and went up to my room feeling like a success. That Saturday night's wild partying ended. My suit, shoes, shirt, tie, and other clothes for the morning was all lay out. I

put on my shorts and left on the one dress sock with the Nicotine patch on that foot. I took my Ambien, went to bed, and closed my eyes. Then the hotel fire alarm sounded.

The marketing director from the UK based company told me what happened next. He was out of his hotel room which was just down the hall from my room. Yelling 'Fire Fire' as he pointed to the utility closet right next door is when I broke the fire extinguisher glass and took it inside that little room to put out the fire. When the fire department showed up a minute later they had to bring me down to the lobby and give me Oxygen. The smoke and the extinguishing agent had made me pass out.

There I sat on the second to last step on the bottom of the staircase leading up to the second floor ballrooms wearing only an Oxygen mask, my shorts, and the one dress sock with the Nicotine patch on that foot. My dad came up to me and in a low grumbling, angry voice said "WHAT......DID......YOU......DO!?! PLEASE......NOT AGAIN......NOT AGAIN! WHY? WHY? WHY!?!?" It was loud enough that many of the people there for the training weekend heard him. All I remember being told whimpering was "It's not what you think. I did not do it...this time." The fire department and hotel said that I had put out the fire but he was still very mad and in disbelief.

A pair of detectives came to my room a few minutes after we were allowed back upstairs to ask some questions. There was nothing claiming, showing, or proving that I had anything to do with starting that fire. There was no need to go down to the police station, be questioned any further, or was considered a suspect of this arson. By the morning, the event and the words from my dad and I had spread to everyone there for the training weekend. This included the UK based company who then had a good excuse to start selling direct to several of our best sales groups cutting us entirely out of that loop. They claimed only I (and their marketing director) was seen around the fire, there was something fishy, and that long term success could not be established with my dad's company due to his questionable heir. Still not sure what exactly happened or why this type of blackout happened again was enough to humble me at least half in size and confidence.

Life and work needed to continue and so did my training sales groups across the country. The only difference is that big money making, advanced, wall mounted gas detection systems were not added to my repertoire. Not even three weeks had gone by before I was up in the Pacific Northwest. There was a large sales group who had been working with us a long time that had offices in Portland, Seattle, and Spokane. I had always been going there about twice a year and flying from each of those cities to train and go on important customer sales calls with those branches. The first stop was Portland, Oregon on this particular itinerary. After two days, I was staying at a hotel near the Portland Airport so that I could take the very short flight up to Seattle the next morning to visit that office. That night it was Thursday, November 3, 1994. That night involved three glasses of Long Island Ice Tea, one Ambien, and the worst blackout up to and since then in my life.

The last thing I remembered was have drinks (and maybe some food) in the hotel bar. The next thing I remembered was having emergency vehicles all around me with lights flashing as emergency workers were pulling me out from behind the wheel of a crashed car with airbag inflated. In between was the hotel evicting me for trying to enter another room window where a couple was having sex. They nicely just got all my things together from the room and dropped me off at the airport terminal where my flight up to Seattle was the next morning. Instead of waiting, I went to rent a car and drive up to Seattle that night. Again...none of this in between do I remembered even vaguely. A car rental company actually rented me a car! Before I made it off of airport property, I smashed into and downed an airport light pole. There was no arrest or major problems because I was not considered DUI due to my size and having 'only' 3 drinks about 2 hours prior. God was watching me because I should have been dead, paralyzed, or at least in jail. American Express paid the $26,000 for the totaled car and my company paid the $1200 for the light pole. Never again did I travel and drink....while taking Ambien.
February 29

#61 (Day 61) Honest Open Willing 2012 Post
Getting past the public school 'torments', then the college 'downfalls', and then finally facing the 'realities' of who I was and who I was not led to eventual progress. There were always setbacks of large to enormous proportions each time that there seemed to be progress made. When each progress met each setback then everything was gloom and doom. As said earlier, the better things got as I got older meant the setbacks

were larger. Now I was feeling like hope was lost, I was sick of myself, and life had no meaning. This 26 year old felt like an adult failure and again was a little kid. Peter Pan Syndrome was always part of me (and still is).

Life with adults did not make me feel superior, confident, or even that I fit in anymore. This is when my social life started to involve hanging around younger people typically averaging between the ages of 18 to 22. All my other friends while growing up now had careers, started families, and matured beyond me. These younger people did not have these 'problems', were about as mature as me, smoked a lot of marijuana, and we did this a lot together. They even introduced me to people that would sell me large amounts of pot and later on mushrooms and Ecstasy to do with them. Now I was a 'big shot' again because I was so 'worldly and cool' with money to buy pot, food, and other things for me (and for them). It was easy without needing to try, grow, or progress. But at the same time there seemed to be no setbacks either. This would be the gradual way that 1995 began and kept going.

Fun times with my adult friends were getting less and less. The most fun was becoming times I was with my younger friends or the ones that I created and found for myself. All that really mattered was not feeling pain or feeling anything bad. If it was just me by myself then fine. If others were there having fun and without it affecting me (or getting in my way) then that was also fine. One example was that a large group of friends my age went down to New Orleans with me and my wife from Wednesday, February 15 until Monday, February 20, 1995 to party. This was about one week before Mardi Gras week started. It was still wild and packed even though we got out of Bourbon Street, the French Quarter, and New Orleans about 8 days before Fat Tuesday. Most of these people (once my closest of friends) were my age but now seemed like very old, boring, whiney, party poopers, and drags to be around. This trip was not as great as I had anticipated and was more of a bummer.

My older friends (the same age as me) were not as 'fun' as I wanted them to be. My newer friends (much younger than me) were not always around or as 'reliable' as I wanted them to be. When I was by myself and wanted to get high then there were no other choices at times but to go and get marijuana all alone. One time I was robbed at gun point in my car while in Spring Valley NY looking to buy marijuana. The man had gotten in the car, pulled out his gun, and took all of my money (that was not hidden in my sock). Even after he left the car my only thing to do or say was "Can I at least please have some pot?" Then he turned around and handed me a nice size joint which was not smoked. I...thanked him...and left?!?!

This location in Spring Valley NY was a very notorious location for drugs (and crime). Another time a younger friend was driving me and another younger friend there to score pot. Just as a drug dealer leaned into the car he looked to the side and said "5-0." This meant there was a police car behind us. We just started to pull away as the lights flashed on with the loud speaker telling us to pull over and not to move. The police asked why we were there. All we had quickly thought of (before they approached the car) was saying we got lost heading to River Vale and were asking for directions. He knew we were full of crap saying this is a known drug area and how could we have gotten lost there. There were no drugs in the car but there was a lot of money in my front shirt pocket. He told us how to get back to River Vale and to go there without stopping or coming back. If we did, then he would know why we were back and arrest us. Never ever again did I return to buy marijuana or any other type of drugs....at least from there.
March 1

#62 (Day 62) Honest Open Willing 2012 Post

Not getting caught that day for purchasing or being in the possession of marijuana was extremely lucky. Shortly afterward was the important date of Tuesday, May 23, 1995. Five years had passed and there was something that I was very glad about not happening during that time. At no point was I (caught and) arrested for anything. That day in court where I first received my sentence to five years' probation was now officially over! A lot of big time worries about messing up and going to jail were over. I still needed to be good, but this huge weight was lifted!

My social graces were fleeting more and more as everything bothered me. This was especially so when it was people who bothered me. One of my last times DJ'ing was for a party filled with Hispanic people in the middle part of 1995. It was buffet dinner time and the younger adult couple that hired me asked if I could continue playing music but just a little bit lower. An older woman yelled across the room loudly and sternly to turn the music off because we are eating! I arrogantly and very rudely said over the speaker system 'No Hable Espanol' a few times. There was a lot of instant hostility and threats by many including the older woman's nephews. I was extremely scared to death for my safety, my DJ equipment's' safety, my car's safety, and lastly....the safety for the person helping me with that party. Now my thinking regarding being a DJ to entertain people had changed. This is not at all what I needed in my life. Why do I have to take this crap and play music and do as people want at their parties? Very soon I stopped DJ'ing totally so I did not have to take orders from 'stupid' customers. Now I could concentrate on my 'real job' working at my dad's company to spend more time with my 'real friends' and my 'real life'.

Finally there was another really cool thing to happen (by excellent chance) that gave me amazing memories even up to today. This was the most exciting event that somehow I became part of although not invited or meant to attend. At the time, it made my decision to just focus on my career traveling across the USA training sales groups for my dad's company a great idea. The end was a little bit of a blur because .... I drank too much. Otherwise, I would have even more memories being among all the invite only Hollywood celebrities and other VIP at the movie premiere of "Waterworld" across from Mann's Chinese Theater in Los Angeles California on Thursday, July 26, 1995.

That week involved flights and short stays along California to train sales people on my company's products. My rental car at LAX was picked up (without being on Ambien and alcohol!) and I drove to a hotel close to Hollywood and Vine that was actually rather affordable. The entertainment card gave me 50% off the rack rate which made the one night stay only $150.00. There was not a lot of guests so I talked my way up to staying in a corner penthouse which would be good the next day when one salesman was coming up for his training. My skills at persuasion worked out well whenever I tried really hard at not being a rude, arrogant asshole.

Walking up and down the famous Hollywood strip was cool because I got to see all the touristy things that I had seen before but not 'while working'. The Hollywood Walk of Fame was interesting until I got to a crowd in front of Mann's Chinese Theater. It was blocked off on that side of the road a little before so I had to cross the street and see what the commotion was all about from there. The eagerly awaited, 'blockbuster' movie Waterworld was finally being premiered after a long time of delay, much secrecy, and the largest budget for a movie of that time. Some of the celebrities for the Red Carpet were seen through the crowd until all of them entered and the thrill was gone. Then I got some ice cream and went back up to my hotel balcony.

About two or three hours later there was much noise, clapping, and screaming from the street below. When I went out on the balcony, I saw crowds of people lining the sidewalk as people seeing the movie were leaving. They were going down the one block on my side of the hotel to a large lot across the street. It was a post premiere party! Seeing all the celebrities walking past it was brought to my attention (and by looking down) that it was Joey Lawrence. Some girls were going 'Joey!' and some reporter was asking about his band. Even though I was not drinking (yet) I had a loud boisterous voice and yelled "Joey...Hey Joey...Whoaaaaa....you are soooo talented....whoaaaaa." Somehow the crowd did hear me and laughed...except maybe Joey Lawrence. Then I decided to go down to the street and investigate and maybe get into some more trouble?
March 2

#63 (Day 63) Honest Open Willing 2012 Post

There have been a few really "amazing', 'cool', 'unbelievably lucky' things and events that I have posted about 'happening' or 'attending'. These few things have been thought to be the only high points in my personal 'feel good', 'egotistical', 'big shotism', 'selfish' life until recently when I realized there were many others. All of these 'bragging' things were obtained by deception, manipulation, and felt then the way I expressed them here now. This could have been to make up for my negative thoughts about the world, myself, and others at that time. Even my yelling down at Joey Lawrence from my hotel room to be funny and get laughs at his expense was not really appropriate because he is a human being and has feelings too. He could have been having a bad or difficult time in his life at that moment and it did not help having some schmuck yelling insulting words from above.

Now I mention this last "amazing', 'cool', 'unbelievably lucky' thing that I happened to attend before my life seemed to go back downhill with nothing else being able to ever compare to this experience. Again, this (like the others) was able to take place due to 'defects' and 'immoral' issues that I felt were with me a lot more back then......plus I was always so messed up with alcohol or other things. I can honestly say that after this occasion my life 'seemed' to only be filled with crap and that is one 'excuse' my life went to 'pot' more and more and more. Today, I attend fun things that make me feel good inside for the right reasons without drugs or alcohol and not at the expense of others. Those things may not 'seem' as far out and wild as others things that I have done but they are real and more precious. Therefore......

There I stood on the street right outside my hotel looking over at where all the Red Carpet people went after the Mann's Chinese Theater movie premiere. The car I had rented at LAX was parked there in the hotel garage across the street. It got me past the initial security checkpoint by saying my car is in there and that I am staying at the hotel. The third level of the parking garage overlooked the entire lot where this official, huge, Hollywood premiere party for Waterworld was being held. It was elaborate, crowded, and strictly NOT for the 'normal people and fans'. There were a lot of decorations like the boats, weapons, and other props from the movie. There also on the top level of the parking garage was a photographer taking pictures of the whole landscape from that perspective. He was talking to me and asked if he could have one of my cigarettes. Yes...I was smoking again after only a few months because I figured it was the combination of the Nicotine patch, Ambien, and maybe the alcohol (a little bit) that was getting me into really bad trouble last year. Therefore, with the Nicotine patch and Ambien out of the equation, there should now be a lot less negative situations occurring.

Then the photographer asked me why I was not in there. I replied "My agent lost my invite." Maybe it was the cigarette, maybe it was his mood, or maybe he thought I was a cute kid because of what he offered me next. He had already been taking photographs on behalf of the movie studio from the beginning with the Red Carpet up until the first hour of the party. Now he was done and ready to go back to his home. He looked at me and said....that I could have his very special studio VIP Press Pass to actually get inside the party. There were only a handful of specially authorized press people allowed inside. This was because they really wanted to make this a very private event just for the cast, the movie crew, the movie studio, and pretty much any other A-List (and a few B-List) celebrity, entertainer, or model that was in L.A. at the time.

Quickly I went back up to my room to shower, try to look as good as possible (it took effort), got on my suit, and went across the street showing my pass and getting inside the lot and entered the main party scene.

I was NOT famous, NOT part of the movie or production crew, and NOT part of the press but no one knew or cared...especially me. The rest of the night and who I met and did was not as important as the fact where I was, how I got there, and how great and lucky am I! There was a woman from a few Baywatch episodes that came up to me while at the bar starting off with my first of probably 12 Bay (or Sea) Breezes. She was alone and wanted to know if we can go around meeting the celebrities together. She was not just alone but she was hot and I knew her with me could mean a lot more rubbing elbows with stars. We did go around and she was recognized by several. I took her picture with many celebrities and got to talk and B.S. with many of them. At the end of the night, she was almost as drunk as me and before I got her number she went to find her friends outside the party perimeter. She never got back so I never got her number or contact information. That really was to get copies of the pictures I took of her and the stars to show everyone, gloat about, and keep as memories forever. I do talk about the stars I saw, did used to gloat about it more than I should humbly have, and still do have a lot of the memories that I remember more vividly than you would think I would.

My attitude was again very Bipolar Manic (which I was not officially diagnosed with until a few years later along with OCD and ADHD). Back them I just thought I was either hot stuff on the top of the heap or a piece of crap buried underneath the heap...it depended on the day and hour. One moment I was funny and pleasant to be around and the next minute filled with attitude, hate, arrogance, and many other negative not-so-nice attributes. This was getting me really disliked, messed up, and more into my own self. This type of self-destructive behavior was getting progressively worse in all aspects of my life but especially at work.
March 3

#64 (Day 64) Honest Open Willing 2012 Post
I treated the other workers at my dad's company badly by calling one an 'asshole' from another office. This he heard and got understandably all

pissed off saying he did not need this and was going to quit. My dad calmed him down by saying how I really did not mean it and was just mad in general. This guy was one of the people there that initially (and continually) did not take kindly to have been working there many years only to have their boss' mental 'kid' come in to take over.

Our bookkeeper was usually very talkative with a unique personality. She was the sort of person that repeated herself over and over saying the same type of things again and again. It was wrong but I thought of her as a parrot and a pain that irritated me constantly even though this trait was something she probably did not realize. The other things was that I was very critical of everyone and wanted to be left alone unless I needed something or to say something myself. Most people were usually patient and very nice to her because she was nice and meant well. It was easy for me to make fun of her behind and in front of her back. Eventually, both of them were driven away from the company and quit probably due to the long term sickness called me.

By the mid-1990's, drinking large amounts of liquor stopped being fun and was more of a requirement so life was less intense and being numb was preferred. Twenty years of drinking no longer made me silly, funny, and outgoing. Now it made me more manic than usual greatly intensifying my mood. This meant occasionally I was funny but mostly irritable, cranky, rude, and acted very uncaring about everyone else. The world and all the people in it were stupid, out to get me, and that they were the assholes now instead of me. The only way that I could deal with myself was by blaming everything on anyone I could.

There were many times that I embarrassed my wife (and others) making them ashamed and worried about what I would do next. They felt like being with me in public was like walking on egg shells especially my wife who I loved but just could not stop myself. One wrong word from her or others and I cracked!

My wife had several friends and family members that I was very rude to, yelled at, and treated like crap. When I was and wasn't drunk it still was horrible. Then I tried to stop or control my drinking (and mood swings). The only problem I had was to know when to stop drinking once I started for the night (or day). Self-medication by smoking more and more marijuana (from my new connections and pot dealer) made me better than when I drank alcohol. My mood was much mellower and I felt more relaxed. People seemed to like being around me again and I was nice and numb without the 'negative' aspects of drinking.

But when I smoked a lot of pot where there was alcohol, I would still drink while stoned. Then it was more of a mellower agitation and anger that I felt and projected with this combination. No matter what I did, where I was, or who I was with...I was miserable. Then I realized these problems where not just from alcohol and that there were many other problems. The solution was to smoke marijuana almost all of the time that I possibly could. This even meant bringing it to places so I could smoke up in the car before engaging in family and other events. Then I was 'less stressed' and 'more polite'....for a short while. Breath mints, Visine, and cologne became a regular thing to carry around as well.
March 4

#65 (Day 65) Honest Open Willing 2012 Post
A change of scenery was required because our landlord at our Oradell New Jersey location needed to use the top floor. This was where my wife, our three cats and I were living since my first wife and I separated as of January 1, 1992. On Monday, September 25, 1995 we were officially moved into our new Chestnut Ridge New York apartment which was part of a large historical log type house from over two hundred years ago. Things were the same but now in New York State and for the first time not living in New Jersey or even Bergen County New Jersey. We were about 100 feet from the Welcome to New Jersey sign so I felt a little sad to see New Jersey from the front porch but to be living in a 'faraway' different state.

The day we were allowed to move in there was a horrible accident on the main road. A car full of drunken kids skidded out of control by going too fast around the curve in the road. The car flipped over and hit a tree on the front side by the hood. Their vehicle was destroyed, the windows were all smashed, and all of the kids were badly hurt and cut up. One of the kids had been projected out of the passenger side window onto the street when the car stopped. The police arrived and so did the paramedics who asked him if he was alright. He looked awful and was still drunk. Badly slurring his words he said that he felt nothing at all and could not move. I do not know if he died or was paralyzed but I know the driver was arrested for Driving Under the Influence (DUI). This was a horrible thing to happen 'to me' on the first day at a new place. Maybe I should have seen this as a sign?

I was extremely unhappy (like always) but smoked a lot of pot and hung around younger, funnier people whenever I could. This really seemed to keep me from going nuts or hurting myself. When the pot and alcohol was not enough there was still mushrooms, nitrous oxide, Ecstasy, and sometimes other pills. This helped short term but it took more and more and more outside drugs, excitement, and attention to get me at least content. At the same time, my mind was changing and trying to adapt and deal with all these 'additives'. Long term, my entire mind was indeed changing but to a degree it could not change back without a lot of help. That help was still over twelve years away. Until then, the destruction being done was easy and continuous which made the eventual rebuilding of emotions, mental problems, and spirituality yet to come very hard!

Towards the end of the year (Sunday, November 5 to Thursday, November 9) involved another National Safety Council (NSC) Exposition and Conference in Dallas TX. No offense, it was not as exciting as previous years. Luckily I brought pot with me to smoke in my room like I had been doing, and continued to do, on all of my flights and trips across the country. My wife was with me and so were my parents (but they were in another room on another floor and do not know what pot smells like anyway...I think).

My wife and I took the short flight from Dallas down to Cancun after the exposition was over. She had been there before but it was my first time in Cancun. My fear was trying to find pot down there...so I brought the rest of the pot that I had left over from Dallas. Everything was made sure to be rationed so there would be enough for this part of the trip. I figured they would not check you coming into Mexico as they would when you came back out of Mexico.

There was a lot of wild partying, scantily dressed people, and alcohol galore. My comedic personality and skills at karaoke made me feel like I was part of the party scene. It was cool until we went to Senior Frogs to dance, sing a Karaoke song on stage, and have a 'few' frozen Margaritas. These 'few' drinks were in plastic 16 inch tall containers that were funnel looking on top with a long neck and Erlenmeyer Flask type base. Tequila was one of the few types of liquor that I really did not consume often or in such large amounts plus these were strong drinks. That night when we finally got back to the room, I was so drunk and felt like death.

Our room was spinning in all directions and it got me trapped in the bathroom most of the night. My body was extremely weak and nauseous until the next evening. Then we went out and partied some more but a 'little less' alcohol was consumed that night. Our flight back home was the following day (Sunday) and being sick anywhere sucks yet alone on an airplane!
March 5

#66 (Day 66) Honest Open Willing 2012 Post
A few co-workers at my dad's company were not too fond of me. There were also a few who did say they thought I was cool and liked me. One of these female co-workers paid a lot of attention and compliments to me and laughed at my jokes....all of them. She was treated special by me in return for treating me special. That was always my weakness and a problem to be attracted to people that liked me. I did not always find those people desirable to kiss or have sex but desirable to be around to feed my ego and self-esteem. This was more of an emotional and sometimes even spiritual (which was not real) desire. My sympathy and heart would go out to those people that had problems.

One of my personality defects was that it was me (and me alone) that could help those people. After all, if I cannot help myself then I might as well help other people. The bond that usually occurs is still not at all physical but definitely does take me out of myself and my life. It also has taken a part of me away from my wife who I greatly love....then, now, and always. The deceit and dishonesty made this a form of cheating which still hurts me inside because it hurt her in a way like when we met and I did not tell her I was marrying another woman a few weeks later. That was something I swore I would never do to her even if it were not romantic or sexual.

This female co-worker did have some problems with money, being a single mom with a teenage daughter, and having an on and off boyfriend that was physically and emotionally abusive to her and her daughter. The last report was that he was out of her life for good and she was trying to get her life together. Besides talking in the office we also talked over the phone. Twice we hung out at her place but just talked even though one time we smoked pot. That was when she asked for a little bit because she could not afford or find any for herself.

One night over the 1995 Thanksgiving weekend, I was with a friend and called her on his early version of a cell phone. I just wanted to see how she was doing and maybe smoke some pot with us if her daughter was out for the night. Her ex-boyfriend then grabbed the phone away from her and started to yell at me 'Who is this and why are you calling my fiancée this late at night?' My shocked and surprised response was 'Fiancée, I though you two broke up for good?' His response back was 'Yeah, she is carrying our baby!' Then I heard yelling and noise over the phone as it hung up. We were only a few minutes away so I drove my car over there concerned to make sure that she was all right.

The lights were on in her top floor apartment that she rented from the people below in the house. There was fast back and forth movement and yelling that could be heard all the way outside by the curb with our car windows down. Again I called and again he took the phone. All I said was something like look I am sorry and did not know. Please just don't blame or hurt her. We are right outside and want to make sure everything is good and that she is safe.

There was a large bang as I assume his phone made hit the ground. My friend exclaimed that he just ran outside the house and was running up the little hill towards us. He crossed in front of my car, put his hands on the hood, and starred right at me for a few seconds. I was scared to death as he headed over to my driver side window to grab me. Hitting the 'pedal to the metal' I drove away seeing him fall backward into the street on his ass, get up, and then yell at me on his feet.
March 6

#67 (Day 67) Honest Open Willing 2012 Post
Later the next day I was hoping he had left. A third time I called her just to ask 'WTF' and a third time he grabbed the phone from her. More calmly and sternly he told me that I ran him over, he was at the hospital most of the night, and was going to take me to court. A trip to the police station was required for my friend and me to make our statements. She did not show up for work Monday morning and her mom or dad called to say it was not a pleasant work environment for her any longer.

A few weeks later a man arrived to the office to hand me a summons. The boyfriend (fiancé) was taking me to court for 'hitting him with my car and leaving the scene of the crime'. It was requested by my friend that he not get involved which I understood and honored. The year 1995 had ended and luckily so did my five year probation earlier that year from the Bergen County Court. The year 1996 had begun and not-so-luckily was the date set shortly after to appear in front of the River Vale Municipal Court.

Tuesday, January 2, 1996 was the first day in the River Vale NJ court house. That was the preliminary meeting to set the date of Tuesday, March 5, 1996 for the judge to hear both our sides and make a decision. My parents had obtained a lawyer for me from the law firm that our company uses. They thought her boyfriend might try to sue the company since it was a company car and she had worked for us.

On the court date it was just her, her dad, and him representing himself. He presented his case but had no medical records, no pictures, and no proof. He did have one picture of skid marks on the street in front of her place. It really seemed like a joke and the judge was asking him questions when he yelled at the judge. My lawyer told me not to say anything but to wait for the judge's verdict. I guess he knew that the boyfriend incriminated and hung himself before the court. I got off without any fines, penalties, or jail time even though I really did not hit him at all.
March 7

#68 (Day 68) Honest Open Willing 2012 Post

This post and point in my life (1997) has been one of the hardest to come up with in words. It still really confuses me exactly why this year, and then each consecutive year, began my reeling more and more down a spiral whirlpool (or toilet). My life went deeper into a place that was scarier than anywhere I had been. This may sound overdramatic but it is a place that maybe I should not have gone back to alone. This was in my own head with all the crap of the last 28+ years. The mixture of all of the prescribed drugs, illegal drugs, alcohol, and now full time marijuana habit made my brain a different place than even 10 years ago. I needed to maintain myself on daily marijuana just to be content, sane, and feel normal.

Little by little that changed and the tolerance of the drug clashed. My mind would adjust (and change in many ways) shortly afterward whenever the THC potency (and price) of the pot increased. My reason for getting into these below, rehashed divided times is that it shows who I was, where I was, what I did, and how I felt at each of these crossroads. Those always affected which path I took at the fork in the road.

From birth in 1968, there were not really any 'ups' in my life as far as I was concerned. The awkwardness, reacting to things wrong, impulsivity, parents not knowing what to do with me, being bullied, not fitting in, and wanting or trying to kill myself were pretty much over by 1987. Everything until then was not intended to be bad but was still 'my fault' (to me). The next 10 years were filled with many ups which made many of those earlier traits and feelings change. This started around May 1987 when I was accepted to college, declassified Emotionally Disturbed, and graduated from high school. My parents had really worried that I may be in jail or not be alive yet alone where I seemed to be right then in my life. Dad hugged me and said how proud he was of me right after graduation. He was normally not a big hugger or expressed himself like that. It really made me feel like it was the end of the old and the beginning of the new. Therefore, that June graduation day was the start of the ups which still had a lot of downs (that were really down). Not everything on the downs list was 'my fault' or in fact had anything at all to do with me or what I did. Stage 1 from 1968 to 1987 was over and stage 2 had begun.

The high from June 1987 until my February 1989 downfall with the college and court trouble was a good run. Cockiness and allowing myself to put my guard down almost entirely bit me in the butt big time. Paying my dues and pulling me out of that hole was a good effort to help myself for the first time. Doing the right things and getting probation for 5 years was a relief that made me think now I had to move on. That got me to believe my girlfriend was the future because she was the past and the present. False reality had me ask her to marry me for the wrong reasons. By the time I realized it was not for the right reasons it was already August 1990 and too late to change anything (as far as I was concerned). I was determined (because I felt there was no other choice) to make the best out of this future. That soon caused resentment, anger, frustration, and many other feelings which were actually inward towards me.

That short period had me doing anything I could to escape and not face reality. When I did finally face reality, it hit me hard in the face (again) and I knew what had to be done. Being semi-honest and semi-real, I did not want this to go on anymore. It was not fair to me and especially not fair to drag my first wife into my increasing hell. This was not only a good effort to help myself for the second time but to actually help someone else for the first time. Then I felt my life was going to get a lot better with the skies opening up to make me truly happy and free (from myself) starting January 1992. Stage 2 from 1987 to 1992 was over and stage 3 had begun.
March 8

#69 (Day 69) Honest Open Willing 2012 Post

Things again seemed to pick up with all ups again. Now I was not doing many illegal things that were directly hurting anyone (except indirectly me and others). Finally this movement up seemed to be going in that direction from the time I moved out into a new place, with a new woman, and my new outlook on life. There were some problems and troubles but not like the ones affecting me pre-1987. These were mature pre-1992 troubles with little done by me but were done to me. Now I was the peacekeeper, innocent person, or one to comfort others. I no longer looked at myself and what needed to change. I looked at the world and decided what needed to change. Then by the time it was around 1997, all the real family, personal, and work problems were fading away. In their place were unreal things and thoughts working out in hidden places of my head to attack in sneaky ways. I do not know exactly why or how things changed and continued to change with me the way they did...but they did. Stage 3 from 1992 to 1997 was over and stage 4 had begun.

My normal way to be was rude, impatient, intolerant, paranoid, lazy, uncaring, anti-social, and to isolate. When I tried to get more out into the world then there were more times of getting into trouble by also being over flirty, drunk, dangerous, vindictive, lying, and intrusive into others' lives. I hated the world, I hated the government, I hated the law, I hated my neighbors, I hated my friends, and I hated my family. Each year I stopped trying to get more out into the world because it kept turning more and more against me. Each year I got more into myself and 'just' my normal way. After a while that was all I had......myself. Because I hated what I let the world and myself do to my life there was one thing I hated more than anything and everything

combined.....myself. Stage 4 started its horrible momentum in 1997 until it hit a brick wall in 2008 where it then had only two destinations left to possibly go. One of these was a decision changed a moment or two away from the absolute final destination......death. Going the only other destination is why I am still alive, life keeps getting better, and there is no dark future in sight. Please let me keep going from the beginning of 1997 until 2008 where I did continue from there with stage 5.
March 9

#70 (Day 70) Honest Open Willing 2012 Post

My trips across the country visiting and training different sales groups in their different 'territories' for work continued. It was important to do this because teaching them how to sell our products with me there, meant they could effectively sell our products themselves after I left. This made our company money which allowed enough of a budget for all these necessary travel expenses to continue every other week or so. Everything was entrusted to me for planning my trips and all the details since I was now responsible and all I had to do was stay within budget each month. This gave me a lot of leeway when planned correctly.

This also allowed me to go anywhere I wanted to regardless if it was a place that I had to go or a place where anyone even wanted to see me. Some sales groups were doing well without any further visits and did not even ask me to go out there. However, there were a lot of places with cities, things, or people that I just wanted to see regardless if needed or wanted there. I just had to tell the sales groups in those places that I was out there anyway for a different reason so I might as well visit. They tolerated that excuse and would arrange training sessions or sales calls to important end user customers. This gave me an excellent purpose to get away from the office and have fun elsewhere.

Beefing up my expensive accounts for reimbursement checks each time I returned was another bonus. Not all monetary records required an actual receipt. There was always a decent amount of extra money (profit) so I can buy marijuana. That marijuana was used not just at home but also brought to friends' houses to smoke so it would make things more fun and make me popular as the well-off older guy that had and shared his pot. This marijuana was also brought to relative's houses, events, parties, and everywhere else regardless if allowed or not. Smoking up in the car before, during, and afterward was needed to have a good or decent time doing anything.

Bringing marijuana with me on all my trips in the car and......on all my airplane flights were a requirement to get by, be effective, and have fun. It was a little dangerous, yet very exciting, to do this and it 'had' to be with me. Even after 300 flights, I knew no one would ever think to look inside my toiletry bag at the little, white vial crammed with lovely smelling potent pot. No one ever did look inside and this container was normally used for different reagents or chemicals and thus odor proof. Drug sniffing dogs could not even smell the hydro quality marijuana in there. This was good because I occasionally needed to travel into Canada and the UK as well. Those K-9s were extremely sensitive but always passed right by me. One time coming back from Jamaica there was a unique experience my wife and I got to see.

There was a large Jamaican looking woman behind me on the airport customs line wearing a very tropical looking hat and outfit. Her hands were both occupied each carrying a suitcase. All of a sudden, one of those K-9s was heading right to her like it was on a missing or was a heat seeking missile. Right up to her with top speed, and full force, went his nose between her legs into her groin. The police escorted her away to another room because we think she was hiding drugs in her...ya-ya. The scene was quite hilarious and surreal. It seemed like everyone had stopped moving and talking while happening and that the sound of impact was 'HONK!!!!' Since then I have called those specialist K-9s....crotch sniffing dogs. I still brought marijuana all over and out of the USA but never into the USA. There was also no reason to bring marijuana into Jamaica since it was always waiting for me there cheaply.
March 10

#71 (Day 71) Honest Open Willing 2012 Post
Sadly, Sunday, March 30, 1997 to Saturday, April 5, 1997 was the last time my wife and I vacationed in Jamaica. We had met there at Hedonism II in Negril back in 1991 as individuals not knowing each other. Together we went back as a couple in 1992 and got married there in 1993. Then we went back once a year in 1994, 1995, 1996, and now 1997. Every year for seven years this was our annual Hedonistic trip to Jamaica and at least a few nights stay at Hedonism II. We bought our house later that year in November 1997. There was no more money or time to ever go 'back to Jamaica' again. That was fine in many ways since I had the best marijuana at home in NJ and knew where to karaoke, party, and get enough attention from many other men and women nearby

and across the country. They all thought I was cool and loved to hang out with me until they got to know the 'real' me.

In late June, one of my 'necessary' sales visits brought me down to Birmingham Alabama. There was a woman that I had met in Dallas Texas earlier that year at a trade show / exposition. She worked professionally for the University of Alabama Birmingham (UAB) and was there with a bunch of other college faculty members. We all drank, danced, sang, and laughed the last two nights of the exposition in Dallas. Her department needed to get a type of gas monitoring unit we sold and probably would have just bought it anyway. The 'important reason' for going down there was to spend 15 minutes showing my demo unit to her boss before they issued a purchase order. The next two nights were spent drinking, dancing, singing, and laughing again with 'my audience'.

When we went to her house for a BBQ there was no pot or any other drugs except just alcohol. While in her bathroom, I found an unopened bottle of Robitussin DM. This was in the bathroom closet which accidently must have been opened and fell out. Someone once told me that the D part of the DM in that particular Robitussin was the same D part in LSD. Supposedly drinking an entire bottle would give you a slight high (or trip) different from alcohol or downing any other type of cough medicine. I chugged the whole bottle quickly and got rid of the evidence. Maybe it was psychosomatic but I felt a little groovier than just drunk although not so much high or tripping. My thoughts afterward were hoping she or her kids did not need that particular medicine anytime soon.

We moved into our first (and current) house in the middle of November 1997. My 10 year high school reunion was a few days later in East Rutherford. It was my intention to go back and see all these people that made me feel like an inferior reject and outsider. Then again, feeling like an inferior reject and outsider was 95% in my head but it was easier to blame all this and my other insecurities on my classmates. Now I would attend to show them all how great things were with me and in my life. Here I was happily married to a beautiful wife, living in a beautiful house, and with no pesky kids to keep us tied down. Here I was having a successful job that allowed me to travel the USA, Canada, and even the UK a few times. Yes, here I was no longer a reject and was now their superior!

Of course, no one at the reunion really thought I was ever inferior, a reject, an outsider, or very negative of me back in high school (as far as I know). However....me acting like an asshole there at the reunion did give a negative view of me now regardless how they thought of me ten years earlier. Smug and trying to be extremely outgoing got worse with each glass of wine that I drank. The low point of the night was being rude and insulting one of the women who I thought was hot in high school while at my drunkest moment. 'You think you were so hot back then didn't you?' is probably one of the stupidest things I could have said. In fact, this person was always down to earth and nice to me. Now she was dealing with a dick head who she maybe once thought was a nice guy back then. Leaving drunk and bitter, I quickly took a big class picture and a class banner in the hallway as a souvenir of the event to show how...I won?
March 11

#72 (Day 72) Honest Open Willing 2012 Post

There was a convenience store that I used to frequent quite often. Munchies were pretty much under control but sometimes I just needed a healthy-ish sandwich, healthy-ish snack, and/or French Vanilla Cappuccino which was the only type of coffee I started to like. Never was I a coffee drinker until I once tried the fancy cappuccino and coffee self-serve machines with the button and cool sound dispensing the stuff. At one point I would have 3 to 5 of these large caffeinated drinks each day to stay awake from all the marijuana.

There were two girls there that clicked with me and we would laugh a lot together. One day I said they should come over to smoke pot with me and some friends. They eventual did. One of the two girls told me something while extremely stoned about her dad. He was a professional orchestral musician in a philharmonic ensemble somewhere in the USA. She said he used to allow his senior orchestral members to go into her room when she was in her early teens to do inappropriate things with the door shut. This she claimed was to get him more into favor with the philharmonic group. It sounded like a sick way of pimping your daughter to get in better at work. Now in her early 20's, she was a little messed up because of this and other things that had happened to her growing up. There was also concern from her that her younger sister might now have taken her place!

'Righteous Steve' (me) had to then find out the e-mail addresses of many fellow musicians in his group. I wrote an e-mail to them about a father allowing fellow musicians to molester his daughter. The content was exactly as she told me what happened. I did not elaborate, name any other names, nor add anything else.

Then a day or two later, I called this orchestral company and apologized for the manner of me sending these e-mails and explained why they were sent. The woman on the other end of the phone freaked out much more than I had expected. They contacted the local police who then asked me to come in and explain why this occurred. If I did not cooperate then they said they would take my computer (at work where the e-mails were sent) to investigate the hard drive themselves. Because this was done at my workplace, my company would get into trouble.

Everything was explained to the police detectives (down at the station) about how she told me all this that happened, we were friends, I empathized with her, and just wanted this to stop. The next day they said that I am no longer in trouble because they strongly believed I was somehow tricked or conned into doing this by her. That really flabbergasted me as I never thought this was a sneaky way for her to get her dad into hot water. Although our friendship ended, I later found out she was kicked out of his house. The father was not fired from the orchestra but was told he would never get promoted to a high class or rank within the philharmonic because of this unsolved but closed 'scandal'......

Now this girl and also her friends no longer hung out with me to feed my ego and self- esteem. My other younger friends had grown up or were no longer interested in hanging out with a 29 year old pot head that was not only becoming more and more manic but also compulsive and irritable each day. So I started to smoke by myself a lot in my house's finished basement / rec room. There were still places to travel for work with other people to possibly meet and want to hang out with me to feed my ego and self-esteem. It was always good to impress and party with others who thought I was cool and hilarious (at first). Here was a guy from the New York area that was 'worldly', smart, had a great sense of humor, and could dance and karaoke. This usually felt like a great symbiotic combination of me entertaining them (and 'letting' them have a good time) while I would love and feed off entertaining them.

The attention and boost to my self-esteem was needed and received by proving and having them think I was great (until they got to know the real me). Otherwise, my self-image was at its lowest and this got me extremely depressed. Then I would need to drink and smoke pot even more in order to just feel 'normal' and not crazy or manic. Again....the more life sucked....the more I was puffing....when anything went wrong....the more I was smoking....when nothing ever went right....the more I was toking. There was never an end to this vicious cycle which was picking up momentum with every disappointment when things did not go the way I had planned. It kept getting worse and worse as further and further I was getting out of my life and losing my grip on reality. This once more may sound over dramatic but I really was losing my mind and everything else as I solved all my problems with alcohol, pot, and any other drug I could obtain.
March 12

#73 (Day 73) Honest Open Willing 2012 Post

Monday, January 26 to Thursday, January 29, 1998 there was a Petroleum Safety type exposition and conference in Houston Texas. Pretty soon there were a handful of other exhibitors who wanted to go out each night to party. One of the women drove 3 of us down to South Houston for 'exciting' nightlife. She was rather drunk driving this 40 minute trip which was a little scary. At one point she pulled the car over to the side of the road. Then the woman in the passenger side seat had to come into the back with me and this other guy. The driver then squatted down over the side of the car to pee rather intensively. Some splattered on us and the car which was now gross but it was only a little urine.

We survived the ride down and finally got to the dance clubs near where she lived. Soon all of us were hammered and she got even more trashed. An old boyfriend of hers arrived and after an hour there was no sign of her or him. Another hour had passed when we realized that we were now stranded there. The three of us were staying at hotels in downtown Houston and had to work the next day. We split a cab ride up from South Houston back to Houston and the fare was about $90. Each of us paid $30 plus tip and learned a few valuable lessons from this bizarre experience. Always be careful of who you meet, who you trust, and who you go with. Also, make sure their blood alcohol level is below 0.20 and that they go to the bathroom before you leave with them......especially if they are driving!

The next day there was major apologizes from her to each of us. She was extremely sorry and offered to pay us back but did not have a lot of money being a single mom with little income. Another girl was also at the show that did not go out with us the night before but showed interest in hanging out with me. The next time I was in Houston then both of these ladies and several of their friends would take me out to their favorite Karaoke club! Within a few weeks, there was a sales call required down in the Houston area with one of our sales groups and a customer. Work was only during a few hours of both Thursday and Friday. Those two nights and Saturday night were spent partying with this huge group of men and women that loved my company and entertaining personality. It was a shame to return home and leave my audience but then again I did miss my wife, my house, and my nice private basement to smoke marijuana and watch TV.

Within a few weeks, there really was more business in the Houston area and a safety show in nearby Austin. So I alerted 'my fans' or 'groupies' (as I thought of them) that Steve was coming back to town! A quick 20 minute flight from Hobby Airport in Houston to Austin made that show (as an attendee not an exhibitor) a one day event. Then I flew back from Austin to Hobby Airport to party two more days with my peeps. The big Karaoke club was also wild with everyone dancing, yelling, singing, and getting very drunk.

The one drunken girl from the Petroleum Safety type show who drove us down to South Houston and pee'd on the highway was there with everyone else. She was dancing on a bar table when she yelled for me to catch her as she fell backwards from four feet up. I had to catch her or she would have gotten seriously hurt. Just as intoxicated as the last time, she thought it was funny and thanked me. Meanwhile, that 'stunt' physically hurt my back for the longest time and still does but it could also be from other things. 'Those people' stopped being fun as they were mindless, too easy to entertain, and did not care about the well-being of others such as myself!

May 9 to May 15, 1998 was one of the two yearly shows our company attended as an exhibitor with a booth to meet and greet the thousands of people walking up and down the aisles. There were a lot of competitors that also exhibited at these two shows even though portable and wall mounted gas monitors and sensors may not sound fun and exciting. Instead of being nasty and ignoring them, I was friendly and showed them our products which usually got them to show me their products. This was always found out anyway through backward, sneaky ways so why not be open and social. It was always a little surprising to some of their other co-workers and guests that the 'competition' was invited to their company's evening hospitality reception parties. There was always food, entertainment, and endless drinks with these sometimes being held in pretty cool places. These would cost their company a lot of money but they were much bigger and richer than my company who never had any receptions.

This year's show was in a city where my favorite competitor group had their worldwide headquarters. They had a really big, private hospitality party at Planet Hollywood and invited me. Drinking was not enough so I brought a few special cigarettes that earlier had their tobacco unrolled out and put back in mixed with some marijuana. These cigarettes looked exactly like normal cigarettes and smoking in public places was allowed 'in those days'. I lit one in the hallway and then reentered the room while walking around. This was humorous to me because I felt like I was the one being sneaky. Many people sniffed the air and thought they smelled pot but had no idea where it was coming from. The party was now more interesting in general and more fun to me being there both drunk and stoned.
March 13

#74 (Day 74) Honest Open Willing 2012 Post

My wife and I did get a chance to occasionally go to a few other vacation destinations even though none of them were ever anything like Jamaica. In July 1998 we went to Cozumel Mexico. A woman came up to me while in the pool area of our hotel. She noticed my Gold's Gym Paramus NJ shirt. Even though I had never worked out in Gold's Gym, it indicated that we probably lived near Paramus NJ. This was rather close to where they were currently living. My wife and I got along very well with them plus they also smoked pot a lot like me (and occasionally her back then). Quickly we all became friends and the four of us experienced Cozumel together....and got into trouble together.

There were buses and taxis to go from the hotel to many places downtown and locally. This guy rented a car for one of the days and drove us all around the island including one of the nicest beaches on the other side of Cozumel. We went to an extremely horrible petting zoo area with rather pathetic looking parrots, ponies, monkeys, and other badly treated animals. If you took a picture of anything (alive or not) then you had to pay the owners money as royalty rights. It was really sad but there was nothing we could do but think how inhumane they were just to make a few bucks at the expense of other living creatures. Our impression of this foreign tourist trap island filled with con artists and 'cruel people' out to take pesos from gringos was about to get even worse.

The car had to be returned at the end of the day with the gas tank filled or the price per liter that he would be charged was four times the price of gas at the local petrol stations. However, we could not find any place to get gas so we stopped to ask a nice police officer there in the downtown area. His English was very good and told us to go up one block and make a right onto 'that street' where he was pointing and even said the street name. Then we had to go all the way down to the end and make a right to soon see a petrol (gas) station a few blocks down. We thanked the officer and did exactly what he said turning right onto that particular street. One block later there was another police officer waiting for us with his hand up saying this was a One Way Street. There were no signs anywhere until that point and rather hidden.

The other police officer came running up from behind. We offered to just turn around and go back the right way since he had told us to go up this exact street. Now he started to play dumb really well and his English became really bad. They said we had to go down to the police station with them to fill out forms and pay a large fine for going the wrong way on a one way street. These two nice, respectable officers of the law were willing to help us out. We can just pay them a certain amount of money right there and then to look the other way about our illegal activity. The 'bribe' was the equivalent of about $60 right away instead of about $200 and an hour or two of time. We did eventually find a gas station to fill up the car gas tank and then went back to the hotel rather pissed off. There we danced, enjoyed karaoke, drank, ate, and smoked pot but the island had already given us a bad taste in our mouths.

Another problem facing us was the marijuana supply had started to run low. We would need to get some more the next day from the downtown area. Walking along the streets of downtown Cozumel asking for drugs was neither great nor fun. Not many seemed to speak English or know what we were looking to purchase. A man near another outside car lot and rental booth sat down to talk with us. He said that he had a lot of connections and could get us marijuana but it would take an hour. There was no choice but to trust him with $50 now and then $50 when he got back with the 'merchandise'. This guy was our only hope so we waiting in an air conditioned pool hall for him to return within the next two hours. We became bored, drank beer, got paranoid, and then increasingly wondered if we were the stupidest people in the world for possibly falling for another con or scam. The people in the pool hall said we had to eat or drink more to stay there. With everything going on the last two days, we just had it and were going to f'ing leave after I went to the bathroom.

March 14

#75 (Day 75) Honest Open Willing 2012 Post

My frustration and feeling of being dicked over and with low self-esteem and rage had me kick in the bathroom stall door as I was leaving the men's room. An attendant rushed in to see the door was barely on one hinge ready to fall off. Guess I kicked it a little too hard but those Hulk Gamma rays were filled inside me. They said I did it because they saw I was angry and the only one in there as the sound was made then the door was seen. Another policeman was brought in by the establishment. The bottom line was $100 would solve everything for the pool hall and the policemen (probably $50 to him and $50 to them). Then they can fix the door and he would not need to take me and the rest of us down to their police station.

Extremely pissed off, we started voicing our concern that bribes and sucking money away from tourists would hurt Cozumel's reputation. None of them cared. We paid the $100 and left disgusted like the other few negative experiences in 'that place'. I had denied to our friends, my wife (whom I later disclosed the truth), and especially the pool hall, their employees, and the police officer that I had anything to do with busting the men's bathroom stall door. Either way, our little NJ group (and especially me) thought many of these people (not all of course) sucked crap.

Then we were heading to the bus stop in order to catch the bus from the downtown area back to our hotel. There we ran into the man from the rental car booth that was coming back to the pool hall! He sincerely apologized for the delay and covertly gave us the marijuana while we paid him the remaining $50. All the time and aggravation, $100 to the pool hall, and now $100 to this 'dealer' still made the ride back to the hotel exhilarating....we got more weed! It was rationed, smoked, and well enjoyed making the end of the trip much better.

The four of us wanted to get together shortly after we got home to New Jersey. It was like that date etiquette thing where you don't want to call the other person right away looking over eager. That was B.S. and I think it was me that called them that night to say thanks, they're cool, and let's hang out soon. We did and they became our closest fun friends to talk to, go out with, and hang out with to smoke major amounts of high quality marijuana. There were also massive amounts of alcohol consumed. Big boxes (and bottles) of cheap wine and big bottles of 'crisp, refreshing, & delicious' (and cheap) Arbor Mist type coolers helped get things rolling along. All of this made us both totally stoned and drunk on many occasions. This rocked because my tolerance was so high but these nights got me past my tolerance level (for now).

They also became our travel partners in a few places throughout the Tri-State area, New England, and one other place that was disastrous in many ways. However, there were quite a few other important things that occurred before this 'October 1999 disastrous' trip.

One Saturday night around November 16, 1998 there was a semi-surprise birthday bash held at our house. It was planned by my wife and our new party friends. This was for my 30th birthday and a lot more of my friends were there than what I expected! It was overwhelming and got me emotional to know so many of my friends still cared. This was probably one of the best birthday parties ever and a truly awesome day which did not occur too often. The rest of 1998 ended without anything horrible or fantastic happening.

The year 1999 started off with a 'WOOF'. Our first dog Harris was originally named Attila because of his wild, attention needing, sometimes destructive behavior (sounded familiar but not sure why)? With a name like Attila, you were bound to be ...Bad To The Bone. This half Spaniel and half Welsh Corgi mix was obtained at Petsmart by the 'Save The Animal Rescue Team' (START). Attila needed love, patience, and

attention so we named him Harris and fostered him until our hearts were with him to stay permanently. Knock on wood....KNOCK KNOCK...he is still with us as a dear family member into 2012. This was the high point of 1999 and it was only the first couple of months. Before (and after) the new millennium arrived, the rest of 1999 was horrible......
March 15

#76 (Day 76) Honest Open Willing 2012 Post

The first thing in early 1999 that was messed up involved my work. We had a co-worker who was technically a private contractor that did a lot of various things we needed to get done over the past 10 years or so. He would stop by and pick up things, drop off things, and hand in his hour's sheet to get a check for payment of services. He was a very unique, eclectic, eccentric individual. People (including me) thought he was very weird because of his mannerism, clothing, and things he did. One thing that stood out more than anything was his horrible body odor. This ex-ordained minister was a true jack of all trades. There really was not anything he could not do or knew. I did get to know him but it was hard to be near him. Many people said (and he heard) things about how bizarre, smelly, and crazy he must be. I did not even hide my nauseous feelings about his aroma.

Not many people knew he was making beautiful, hand carved violins in his home basement work shop including me. His wife came home one day and found him in the basement. He was not working on anything....he was dangling from the rafters on a rope. He committed suicide by hanging himself. I cannot image how his wife felt to see his lifeless body but it had to have been horrible. Later that day, she called our office to tell me her husband killed himself and would not be working there anymore. She asked that I tell my dad, my chief technician (who was close to him), and everyone else in the office. The 'working here anymore' part was not nearly as disturbing as him ending his life. We do not know why he would want to snuff out his life when it was filled with so much to offer. If only he conformed to society....or if only society (and me) accepted him even with his odor and very few other defects.

My wife and I had our new best friends that we met in July 1998 while staying in Cozumel Mexico. This couple lived together but was not married and did not have any kids. They loved to have a great time, laugh, eat, drink, and smoke pot like us. We hung out at one of our places or went out together at least one to two times a week. They had a lot in common with us and we were alike in many ways. It seemed like we would be friends forever and the four of us went away to many places. Even over the last year my mood was getting worse and the Dr. Jekyll and Mr. Hyde was more Mr. Hyde. The last trip that my wife and I went on with our quickest and best friends over the previous 15 months would be back in Mexico where it first began. Everything bothered and irritated the hell out of me. Even my best friends and wife were not on the same page as me and were out to get me like the rest of the world. I hated doing what they wanted to do and was bitter if there were conflicts or if he made a funny wise crack about me. When I felt hurt then I lashed back harder.

After this trip, the two of them were all fed up with me. It was not just this trip but the last few months. This trip was an extremely intense experience of how bad I had quickly become in a short time. They never wanted to see me again and told my wife sorry but it is not her...it is me. My wife had already grown closer to the female friend and had been doing things often with her. They were willing to still be friends with her if I was not around and this got me very bitter and resentful. I got in the way saying to everyone that there had to be a general decision. It was either going to be the two of us with the two of them (and I would change) or nothing at all. They said neither, my wife reluctantly said me, and I still did not change. My personality was 180 degrees from where my wife first met and loved me. Now 180 degrees later, she did not have fun being around me and I was always distant and cold back. It got to this point where she was entirely (and understandably) disgusted with me and an ultimatum was made. If I did not agree to go to counseling together, and try to help her and me in our relationship, then it had to end. We went to a Psychologist to talk about our problems. After a few visits, we discovered our problems were not with each other. I really did not have any problems with her. We both realized that our common problem was just with me.
March 16

#77 (Day 77) Honest Open Willing 2012 Post

Now the focus was for me to get better because I loved my wife so much and wanted her to love me (and like me) the way she used to before I changed. That would be the only way we could be happy again like years past. This Psychologist was great and helped a lot but could not prescribe medication. He recommended a Psychiatrist who he had worked with that could get me on some medicines to assist in getting better. The last medicine I had taken for my 'disorders' was Ritalin as a kid for ADD. Now I was diagnosed Bipolar 2 and OCD by this Psychiatrist and the journey with all the many different pills started even though he knew I was still smoking pot. He did emphasize that I could not really get the full benefit of the medications while getting stoned all the time. It may help a little but he was not adamant that I stop 100% or he would not be able to work with me any longer. However, the medicines would not be good to my body, organs, and health if I drank as much alcohol as I was doing. So I tried to reduce the amount of alcohol and stuck with pot but there were many times it just did not 'help' me enough. Those times (and whenever I could not smoke in public) I still had to drink even with all the different medicines.

New Year's Eve on December 31, 1999 was spent at home with my wife awaiting the Y2K problem and ringing in the new Millennium just the two of us. Each time zone celebrated without tragedy and it was cool to see the world slowly become 2000 each hour including Hawaii at 5 am our time. This was my goal to become 'Steve2K' starting in 2000. I was determined to work as hard as I could to get back the good things in my life and positive traits that I once had. At the same time, all of the bad things in my life and negative traits that I currently had would disappear. This was going to be like 'magic'...it had to because I hated myself for all of the pain I had caused hurting my family, friends, and especially my wife. Therapy was continuing for me and the medicines were being changed often to find that right 'miracle combination'. The two of us together can eventually get back what we once had. I wanted her to be happy and not miserable with me so then I could stop being miserable with me. We would just concentrate only on each other forever and ever....until something happened almost 100 days into the 21th Century.

It happened on the morning of April 7, 2000. My wife and I were in bed when she rolled over to gently wake me up. She wanted to show me something very interesting that would (and has) change her life, my life, and (more importantly back then) our lives together....forever and ever. Who would have known that peeing on a stick and showing me 'positive' results would initially make me sick to my stomach? She was pregnant.

There was no way I could panic or show how uneasy I really was at that moment, that day, and for a long time. This was not our plans since we first met and agreed that neither one of us wanted children. We later concurred that bringing a baby into a world like this is not fair for a child. It would only be for selfish reasons to have a kid. Part of this selfishness is having someone to be there for you when you get older. Being lonely and with no one to care or love you in your old age is scary. That would not really be too scary because I always thought I would grow old alone and die alone (if I lived past 30). The scariest thing was not that I was now going to be a dad. What scared the living hell out of me was being responsible for another living human being. How can I take care, provide safety, and raise someone correctly when I could not do that with myself.

The upsetting thing with me was that we were both working together to make our relationship work. Yes, we did agree to try and conceive a child because she was not sure if she could or if 'my boys could swim'. It would have been God's will if she had become pregnant and it was a chance I was willing to take. This would be destiny, get us closer with hope, and never did the reality hit me it could and would happen. I had to deal with this because we would deal with this as a true couple and it could be the best thing to happen to me and to us. Now I just had to figure all this into the equation and reevaluate how I could become Steve2K+1.
March 17

#78 (Day 78) Honest Open Willing 2012 Post
Exactly 8 months later was Thursday, December 7, 2000. This was "A Date Which Will Live in Infamy" because it was Pearl Harbor Day. This was also the date our son was born. She was lying there on the delivery table having an unexpected C-Section because our boy was not facing the right way. I was allowed to be in there as long as I remained sitting in my chair near her head and stayed out of trouble. My wife was all drugged out and I was jealous. At no point did she know what was going while being sliced opened and looking like a fish being gutted. That is a very vulgar way to describe it but if you are a man watching this for the very first time then you would know it is meant in the most special way possible.

Every few minutes she would ask what the doctor was doing and I did not want to freak her out. My response the first time was that they were just planning and getting everything ready. Then she asked again and I said they are prepping the area. Then she asked again and I said they are about to make the first incision. A few seconds later, the doctor pulled out our son from her belly. I exclaimed "O my God...he's got so much hair...he's beautiful!" My wife said "Who, the doctor?" That was and still is hilarious. I then told her that the doctor had already been inside, working for several minutes and it was our son that has so much hair and is beautiful. The cool thing is that I meant it while feeling truly wonderful and proud. There was nothing at all to be nervous or scared about. Then we had to leave the hospital a few days later to return home with our baby and be parents without doctors, nurses, and our own parents' constant help. Reality immediately set in along with my own fears and insecurities.

*** Here I just wanted to note something important with a slight flash forward ...... I did, I do, and I will always love my son more and more each day. Even though he may not always listen, even though he may not always do what he is told, even though he may not always 'agree' with my wife and I on several issues, and even though he may not always use nice words to describe and yell at us, and even though I often get frustrated, angry, depressed, and cry....I no longer have any regrets whatsoever about his birth. Now in my life, I continue to try my hardest to see things on the flip side. Very often he does listen, do what he is told, 'agree' with things, and says heartfelt adjectives about us like wonderful, cool, great, the best, and tells us he loves us. He means it. I very often get serene, proud, overjoyed, laugh because of him, and say these things to him along with "I love you." I mean it. Today, he is one of the very best 'things' I have ever helped to 'create'.

Every single thing that I have mentioned about him then and now applies equally to his sister born a little over five years later. My life would be empty without either one of them although I cannot say that until several years ago when I decided to change and have not stopped. There is nothing I would not do to save either of their lives even at the expense of mine. My greatest fears, insecurities, doubts, and more are not as much about me as a parent versus them growing up. I do not want either of them to experience any of the horrible things that I did or happened to me and loved ones. Unfortunately, there is not much I can do except be honest, open, willing, and supportive to them and hope to God they don't get hurt or hurt others as much. I have always wanted them to grow up only like their mother. Now I would not mind (as much) if they grew up to be a little like me today but definitely not like me back then...... End of note and slight flash forward. ***

My son was born at the end of 2000 and it was now 2001. (2001: A Space Odyssey....there is an ironic similarity to how I felt back then and that movie title!) Work phone calls were able to be forwarded to the basement office of my house which was only 1/2 mile away. Work e-mails could be responded to from the computer there as well. Eventually I stopped traveling across the USA and isolated myself in that basement. That was where I 'worked' from 1 pm to 5 pm Monday through Friday in between smoking constant amounts of marijuana while watching 'important things' I had taped on my VCR. It took a lot to get me high and keep me high. Drinking a little alcohol was also needed but usually 3 to 4 beers or half to a whole bottle of wine did the added trick. It would have been a lot more beer and wine but my medicines would not mix well with 'too much' alcohol. I also stayed down in my basement office often at night and weekends to 'work' on the computer or watch 'important' TV shows. Rarely leaving my home meant I was staying out of trouble. This also afforded me precious time to spend with my wife and my son when I was not busy doing other things down in my precious basement. Life was still happening outside my house but I did not care until Tuesday, September 11, 2001.
March 18

#79 (Day 79) Honest Open Willing 2012 Post

When this portion of my daily posts is being written, September 11, 2001 was just over 10 and 1/2 years ago. The events of that day was, is still, and will always be a very sensitive topic to many people including some of my closest friends and family for several different reasons and their experiences. Not to mention 9/11 even briefly would be an injustice to the memory of what happened, what it meant, and who we lost. Being isolated and messed up with drugs, alcohols, and in my own selfish mind made this one of the few events that initially happened to me! OMG! Please preserve the fond memories of all those who died without extreme hatred for those responsible who had either had a sick soul, were brainwashed, or had twisted emotions. Also, please preserve the fond memories of all those who died without extreme depression and tears but with a little sorrow and great remembrance of who they were and still are up in Heaven. None of them would want to see anyone (especially their loved ones) fill up with anger or depression from that tragic day. Lastly, please forgive me for making anyone relive horrible feelings from this time in their lives. It is very important to know how twisted I first felt and now feel about that day. Otherwise, I would not have written this as an amends to everyone who was affected including one very dear friend who is no longer with us and his family and friends left behind.

In the morning of 9/11/01, I went to the office at 8:30 am. AOL said something hit one of the World Trade Center Twin Towers but did not know what. They first said it was a small airplane or helicopter which was really messed up. My wife dropped off our son at day care on the corner. She and our bookkeeper came in a little before 9:00 am. I was not listening to the radio but they were. They said it was a regular size airplane that hit one tower. Now the two of them did what many then did and started to do...turn on the TV to CNN. When the second plane hit the second tower is when we all knew it was not an accident. My thoughts went to a friend who had been proud to be working near the top of one of the towers for many years. I called his wife hoping to God he was not there that morning. He was and had spoken to her very recently telling her everything was alright, he was safe, and was going to find his father who worked a dozen or so floors below him in the same tower. That was the last thing that I was told and waited. Then we all know what happened to those two towers.

Nether he, his dad, nor almost 3000 people survived that day from the four hijacked airplanes. Again, my selfish, self-centered thoughts were that one of my most dear friends was dead. He was married with a newly arrived little girl working to make a very decent, happy life. Those bastards took him away from me and everyone else! My hatred towards those 9/11 terrorists and supporters were as intense as my sorrow for myself and for my friends. The thoughts in my head (which affected my heart and the rest of me) were 'How could this happen to me?' It happened to everyone and realistically affected many people a lot worse than 'poor old me' but that was not how I saw things. Back then my heart went out to what was happening to me and how it was affected my friends which was a horrible thing to happen to me.

That night my wife and I stared at our son who was now a little over 9 months old as he slept peacefully. We both could not grasp how something so horrific and evil could have happened like this while something so sweet and innocent could be in our lives now. In many ways, our son gave us a little bit of hope about life instead of just 100% dread. This was ironic because just a few years earlier we had believed bringing a baby into a world like this is not fair for a child. Maybe a world like this needs more children who are sweet and innocent to make it a better place for the future? I stopped beating myself up about those twisted feelings of reality because I was and still am sick but got much better. Several years later, my heart first goes out to everyone directly affected and their pain. Then my heart aches for this loss of my friend and also primarily because I care and sympathize deeply for those people he left behind.

March 19

#80 (Day 80) Honest Open Willing 2012 Post

The years after 9/11 brought back all the crap about the world and I decided again to forget the world which was cruel, stupid, and out to get me. The difference was now I had convinced myself that the world was also out to get my loved ones (wife and son). This gave me the rationalization to try extra hard not to hurt them or anyone else by staying away from my family, events, and friends a lot more. Maybe time would heal me? Maybe I was an alien? Maybe I should move to Jamaica and just be at peace growing, smoking, and selling marijuana for the rest of my life? Thinking too much made me think I could figure out what to do while still taking different medicines that kept having awful side effects. However, sometimes a change in medication gave me better clarity, more energy, feel happier, and other great, wonderful, hopeful things! Even then, it eventually wore off and I was more depressed and hopeless than ever.

Sometimes a change in medication was initially a nightmare. Certain prescribed drugs gave me too much nervous hyper energy, no energy or motivation at all, made me gain weight, lose hair, get rashes, or caused dizziness and light headedness with fainting when standing up too fast. The worst thing that happened (with two medicines called Paxil and Zoloft) was one of the worst things for anyone to experience (especially a man). The mood was there, the equipment was ready and sprang into action, but it was like when the tide comes in. The waves would crash onto the shore...but then go back. Then the waves would crash a little further onto the shore...but then go back a little less. Then the waves would crash even a little further onto the shore...but then again go back even a little less. Now picture that 800 to 1000 times until it got where it needed to reach like off the beach and down a drain pipe. The frustration of this was crazy and really screwed me up even more. Smoking a boat load of the best marijuana helped a little in the wave crashing to where they need to go department.

All of these major, constant, daily, smoke-a-bowl or smoke-a-bong marathons were not helping my mind. The medications were not working either (under these circumstances). I was persistent (to myself) that the pot was helping keep me at the 'normal' line instead of below. There was no more real high above the 'normal' line like 10 years or even a few years prior. Denial would not allow me to think I had any problem or problems out of my control. Having the power to manage everything in my messed up life was something I could do myself and needed no real help. These 'professionals' never had any power greater than mine to restore the insanity within me. My Psychiatrist would usually just tell me to wait it out and see if the emotion and mental aspects improved where needed and the negative mental and physical aspects tone down. Eventually, I would get switched to another medication.

Now I wanted to just be alone and was afraid of getting messed up away from home and feeling or doing bad things. When I did go out, and drank, I usually drank too much and became angry, anti-social, tired, and wanted to go home to be alone. My wife again had a husband who was Dr. Jekyll that always had to hide in the basement else become Mr. Hyde. If he was already Mr. Hyde then he would need to go or would be asked to go into the basement to 'get better'. It was a full time job to remain not as bad as Mr. Hyde but could never get nearly as good as Dr. Jekyll again. She was now trapped in a house with the grumpy, resentful troll in the basement even worse than ever before. Where could she go now that she had a kid, no steady job for her own income, and nowhere else to live? She tried as hard as she could and I now give her so much credit, strength, patience, and tolerance to have put up with me as much as she did.

My hostages were held close by and I thought they could be controlled (by me). At this point....there was no God. To me, I was the closest thing to God. Nothing and no one mattered to me even a little bit. When I stopped believing in God and letting him in and having this last transformation is when few things happened. But when they did happen it was not to Steve. These things were happening by idiots to me their superior. Conversely, these things were happening to this idiot by everyone who was my superior. This depended on the day or hour.

I stopped seeing my Psychologist every week for an hour because the money and time was too much to give someone that could probably never help me anyway. Instead, I had just been seeing my Psychiatrist for 15 minutes once a month to discuss medicines but not my problems. The term inferior/superior complex was introduced to me from my Psychiatrist. Soon afterward his office stopped accepting my health insurance. Now it was around the middle of 2002 and had no Psychologist, no Psychiatrist, no therapist, and no one else to help me control life or at least myself. My general medical doctor was told the medicines that I was on and was now the one that renewed or would change what I was taking usually at my advice. Pretty much I was free to help myself alone. The worst person to talk things with to obtain a solution is you. They say a man who represents himself in court has a fool for a client. My thoughts now (but not then) were a man who psychoanalyzes himself in his head has a psychotic person as a patient. March 20

#81 (Day 81) Honest Open Willing 2012 Post

It was about May 2004 when my wife was driving home back up from her parents in the Trenton area on a Sunday. She went down there with our little boy every 2 to 3 weeks so her family can see them. Meanwhile the terrible troll stayed home to be miserable by himself. The phone rang earlier in the morning than usual as she would normally 'warn' me that my 'privacy' was about to be 'disturbed'. This troll was still asleep in bed from a long night of doing nothing but self-partying. Her voice and phone mannerism was different. There was a funny feeling that she had at her parents' home which woke her up while everyone else was still fast asleep. The sun was not even ready to rise and it was still dark when she went out to a 24 hour pharmacy. Her body was telling her something that was confirmed......by peeing on another stick. She was pregnant a second time.

The poor sweet woman was nervous and scared to wait until she got home to tell me. There was horrible, awkward silence from me as I felt my mouth open and my jaw drop to the ground. I just know the support and comfort that I gave her during that phone conversation in her car and when she got home was probably unlike any husband would give his wife. Most husbands would have compassion, sympathy, and empathy with their spouse in times of need but not me. This is really going to affect me even worse as I was just getting used to dealing with a son no longer in diapers that required so much dependence and attention. It was my turn again to get some dependence and attention. Now that went out the window.

That was the second to last time that suicide entered my mind and tried to get out. I just could not imagine my life with two kids especially the way I felt about life and the way I felt about myself as a parent and as a person. Obviously, I am still alive and any thoughts or fleeting moments of trying to end my life (again) went away. That would have been the most selfish thing to do and obviously the most selfish of all my previous suicide attempts without a doubt. This hopelessness that I 'felt' was all just because I wanted as few people in my life and gave a crap about anyone even my family.

Now there is not a day that goes by where I regret the pregnancy, birth, or life of either of my children. There is just the regret of feeling that way, several years ago, when all I thought about in my twisted, sick head was me. I have said this before about my wife and I have said this before about my son. They are two of the dearest people in this world to me that I will always support, protect, and love. On Friday, January 7, 2005 is when my daughter was born. My wife, my son, and my daughter are three of the dearest people in this world to me that I will always support, protect, and love. All I could do today and each day is remember how I did not feel that way once and try my best to be a good husband and father to them now and forever!

That is now...but back then there was no one else to take out my frustration and anger at life never giving me what I wanted...except everyone outside my home. This was increasingly so with different authority figures including my dad and with people in charge of other companies and groups that we had business relations. No one (usually) likes being told what to do. There was one other profession that I was starting to have conflicts and problems with which is the worst to have as your enemy. That was the fine men and women of law enforcement. March 21

#82 (Day 82) Honest Open Willing 2012 Post

The police tell you to do things for good reasons such as safety or it is the law. They are not really out to get you and it is a hard profession which I have learned to respect more and more over the past few years. If you tried to tell me that a few years ago I would say that they love the power and love making people do what they want. They demand respect and get mean and vindictive if you go against them. Every time, I 'felt' that a police officer was not being fair was when I made a loud, noticeable fuss and of course it would always only hurt me. I did not feel like I was a law breaker or a bad person. I felt like someone needed to keep them in their place like checks and balances. That someone was your local neighborhood had-to-always-get-his-nose-where-it-should-not-be-involved, over righteous, pot head. Hey, I was not a kid getting in trouble doing bad things anymore and was now a responsible home owner and parent so it was my job to be responsible for making everything 'fair'.

Because people would 'peel out' at the stop sign in front of my house meant it was totally acceptable that I could do that too. The dirty looks from crossing guards, parents, and other people was not deserved because there were many others that deserved those dirty looks. Some things are not worth the trouble and I was occasional one of those 'things'. But if there was a good reason to 'get me' then why not pack everything on all at once. After all, the world was just waiting to get me. One police officer had told me to 'get my dog out of here' when some German Shepherds were barking ferociously at him from behind a fence during a block party. Otherwise, I was warned they may get out and attack. That is some nerve to tell me to take my sweet dog home because some vicious dogs were upset! This person was not even in uniform or on duty. My attitude was really bad ....with her.

Now being a police officer is tough and has to be. To be a female police officer is even tougher for many reasons. But to be a police officer and a female both authoritative 'to me' was way too much back then. One day I saw this police officer in her patrol car going the other direction and decided to be the big shot. My car horn honked, my arm went out the window with a defiant wave hello, and I 'accidentally' swerved the car. That shows her who the boss is. Then the lights went on, her car turned quickly around, and her siren had me pull over to the side of the road.

Smugly I rolled down my window to say hello and see what the problem might be. She told me that I was going fast and swerved. I responded that I was going the speed limit and just wanted to wave hello when I saw her which made me lose control of the car for just a second. That was when she mentioned how there were complaints about me "screeching my tires" at the stop sign the other morning. My response was that it was wet and loss of traction. Pretty much I had an excuse for everything as far as I was concerned. Then she went back to her patrol car for a few minutes as I impatiently waited for her. She came back with a ticket for careless driving! I started to argue and said look I just have my child in the back car seat and wanted to get to the daycare center before work. That is when the 'fun' began. It was not known to her how there was a small child in the vehicle so she 'had to let me know' that DYFS would be notified.

That was when I just went berserk and started to vent my complaints in fast, high pitch squeals. First I told her that she had it out for me saying that I screech my tires and am a bad parent endangering my kid by telling me how she would call DYFS! She also had it known that I did not like having her tell me to take my dog home or other dogs will attack him. Basically I said just about everything except saying she had a bad, corrupt attitude and was very masculine. That would have gotten me in more trouble. As it was, I took the ticket and peeled away to drop off my poor child at daycare and go next door to work. My wife was working there and listened to my side of the story which had her agree there might be a conflict between this police officer and myself. Finally a meeting was arranged with the police Captain so that the police officer and I could sit down and discuss things with a mediator. All this was just a few misunderstanding on my part so I 'apologized' and that 'got her off my back'.

When one door closes then another door opens. This opened the door to have conflicts with a younger, newer male officer who started working in 'my' town a year earlier. Now it was 2006 and that is when he first started to 'seem' and have it out for me for no good reason at all. One day he just rang my door bell and wanted to talk with me and ask where I have been all day. I was confused. Then he asked me to come out to the curb for a moment. I did and was even more confused. Then he said something into his walkie talkie and a police car passed by really slow. I could not quite see who was in the back seat. Then he got a walkie talkie message back that it was alright. That is when he explained that two boys were trying to get coerced in to a red small car with the offer of a basketball earlier that morning at the playground and finally ran away.

Several hours later, I was doing my usual walk around the block to smoke a cigarette. Even though I was 'still' smoking cigarettes, it was never done inside the house for my kids' sake. When they saw me walking around the block is when they told their older sister that I kinda looked like the man from a distance. That is when she called the police who then got involved. The two boys were put in the back seat of that patrol car that had passed me slowly after this young, new officer came to my front door and had me stand at the edge of my property. They were going to identify me like it was a one-person line up. However, they got a good look at me and my face. Then they told the policeman driving that it was definitely not the same man who tried to lure them into his red small car. Even still....I was more confused and now furious by all this! March 22

#83 (Day 83) Honest Open Willing 2012 Post

This brand new, very young police guy had the 'nerve' to accuse 'me' of being a predator! Plus, he tried to be sneaky in the manner that this was going about. Why not just ask me? I had been living in that town since 1997 and it was now about 2006. Being a resident there that many years meant I deserved a little courtesy! Also, could he not see that I did not own a red small car, anything red, or anything small? I did not even own a car. All I owned was a Grand Cherokee Laredo (which was not really a car I thought) that was big and silver. I did take this as an invasion of my privacy and felt it was all him. However, at that point I was not quite sober or clean so I shook his hand goodbye politely (on the outside). On the inside I hated him for putting me through this humiliating experience. There were other problems including once when he was being very unfair to me (again).

Around the corner from my office we all heard a big bang. It was asked if I could be the nosy one to go out and see what happened. Everyone else from the nearby offices and businesses was out on the street to also see what was going on. A power transformer had exploded up on top of a street pole. This same officer was there protecting, serving, and staring right at me while I was not even half way up the block. There were people much closer but he chose to yell for 'me' to turn around and go back the way I came. I turned around and walked back maybe 10-20 feet to ask people there what was going on. Then he yelled again "I said to go back the way I came!" That is when I got annoyed and yelled at him "Nice People Skills!" and called him by his first name which was disrespectful. He walked briskly down the block to me as I was (then) leaving the scene. We had a rather non-polite discussion until my 'favorite female officer from the town' was there to ironically play good cop to his bad cop. This was not going to be something I could win, knew it, and thanked her for clearing up the situation in which I was sorry (not really sorry).

The rest of the times when I saw him all I did was give him very dirty, disgusting looks. On most of those occasions he would stop me and ask if I had a problem. I had finally learned to shut my mouth but still had an attitude with him since he had one with me. This was becoming increasingly unhealthy until finally I was given a ticket for something but honestly have trouble remembering exactly what. Luckily I had a friend that worked with the Bergen County Sheriff's department that knew him and knew me. He wanted to intervene before the problem got even worse. Again, he knew me and that I was heading in the wrong direction with a fight impossible to win. Being a good person and a good friend is why he wanted to prevent a full scale escalation of me getting worse. He went with me on the date of my court hearing and spoke to the side with that officer as one professional to another. Then he had me come over and was the mediator like before when the police Captain was the mediator between me and the female police officer. I shook his hand and all was 'forgiven' by him and all was 'ceased' by me in my mind. The ticket still had to be pleaded as guilty and paid but at least the case of the new town officer and the old town idiot was closed. This situation would not have gotten better on my own and I thank my friend greatly! No longer did I have any problems with police officers or any members of law enforcement from my town or from any other town...at least on a municipal town level.

There is a direct street I took every time that I went back and forth between my home and my office. A one way trip between the two places was less than one-half a mile and took about three minutes but my judgment of time was always off. That direct street has a speed limit of 25 MPH which seems really slow for those few blocks. I would go 35 or 40 MPH when I was late (usually always). While heading to work one morning, a truck pulls out from a driveway and a man comes out telling me I drive too fast and crazy. He was in regular street clothes and claimed he was a policeman but never showed me a badge or any identification which I had to see to believe. It 'seemed' like he was being arrogant and we got into an argument. Finally I drove around him and his truck to go to work. He got into his truck and started to chase me. For several blocks and around several buildings I tried to lose him but he kept finding me. Then I saw my parents pull up at work and drove right there with him behind me. He then finally and calmly showed them his state policeman badge and said that I need to relax and drive slower or else. Threats from him were not tolerated by me so I started to yell back which got my dad to 'nicely' quiet me down for my own good.

Every time I passed his house for the next few months I made sure to slow down to 10 MPH while either waving and/or honking my horn. That was my way of saying 'see I am doing what you wanted me to do and hope you are happy'. That was done every time I went back and forth to work which was sometimes twice a day. He then wanted the local police to give me a ticket or he was going to 'take care of me personally' as a state policeman. The town police had no real problem with me driving slowly or honking. This person really thought (and was right) that I was disturbed. His wife contacted a mutual friend of my wife that her husband was going to 'take care' of me if I was not intervened. That would not be good if the state police invaded my house and found all my paraphernalia and drugs. Reluctantly, I drove normal and went a different street to make sure I did not screw myself anymore that I already had been doing. Again, and like always, they won and I lost.
March 23

#84 (Day 84) Honest Open Willing 2012 Post

Traveling between my work office and my home office was becoming more of a problem now that I had to take 'the longer way around'. My commute each way increased to over one-half a mile, involved a traffic light, and sometimes took five minutes! There were some days that I smoked pot before I went to work and there were some days I would go home for a short break to smoke pot and go back to work. It was easier to just smoke before work and get there before I was too messed up. Then at about 1 pm would be my formerly 3 minute and now 5 minute commute home to go in the basement, have the calls forwarded, and my dad and the secretary could close the office and go home. It was at that point that my pipe and bong came out to get as much 'done' in the time that I technically had to return upstairs to my wife, son, daughter, and 'reality'. When it was a bad 3 or 4 hours in the office then I would really want to get out of there and get home to safety and to 'relax' as quickly as possible. One afternoon, I had to stop and get gas for the car (not me). Then I realized it was almost time to be stationed at home and all ready for work mode and marijuana mode.

My house was about three blocks ahead of me on the main road. However, I saw a fast moving, pushy person who was 'out to get me' approaching from the opposite direction. Without any good reason, I turned my car and made a sudden left while also going fast just to beat this other car before it got to that street. My car jumped over the curb, knocked over the corner street sign, and crashed into a large tree. This was on the municipal building property which also housed the police station. I was a little stoned when this occurred and my judgment was off. Thankfully I was not stoned enough to smell, act, or have red eyes like I was under the influence of pot. The car was towed away for over a month to get major automotive work performed. Our insurance company paid for a rental car and my work paid for the automotive parts and labor of my greatly destroyed car. That was not the most destructive thing that I did that year……

No one knew what to expect at any time with me in the office. Most of the people had left because of my personality disorders. Now there was just my dad, occasionally my mom, my wife, and my sister working there with three other non-related employees. My sister and I always fought but usually it was kidding around or if serious always resulting in an apology (always from me). Then we made nice and got along with our lives in and out of the office. She was the one that I got along with the best out of my three siblings. Was it their fault? No it was my fault for ruining any chance of a relationship with them as a kid considering what I was like as a kid. It was still my fault for ruining any chance of a relationship with them as an adult (or now older at least) considering what I had been like the last few years and especially since my son was born. My wife and her were close and would talk to each other over the phone. There was one time shortly after where my sister asked how she can stand being married to me and put up with me. Neither my wife nor I really knew.

Maybe it was a week or a few weeks after my latest car wreck when the inconvenience of having to wait and wait for my car to be fixed affected me. My thoughts were that it was not my fault. It was the jerk who tried to beat me to that intersection and 'made me' have this accident. Now this asshole fixing my car on the corner was taking his sweet ass time getting my car done. Everyone was being unbelievably stupid, irritating, and I had no choice but to deal with 'people' because of this accident.

This sister working with me was the younger of my two sisters. My parents had originally asked if she would like to come and work at their office with the thoughts her and I can run the business when they retire. My sister would run the administrative, accounting, and office managerial aspects while I would run the sales, marketing, and technical aspects. My mannerism one day in the office was really more bizarre and ranting against the world and everyone in it greater than normal.

She tried to calm me down but I was too much on a tangent. Finally she had it with me and said something like "You really do have some major mental problems!" Usually when I was hurt I would immediately think of, and immediately blurt out, the worst possible things I could say to be vindictive. Never have I ever screamed out words more hurtful than the ones directed back at my poor sister.

It is so true that the tongue is mightier than the sword. That is one reason that repent of tongue and pen is a very wise expression to keep you from saying stupid or hurtful things without thinking them through first. Right away my sister got up from her desk and ran out saying I need serious help. After being there for so many years, she quit work. My dad could not convince her to come back while my mom was very upset that I could say such cruel, angry, (and manically crazy) things like that to my own sister.

It was over a year until she wanted to have anything to do with me. That was only after I did finally get help, admitted my problems to my family, and that I was truly ready to make my amends to her. That comes later and I do not want to get ahead of myself (like usual). It is just important that I eventually accepted this as something entirely my fault that had no excuse whatsoever. Those were some of the absolute worst things anyone could say to another person especially a brother to his sister. When the time arrived, I was more sincere and humbly sorry than almost anything I could have been. She understood and recognized how much I meant it with all of my heart and found it possible to somehow forgive me. The two of us have been closer now to each other than even before in our lives and for this I am extremely grateful!

This was the past, I was really sick, and she had forgiven me. There is no way to go back and change anything in your life. If there were, this is one I most certainly would want to do because no matter what... I did say those things and that alone eats at me often. However, as my 'mentors' in the present would say, that was a different person in the past which cannot be changed. The best amends is trying to be the best loving, supporting brother possible now for each and every day.
March 24

#85 (Day 85) Honest Open Willing 2012 Post
Now it was 2007 and was still about 396 more days until the next year when it became that pivotal day in 2008. Until then, 2007 was the most insane years ever as my destructive behavior and voices in my head were getting worse almost every day. Much of that year and January 2008 are like a blur and bad dream / nightmare. There was nothing I did, drank, smoked, or took to help. My wife always seemed to complain and take interest in her other female and male friends that were nice to her. I did not care or notice that I was not fun or even tolerable to be around. Now I felt other people were turning my wife away from me. Those people were either superior or inferior to me depending on the weather.

Either way made me feel rage inside like a bomb waiting to explode or like Popeye after he eats Spinach. It seemed to me that she wished I were more like them and less like myself. People that were good with kids, got along with people, did not lose their cool, and were talented in many fields that I lack such as automotive, carpentry, gardening, and much more were resented because that greatly affected my self-esteem. Their negative traits are what I focused on and made comments about and pointed out to make them look less positive. Road rage had always been bad with yelling, cutting people off, and giving them the finger. This had constantly gotten me into a lot of trouble, arguments, chasing, and (of course) the police. No one at all by this point was safe from my insanity.

Everyone (again) was to blame because the world changed and I did not. Actually, the real problem was I needed to change and grow as life and the world changed. Both ways, I was right and the world could blow up for all I cared. That might have been better to me back then because I blamed and got mad at all the people that got in my way or near me innocently. It was not just that I saw and felt the world changed. My lack of reality had me see and feel that all the people I knew had changed including my wife conveniently after my kids entered our life. It was not like this before either was born. Now they are great and I have expressed my love to them and everyone in my life. Now I regret feeling that way I did back then like they were annoying, noisy, needy, life-sucking rats upstairs.

Pre-2000 was bad but was going to get better until 'they' got in the way of happiness for me and my wife. However, I was ignorant and saw nothing real. My wife was happy with them although they were a lot to handle when you really have three children and not two. Then again it would not have been as bad if I were like a third child instead of an immature, miserable acting, person living in the basement like a tenant that you had no choice to deal with because of a forever year rental agreement. Now, I was the completely opposite of how I felt then to my kids. The resentment was intense making me bitter, neglectful, and uncaring. All this was probably starting to emotionally harm them but I did not care nor even realize it. My son was older so a few more years at the way I was going would have possible done irreversible emotional and maybe eventual physical harm. That is something I do not even want to think about at this point in my life. The idea alone that I 'could' have gotten worse in many ways to my wife and kids from 'just' the things I was already doing, saying, and acting is scary now.

When they were younger I 'had' to watch them as babies in their bouncy chairs downstairs while I watched TV. Even I knew smoking marijuana in front of them would be wrong on many levels especially second hand smoke and contact high. (Thank the Lord that I did actually care enough they were babies who were not fully developed yet). So I would go on the other side of the door when they napped to take a quick few hits outside the room and around the corner making sure no smoke followed me. If they were not asleep and were crying then I would get upset because I wanted them to stop crying and sleep so I can have peace and go through the door closed behind and just right around the corner to smoke my pipe. They were not only 'keeping me' from my marijuana but keeping me from going outside the house to have a much needed cigarette (which 'that' I did not really do inside as I did smoke everything else in the house downstairs). This lack of freedom and my selfishness added to the resentment and frustration already there.

One time something happened that proved things were starting to get bad. My 7 year old son was having a fit carrying on and screaming. He was not listening to me so I picked him up by the shoulders and started to yell loudly at him. Quickly, I realized having him in my grip while angry was dangerous because I felt my dad was violent with me (even though he was not and I realized this once I grew up...at age 39). Letting go of my son, he ran away into his room. My wife was scared at what I did and what this monster could become. Finally, I myself realized that I had a problem with my temper no matter what medicines, no matter how much self-medicating with marijuana, and no matter what I did.

Even though there were weeks where I did not drink any alcohol, there was almost no day that went by in over 10 years without smoking pot. There seemed to be no difficulty avoiding all other recreational drugs like mushrooms, nitrous oxide, and Ecstasy. What I needed to do was try and stop getting messed up so much and wait for my mind to heal (uhhh...ummm right)? Simply skipping pot every other day and no longer doing anything else except occasional drinking would help (is what I thought).

However, even one day without pot (regardless of alcohol or any other drug) gave me psychotic illusions and depression so I would 'need' to smoke again to stop the pain, voices, and thoughts. Once pot made life happy and fun and then it made life better by numbing it. Now pot did nothing except making it a daily necessity to live life and do anything at all without it being painfully intolerable. I always heard, believed, and then told myself that marijuana was not addictive in any form. This was a very unpleasant reality to know my friend marijuana was no longer my friend and severely turned on me affecting my mental capacities and mood swings beyond my control.

The last little bit of power I thought within me was extinguished. No longer can any doctor, medicine, drug, or person help me manage anything in life. My chance at any future was hopeless. The different

paths that I took over the years were either given or chosen by me. Never did I expect that there was eventually going to be only one end destination on my journey...despair.
March 25

#86 (Day 86) Honest Open Willing 2012 Post

All I really could do was stay entirely away from my wife and kids before I hurt them worse. That scared the crap out of me because I had 'felt' that my parents' 'upbringing' made me into who I hate and despise now. Of course that was not true but it was a good excuse to blame someone except me. I could not even blame God because I had given up on Him a while back (although I later learned He never gave up on me). So right then I felt so hopeless that the only 'reasonable' option was to stay entirely away from my kids to 'try' and avoid happening to them what I was going through now as a failed adult. Everything had been tried, changed, and attempted to 'get better' that was within my control and power. If only I could succeed in doing something proving to myself there was some power or control in me a little bit. Maybe that could be what was needed to start and get out of this painful cycle?

On February 20, 2007 is when I had my last cigarette and never went back. That was something I needed to do for myself. If I had the power to stop for good then maybe I had the power to stop other things for good. Since that day, I have not picked up or had one little puff of a cigarette ever again. The smell and knowing what it did to my body and even now the addiction taking over my head upsets me. It has been over 5 years (as of March 25, 2012) and I feel healthier because of that. My wife did say back then that if I had to stop one thing it be cigarettes now and pot later. That I figured was realistic because if I could stop with cigarettes that I could eventually stop with pot. Now I knew pot was something I could not do the rest of my life but always felt like it was too late to stop at various points. I had starting cigarettes at age 19 and except for a few periods of 'quitting' for a few weeks or months, had been smoking half to one pack a day for over 19 years.

My personality and mood swings were still there but my addiction to Nicotine was bad for my lungs, throat, heart, and those many other organs and body parts that could get messed up. I was exactly the same in many ways except not being a slave to needing a cigarette, dying on long airplane and car rides to immediately find a place where you can smoke, hiding in places to have cigarettes where you should not smoke, going out in the middle of the night or 2 feet of snow or hurricane to buy cigarettes because you had to have them. I already had bad mental illnesses (and still do), physical and addictive OCD natured mental case addicted to anything. Finally, I felt like this one addiction was no longer keeping me controlled and trapped into a confined world. It was a great feeling that got stronger and better each day. This is fine with me that there are still many people that smoke and I am not an anti-smoker crusader. Most people want to stop and can with the encouragement and support (and with the patch as directed...for me).

Maybe my physical health was a little better without the chemicals and addictive nicotine in cigarettes. Constant pipe smoking and bong hits of marijuana continued to have me cough up lungs in the morning and every day. It was hard to breathe even with just smoking pot. The brick wall was fast approaching and it looked like there was nowhere to go. My power over cigarettes was great but now I realized there was more to my problem. Quitting one problem is not something to settle for when there appears to be one or two (or 20+) more. This did give me a little hope that maybe my unmanageable life could be managed but maybe I needed some help to have the ability (or power) to stop or at least slow down the pot. All of my family (and the few friends that I still had) were so happy, proud, and grateful I stopped cigarettes mostly for one 'selfish; reason....so I can live longer and be healthier for them and my kids. How could I not have felt somewhat touched by this?

Now it had just become 2008 and my last cigarette was over 10 months ago. I was going to turn 40 in November which was only 11 months away and still knew I had to get some sort of support group for the marijuana. I searched the Internet for a very long time to research and find something geared to help heavy hitting pot smokers. There was a website that I found which mentioned a meeting that met once a week at Bergen Regional Hospital in Paramus NJ. This place used to be named Bergen Pines and is known by many as the county's mental health hospital. There was a phone number to call for more information. The strength and courage somehow come to me just enough to dial that number, not hang up, and talk with the person on the other end from Marijuana Anonymous (aka MA).

This fellow marijuana addict knew and understood what I was going through and exactly how I felt. The 'correct' and 'acceptable' kind of encouraging words got me on Sunday, January 20, 2008 to attend my first MA 'support group' meeting. This was not Narcotics Anonymous for addicts with major drug problems and it was not Alcoholics Anonymous for drunks that only had problems holding their liquor. This was maybe the first beginning of approaching the First Step to recovery but not the entire First Step...yet...because I was still smoking pot and thought that was my only problem. I could identify with pot heads but did not see myself as a person with drug and alcohol problems.

Sunday, January 27, 2008 was my 2nd MA meeting and it was suggested that I stop smoking pot at least 'one day at a time' (WTF is one day going to do?), get a 'sponsor' (another man telling me what to do?), and work some 'steps' (after reading them I was like WTF)! My thoughts were what the hell is one day going to do, why would I want to have some other man tell me what to do, and the 12 Steps to Recovery from Marijuana Addiction made no sense. I did not need or want to follow their suggestions because this was something they might be able to help me with but it would be on my own terms.

No one would tell me what to do but I did at least listen to the suggestions. The money in the basket I understood quickly because it was voluntarily and the money was to pay for the room and supplies since none of 'us' likes being supported by outside people or groups. The spiritual aspect still sounded like religion and was not too 'Jewish' although I was no longer too 'Jewish'. Holding hands and looking at each other in the face while making eye contact seemed like a 'cult' or maybe the men liked other men in 'that way' which I had long gotten past the phase decades ago. Yet, I agreed to come back each Sunday night, once a week, since that was only every 7 days and not too much inconvenience or out of my busy schedule. It was a few days after my second meeting when I ran head on into 'THE WALL' which wacked me in the face so quick and so hard that I panicked.
March 26

#87 (Day 87) Honest Open Willing 2012 Post

My parents were taking the entire family on a cruise to Bermuda to celebrate their 50th wedding anniversary. The trip was scheduled for Saturday, June 28 until Thursday, July 3, 2008 and was planned for well over a year in advance. I did not think about any real bad aspects except being trapped with my entire family five days on a ship in the middle of the Atlantic. That was something that I could try and make the most of for my parents' sake. As it got to be the end of January the thought occurred that it was an international trip with customs and luggage searches. The smell of pot would also be extremely noticeable on a little boat. What could I do? Not one day could go by without me needing to smoke a lot of this stuff that I could not bring with me! Holy crap!

My fear was expressed to my wife who wanted me to be less stressed on this trip and for all of us to enjoy ourselves. The advice she gave me was to maybe not take all my medicines that would interact with alcohol (gets me too drunk or can harm my internal organs) and basically to just drink a lot instead of smoking pot. That may not be exactly how ('HOW') she said it and it was not to enable anything but just to ease my mind. She had tried to support and encourage me to reduce pot and to stop other drugs for over 10 years but I was stubborn, not going to listen, and resisted each piece of help offered every so often without being pushy or demanding. Being honest, open, and willing much sooner would have made the inevitable easier to do than continuing year after year after year.

This idea that I needed and must have 'something' to depend on as a crutch or trapped like in a cage is what exactly made me finally (and I mean finally) realize that it was much more than pot or any 1 to 12 addictive or negative aspects. It was everything about me and my entire life going deeper into the woods getting lost forever or going down into a whirlpool dragged to the bottom of the ocean to die (and I was going on a cruise on the ocean soon)! There was no other way to go but admit...that I was powerless over many things in my life and must get real, professional assistance to help me work out a way to manage my life again and 'be normal' and stop hating myself...for me.

What I did that afternoon was completely freak out. My mind and my heart were really racing like a desperate animal. It was impossible to be calm, cool, or collective and even to breathe. This sounds weird but I called my pharmacist and my medical physician to get advice on who to contact and where to go. There were three places that I was told about and immediately called them one after another. The first place was not taking any more people right now. The second place was part of a hospital program that I would have to apply for and it would be a longer term inpatient rehab type place. However, if I was 'just' a pot head then it may not be at all appropriate. The last place (like the other two) did not accept my insurance. The cost would be outrageous if out of pocket without coverage. Thankfully, the last place recommended another outpatient treatment facility in Paramus. Although getting very discouraged, I called this last place with little hope of finding anywhere or anyone to help me now that I was desperate to be helped.... They accepted my insurance, accepted 'pot heads' and gave me an intake interview for Friday, February 1, 2008!

The day before we interview at this outpatient facility in Paramus was Thursday, January 31, 2008. My last drink or drug was (of course) puffing heavily on my marijuana pipe to 'prepare' for the meeting in the morning. At about 9:58 pm I was about done watching Lost and going to watch Celebrity Rehab at 10:00 pm. They were both being taped on my VCR. But at 9:58 pm is when the baby monitor and yelling from upstairs required my assistance. When I came back down minutes later my pipe was already all smoked out. It was not repacked and nothing else was done (like a drink or inhaling nitrous oxide from the whipped cream cylinders). The last few minutes were watched of Lost and I went upstairs to sleep. Again, that last puff was the last of anything to prevent me from being (and remaining) both clean and sober.

Interesting thing about that episode of Lost was that it was titled 'The Beginning of the End'. Charlie (the heroin addict) and another island survivor are inside a self-contained underwater science station. Charlie is inside the little communication room down there which has a big metal hatch door. He had just pushed a button that allowed his fellow castaways to contact the outside world for help with a satellite phone. After the button is pushed, he sees that there will soon be a grenade detonated from outside that window. He rushes to close and seal himself inside the room just as the explosion breaks through the wall and the ocean water rushes in. This was done to protect his friend down there with him who remains unharmed looking inside that sealed room as the chamber is quickly being flooding. His friend, the hero, seems calm and at ease with his destiny and impending demise.

Charlie helped all of his friends, expressed true human love with one of the pure hearted women, and was clean for a few days. Then they show him drowning in the water filled chamber as he dies floating there with his life snuffed out as he surely goes up to Heaven. He had originally been selfish and self-centered caring for no one else. In the end, he was starting to 'recover' and 'get better' while experience a spiritual change that allowed him to sacrifice himself for his friends. That is something very deep (at least to me) because I loved that show and his death made me cry. I was proud of his character (although fictional) for many reasons including being 'a role model and inspiration'. Never will I forget his sacrifice and death right after my last dealing with marijuana before I went upstairs to (not as heroically) help my wife with one of the kids that needed assistance. There was no reason to ever watch that episode of Celebrity Rehab because I knew my 'Rehab' would not be as glamorous or unrealistic as theirs and I was right.

Tonight is when I officially said goodnight to the end of the old way and got off the wrong path which led me into the brick wall of despair. The next morning is when I officially said good morning to the beginning of the new way and got on the right path which would lead me in the direction of hope. This was 'The Beginning From The End'.
March 27

#88 (Day 88) Honest Open Willing 2012 Post
The appointment that following Friday, February 1, 2008 morning consisted of two women that were experts in the field of psychology, chemical dependence, and the combination of mental illness with chemical addiction. This intake interview lasted over two and a half hours with many questions that were very personal and psychological. They told me I was definitely Bipolar 2 (still), OCD (still), and had an overall addiction problem (which was confirmed). I was accepted and told to start that upcoming Monday which was the day after the 2008 Super Bowl. My program there would be four days a week, three and a half hours a day, and my insurance allowed something like 10 weeks. My co-pay was $20 a day but that was a bargain since $80 a week was much less than half of what I was spending for marijuana each week. I told them that I only had a little bit of pot left at home and would make sure to smoke it all so it is gone when I start on Monday!

The two people doing the evaluation were extremely nice and asked if I did any mind or mood altering substance today. I said no and they said please not to smoke any of that 'little bit of pot', drink any alcohol, or do any type of drug so I can come in Monday four days clean and sober. There was some confusion because I had a problem with smoking too much pot and did not really have a problem with alcohol. My concern was stated to them and this is when they told me that all drugs are bad if you have an addictive problem and that alcohol is a drug. When you stop with one type of addiction it leaves a hole inside you that usually must get filled back up again with that addiction or with another addiction. This would continue unless the right help is obtained to stop that vicious cycle.

This is not what I signed up for but was willing to do as they asked. That would be difficult (again the Super Bowl was in two days) but I knew if I could do this much by myself that I could do a lot more with this place that might restore me to sanity. Afterward, an extremely long stage fright episode was endured to give them a supervised urine sample (to get a baseline of my chemical makeup or something). My peeing was always private and done in a stall or room alone. It was an effort to just get relaxed enough to give the amount needed although I really had to go. Once that was over it was time to go home and 'be good' until Monday……

That Super Bowl Sunday (February 3, 2008) there was a meeting of Marijuana Anonymous. There are meetings for all support and anonymous groups usually always even on holidays like Christmas, Thanksgiving, New Year's Eve, and the Super Bowl. This was my third meeting with this group and my first meeting where I was not stoned a few hours before or even that day. There were three days of no pot or anything else under my belt. This was probably the longest amount of time without pot (or otherwise alcohol) in over 20 years. I was thankful and proud to tell this group, who gave me the initial assistance, that they helped me make my own choice, and was starting my outpatient program the next day. The support and pride from them toward me was such an unbelievable (positive) feeling!

Monday, February 4, 2008 was the first day attending 'my new school' classified as CD (Chemical Dependency). Ironically, every time I had started a new school growing up I was classified Emotionally Disturbed (ED). This was for four days each week with Friday, Saturday, and Sunday off. They highly recommended going to AA, NA, or MA meetings at least on those three days there was no outpatient classes. They also recommended finding a sponsor at one of the meetings that we could relate with. My MA meeting each Sunday is the only anonymous group that I attended. There were no other MA meetings often or nearby. That would be a problem getting to an MA meeting Friday or Saturday.

Going to NA and AA meetings were highly recommended to me since any drug or alcohol goes against their program. If pot, alcohol, or any drug was used then we would be expelled. They tried to teach me that I was more than just a 'pot head' and these other fellowship meetings would be good to keep me clean and sober from everything that would negatively affect me. Still, I could not get myself to go with the addicts and alcoholics although I soon realized they were just like me too! At my once a week MA meeting there really was not anyone that seemed 'sponsor-able'. I did very little extracurricular things that this outpatient center asked or highly recommended. The things they taught and the literature handed to us was thoroughly studied and memorized. However, I soon discovered that book smart recovery just by itself is not the right way.

Getting deeply depressed and weeping out of control was constantly happening several times a day. I was too emotional and acted crazier than usual without anything 'to help me'. Sleeping at night was difficult since my marijuana sleeping aid was discontinued. There was no more numbing life and my experiences handling feelings were minimal. The outpatient center's psychiatrist did start me on a prescription of Seroquel to take each night before bed. This medication would knock me out cold to sleep all night. It was also an anti-anxiety, anti-depressant. This was not enough to help.

One week after I started they moved me from CD (Chemical Dependency) to MICA (Mentally Ill Chemical Affected) on Monday, February 11, 2008. This felt a little better because now it was with people that had mental problems and substance abuse just like me. There were still difficulties and interaction problems but all was going decent for about two weeks until Friday, February 22, 2008. One of the other patients had gotten me upset and verbally I lost my temper. The counselor asked me to go outside the room into the hallway to talk to her. Then she had me wait inside a smaller session room while she had a short meeting in the supervising therapist's office.
March 28

#89 (Day 89) Honest Open Willing 2012 Post
I think it was within the very first few days of starting my outpatient

program that I asked my parents to come over my house. Everything was told to them in person about what was going on. This was not just because I worked with them and they needed to know my temporary new work hours. This was because they were my parents and deserved to know what was going on in my life for the longest time and what was going on with me now. This was not easy because I knew my mom would cry and my dad would get very upset. It was asked of them to please listen without getting too sad or mad. They were both much better than I expected and gave me their continued love and support as always. Then my journey continued as previously discussed.

After about two weeks, it was time for my brother and two sisters to know what was happening. This would be harder than telling my parents in many ways. All three are older and were pretty much fed up with their 'baby brother' at this point. It took a while to word everything correctly without making anything sound like they should forgive, forget, or feel sorry for me. The following is the 'final copy' of the e-mail that I sent to my brother and two sisters. Yes there are some grammatical errors (effected vs. affected and my self vs. myself) and factual errors (my clean date is considered the day of my last drug or drink which is January 31, 2008) which I see now. However, I did not want to correct or change anything to keep this exactly as it was received around the middle of February 2008......

***** E-MAIL BEGINS *****

"Hello my name is Steve and I am a recovering addict. I also have several mental illnesses that many of you know about or have guessed about by now.

This is not a chain letter and I very humbly ask that you read this entire letter with an open mind and heart. I do not mean to cause any further pain, confusion, sadness, or anger from any of you getting this letter. This applies to any of your friends or family that has been negatively effected by me. This is one of the hardest things I have ever admitted or had to do in my life.

On Monday 4 February 2008, I began a 4-day a week 4-hour a day intense program for CD Chemical Dependency at an In-patient Outpatient rehabilitation clinic called High Focus Center in Paramus.

Starting Monday 11 February 2008, they moved me into the MICA Mental Illness Chemical Abuse division for further treatment and help 5-days a week for 3-1/2 hours a day.

I have been an addict for many years using my addictions to 'self medicate', feel better about myself, and/or to relax. At first it was just alcohol. Later I became more of an addict where anything that felt good was what I needed. This included but was not limited to marijuana, which became the largest, worst, and most crippling of all my addictions.

The other major problem is that my mental illnesses include OCD Obsessive Compulsive Disorder and Bipolar, which I have also had for a longer time than my addictions. The OCD controlled my life and made me very compulsive with all of my addictions. The Bipolar made me have very emotional mood swings ranging from manic depression with suicidal thoughts and feeling inferior all the way to superior feelings that I was the only normal person in the world and everyone else was to blame. My anger and hatred for myself was directed mostly to those that I know and know me the best.

Very recently I have learned that my mental illnesses and chemical abuse together were destroying my life and those of all my loved ones. I never knew that marijuana made my previous medicines and therapy useless and that it causes such Psychotic episodes and extremely messes the brain. Over time, marijuana became my only friend and family. It kept me physically and emotionally away from my true loved friends and family members.

Please understand, all my efforts were to still be as loving and active as marijuana would allow me for my immediately family including my wife and kids. They mean the world to me and it is their love for myself that helps me through my new life of recovery wanting to make them love me so I can truly love myself the way I should. There was no room for anyone else and it soon became hard to even focus on my family.

As of February 1, 2008 I have been 100% clean. No alcohol, unauthorized medications, marijuana, or anything else has been or will be in my system. 24 hours was the most I had ever been clean in the past and not by choice. So far, I have also been to several MA Marijuana Anonymous meetings at Bergen Regional Hospital (formerly known as

Bergen Pines) and attend many online MA meetings. The support that I receive as a marijuana addict with other addictions and illness from the other members and from High Focus Center is incredible. I am not alone and never want to be again.

My mind is much clearer than it has been in over 20 years. However, my emotions and mind are very bad and running rampant with my mental illnesses without Pot. All I can think of is the ways I hurt each of you and even your loved ones. This was done because I hated my self and blamed everyone for my shortcomings. Anytime I was hurt I would lash out to hurt back much worse. This was uncontrollable and was not just short term but long term. Not just compulsive lashing but long term built up anger.

It will take time but I want to return to my life and include each of you. All I ask is for your love, understanding, and prayers. Apologizes alone cannot be enough for some of the things I have said, done, or thought. I can tell you that I am receiving and accepting the best care to help me recover and be a positive part of your lives again.

This letter could go on and become a book if I included all my wrongs and stories. There are many questions and concerns that each of you might have. If you would like me to write specifically or would like to talk to me then please let me know especially by phone. There was a time I could not or would not even want to discuss my addictions or illnesses in person, letter, or phone but that has changed recently.

I do not need pity, enabling, anger, sadness, or anything else except patience and love. I love you all and thank you very much!

Steve
Marijuana Addict, General Addict, and OCD/bipolar patient

Now, I have started the Twelve Steps for MA which are very similar to those of AA, NA, and other Anonymous groups. The first one is the most important one and I have already been there soon to move on. By the way, I am still Jewish and the Twelve Steps can be for any HP Higher Power. My Higher Power is 'Love' which includes my family, kids and of course G-d.

1. We admitted we were powerless over marijuana, that our lives had become unmanageable"

***** E-MAIL ENDS *****

Then it was about a week later that there was a major problem. On Friday, February 22, 2008, one of the other patients had gotten me upset and verbally I lost my temper. The session counselor then asked me to go outside the room into the hallway to talk to her and then to wait inside a smaller session room while she had a short meeting in the supervising therapist's office......
March 29

#90 (Day 90) Honest Open Willing 2012 Post
The MICA (Mentally Ill Chemical Affected) Counselor who was working with my group during that session (of only 8 or so other patients) came out of the Rehab Clinic Supervising Therapist's office with her. They told me that starting Monday I would be going into the third type of group there at the center which was PSYCH. That division concentrated on mental problems and not chemical addictions like CD or MICA. I tried to tell them it would be wrong since I felt better in MICA because I had dual problems. The Supervising Therapist went back into her office. Then my Counselor asked that I return to the group for the rest of the day and come in Monday with the PSYCH Counselor. My hostile demeanor towards her is why she instead had me go back into the smaller session room where I had earlier waited. There I was told to journal my current feelings on paper with a pen (or maybe a pencil?) using one of her cool fluorescent, bright colored clip boards.

The clip board was indeed cool but writing with a pen (or pencil) was not my thing. Word processing programs on computers were easier to correct and spell check. Every minute that went by had my aggravation level increase. Thirty minutes later is when my explosive behavior 'made me break' her clipboard (being used to journal) over my knee. Quickly, I realized this was not a good thing. That 'accidentally broken' clipboard was thrown out in a trash can a few rooms away under some garbage and a new clipboard was obtained all without being caught. However, someone must have seen me throw out a clipboard, knew I was with this Counselor, and told her what I had done. She came into the smaller session room rather agitated and asked why I broke one of her clip boards. This Counselor made it sound like it was personally done to hurt her since she had gotten me angry. That was mostly true but I did not admit it and said it 'broke accidentally'.

Another longer meeting was held 'in my honor' in the Supervising Therapist's office. Afterward, the Supervising Therapist told me to go home for the rest of the day and call them Monday morning instead of coming right in. Over the weekend is when I calmed down realizing maybe they were right and I should give what they said a try. Monday morning I called and they had me come in to have a meeting with that Counselor, the Supervising Therapist, and also the Outpatient Rehab Clinic's director! They thought everything over and decided their facility would no longer be a good place for me.

There were too many problems between me and everyone else. I was constantly taking too many inventories and judgments about the other patients thinking they were all too different from me and I was unique. The staff would always try to calm me down, reason with me, and get me quiet but instead I got angry or depressed. The staff and the patients just could not work together with me any longer and it was not doing them or me any good. They official kicked me out of that outpatient rehab on Monday, February 25, 2008. I was told that it would benefit me to get a good psychiatrist, therapist, go to AA or NA meetings, find a sponsor, and basically felt like they were saying 'good bye, good luck, and good riddance because we don't want you.'

This was now my lowest bottom which I did not think could get any lower. Feeling that even a place like where I was attending no longer could help or wanted me meant there was absolutely no hope for me. This level of being desperate, hopeless, and depressed made me feel very much something that I had felt many times and tried to do a few times in the past. This time the feelings were the most intense. This time I was the most determined and would search the Internet but not to find another outpatient program or support group. This time I would search the Internet to find the easiest, quickest, and most painless way to kill myself.

All of the voices and reasoning inside me were unanimously in favor. There were many different websites and videos offering several ways to commit suicide. Every site, every link, and every method that I looked at made me feel more uneasy, sick, and scared with every click. The thought and ideas that I had about ending my life over the last few hours was getting less determined. There would probably be an excellent chance I would fail at successfully killing myself again and that I did love my family too much to do this to them. Then I wept for a long time before I remembered there were one or two 'other last resort' things told to me when I was kicked out of my outpatient rehab.

Looking online under www.AA.org is when I found a more local www.nnjaa.org website of Alcoholics Anonymous. This showed there was a meeting the next day, in the next town over, at 12:15 pm that afternoon. Then I figured there was nothing more to lose and called to get an appointment with the psychiatrist they recommended. This guy accepted my medical insurance and gave me an appointment right away on Wednesday which was the day after the meeting. Now I had a meeting and then doctor scheduled over the next two days. This gave me enough reason to get off the computer, go to sleep, and hold off on finding ways to commit suicide. Tuesday morning I woke up still alive and nervously awaiting 12:15 pm with much anxiety.

There were two other AA meetings which I had gone to in the past but not for the right reasons. One meeting was back in 1989 during the whole college / court fiasco. There was a girl who I thought was hot that wanted to know if I would be interested to go with her to a meeting. She did not have a license and knew I smoked a lot of weed. Of course I pretended to be interested thinking I would score with her but did not. That meeting was totally 'not for me' because it was at night with 'scary, weird, different' people who I would normally not hang out with. They had serious problems but were unlike me (as I thought back then in 1989) when I had the power to help myself....when I wanted to.

Then there was another meeting in 1999 which I was strongly urged to attend at the request of my therapist at that time. He stated that I should try at least one AA meeting before we met again next week. This guy was pretty cool with me so, after 10 years, my second meeting was attended with much reluctance and closed mind. There I went, there I stayed the hour, and there I left feeling like this was a waste of time. A group like this was not anything I needed. They had emptiness, unhappiness, and messed up lives unlike me (as I still thought back in 1999). No one else could really help me because if I was not able to

manage my life then how could these people!
March 30

#91 (Day 91) Honest Open Willing 2012 Post

On Tuesday, February 26, 2008 was my first AA meeting that I willingly attended. Even though I had gone to about six of the Sunday night Marijuana Anonymous meetings that year, this was not the same. This Alcoholics Anonymous meeting was during daylight, at a church, and the people there were older and seemed happier. There were a lot more people and at least half were women and almost all of them looked (to me then) like they were 50, 60, 70 or even older. The general theme was similar with things that were said, 'The 12 Steps' shown on the wall, and a basket that was sent around mid-meeting to collect our own funds to be self-supporting.

This was alright but the AA people asked that everyone only talk about their problems with alcohol (and not other drugs). The meeting seemed very religious and there was no cursing at all. My problem involved pot, other drugs, and also alcohol. I was Jewish and was not interested in joining a church group or a religious cult. Cursing was not a requirement but my impulsive mouth had me very nervous what to say and did not want to offend anyone with a potty mouth or talks of pot. It was not my intention yet to give up on Alcoholics Anonymous after just this first awkward meeting. There were many things I tried in my life more than once before I decided it was either good or bad. Sometimes I still tried things a few more times even when bad just to make sure it was not anything I could like. This included cigarettes, pot, and beer which I did eventually grow accustomed to and....enjoyed (for a while).

After the meeting, I again went back to my computer to give another fellowship a try that was focused on drugs such as maybe marijuana. Looking online under www.NA.org is when I found a more local www.northernarea.org website of Narcotics Anonymous. This showed there was a meeting that same day, two towns over where I grew up, at 8:00 pm that night. Now I can try one of each fellowship (AA and NA) and see where I fit in the most and had less of a problem hanging with 'those people'.

The NA meeting was different from the AA meeting because they hugged instead of shaking and holding hands. They had no rules about profanity (up to a point) and people were allowed to talk about any drug addiction which affected them. Plus, alcohol was considered a drug. This seemed much more of a fit than AA. There was still 'The 12 Steps of NA' shown on the wall which were exactly like 'The 12 Steps of AA' but with the First Step stating "We admitted we were powerless over our addiction - that our lives had become unmanageable." The First Step of AA had said just that we were 'powerless over alcohol' instead of 'powerless over our addiction'.

All this was a little bit confusing but I saw younger people who seemed more like me than the people of AA. One other thing that was cool is that a gallon size plastic baggie was used to collect our own funds to be self-supporting instead of a basket. There was never a basket used to 'get my stuff' when I had my 'difficulties' and 'vices'. However, there was almost always a plastic baggie of different sizes to 'get my stuff'. Still I was going to try these NA meetings along with AA meetings and of course stay with my original Sunday night MA meeting. There were a lot of NA meetings and even more AA meetings in the area several times a day where the MA meeting was only once a week. The variety would be good for me to pick and choose which parts of each fellowship to follow and which parts to leave alone.

My outpatient rehab clinic showed me the door because I was not ready to be honest enough, open enough, and definitely willing enough. That cost me what I thought was my only opportunity at a last chance for help. First, I had finally admitted being powerless over a problem that had made my life become unmanageable. Second, I did come to believe that it would be more than just me alone to get better. Third, I decided to do something about this and allow myself to get help. Those are (sort of) the first three steps out of the 12 steps to recovery. They were not 'worked' the correct way, thoroughly, or consistently. They still would not be until a little while later.

That next day is where I was willing to do a little more of these things out of desperation. Both of these two different meetings of AA and then NA were on that Tuesday, February 26, 2008. Then I decided to continue and go to more of these meetings. That next day Wednesday, February 27, 2008 was most certainly NOT my first appointment with a psychiatrist. This was probably the first appointment with a psychiatrist or any therapist, sociologist, psychologist, and similar that I did not want to bullshit, impress, or cherry coat my life and how things were. This was the first time that I decided to try my hardest to work with someone to try and get me a little saner.

It was time to start being H.O.W. with my newest psychiatrist. He was told as much as I could say in that one initial hour. Boy did he get a lot of information within 60 minutes and was probably told more real, honest, deep things about me, my past, and my present than I ever told anyone else in my life. The medicines for OCD and Bipolar were continued by him and he later tweaked them around with different dosages, different times of day, and totally different medications. Now these may work better since I was now willing to get help and willing to stop pot, alcohol, and all other things for good that fought against my recovery.

This psychiatrist was very good, knew about the 12 Steps and fellowships like AA and NA, and got my records from the Outpatient Rehab Center. I did feel comfortable around him. All these things allowed him to start assisting me now that I wanted to be assisted. His role was to supervise my therapy and prescribe the correct medicines. His role was not to provide my weekly, hour long therapy since his sessions, from that point forward, were to meet with me every other week for 30 minutes to review how things were going along. That is why he recommended for me to find a good therapist that was in my medical plan to see each week for an hour.

He was also glad that I already was attending my MA, NA, and AA meetings at least once a day. One of the biggest recommendations in recovery is not to drink (or smoke pot or do other drugs) and go to meetings. This does not mean not to drink and also not to go to meetings which my warped mind kiddingly thought. This also does not mean you should go to meeting each day but just don't drink, smoke pot, or use drugs right before each meeting which is something a few people actually do think in the beginning. New people in recovery should attend at least one meeting every single day for 90 days.

When asked what you do after those 90 days it is usually responded to do it again! That way you concentrate on your meeting for that one day and 'plan' to do this each day for simply 90 days in advance. You are not projecting a future of meetings forever and ever. You simply plan on

going each 'day at a time' for about 3 months at a time which is much less than even one year. The 'One Day at a Time' is the best concept because it is easy to wake up, go through the day, and go to sleep. Concentrate on the day without worrying about what happened yesterday and what is going to happen tomorrow. That ruins the day you are in and does no good in any way to regret or dread before or after your day now living. That is good advice but easier said than done for some people...at first.
March 31

#92 (Day 92) Honest Open Willing 2012 Post

Life continued as I attended several different Narcotics Anonymous (NA) and Alcoholics Anonymous (AA) meetings at least once a day and sometimes twice a day. Marijuana Anonymous (MA) was still considered to be my primary fellowship even though there was only the one Sunday night meeting each week. This was the only Marijuana Anonymous meeting within a 30 minute driving radius from my home. There were three other MA meetings during the week but they were far away (35 to 40 minutes) in Nyack NY and Valley Cottage NY. It was rare that I drove farther away than 10 to 15 minutes from my house if I had to drive even that far. One of my many phobias was driving especially around other cars and people.

Being a member of all three of these fellowships was a little confusing. Yes, they are all extremely similar using the Steps, sponsorship, structure, ideas, and other things like AA which started first in 1935. However, each one had slightly different terminology, practices, and customs. Mixing up words, actions, and expressions happened often which was a little embarrassing. This is almost like your dad having three brothers that are all your uncles who you hang out with. They all have a lot of similar things in common, look a lot alike, and all come from the same parents. But each one has a different name, their history involves different people and events, and they do some things the other two do not.

The day that you had your last drug is considered your Day 1 of being clean in NA. The term 'clean' is mostly an NA term but they also do consider alcohol as a drug (which it is). Even if you 'just' drink, then NA still considers that a relapse, slip, or 'going out' and your clean day will start over as Day 1. Obviously this also applies to doing any other drugs such as marijuana, crack, heroin, cocaine, meth, amphetamines, or even inhalants like nitrous oxide. The myth about people in Narcotics Anonymous still being able to drink alcohol but not using other drugs is false. A drug is a drug is a drug plus one is too many and a thousand is never enough.

The day that you had your last drink is considered your Day 1 of being sober in AA. The term 'sober' is mostly an AA term which involves alcohol. However, AA still considers it a relapse, slip, or 'going out' and your sober day will start over as Day 1 even if you do any of these other drugs. The similar myth about people in Alcoholics Anonymous still being able to smoke pot or 'pop pills' but not drink alcohol is false. Anything that affects your mind or mood is just as bad as taking another drink.

AA just concentrates on 'alcohol' so everyone feels similar, relates better, and does not need to identify themselves differently from each other. There are people who almost never drink but have had problems with other drugs. Those people can join AA because they are not allowed to use those and other drugs. Those people can join AA because there is a huge potential to abuse alcohol when you stop with another drug. The idea in AA is to NOT take that next drink whether you did it often as an 'alcoholic' or rarely but did occasionally drink as an addict. Taking that drink can easily get you back in that vicious cycle of your other addictions. This is how it is for me now but I still had a few more months of being slightly confused.

Later I discovered that many groups of Marijuana Anonymous only considered marijuana as a problem. Some members eventually expressed to me that they would have a drink or two throughout the year because they had no problem with alcohol. Most members did no marijuana, alcohol, or any other drugs because they knew there was or would be the potential for major problems. As long as you did not smoke pot and did not care about doing other drugs or drinking alcohol then you could continue being 'clean'. The myth about people in Marijuana Anonymous still being able to drink alcohol and using other drugs but NOT smoking pot is somewhat true depending on the MA group and the MA person. That is not totally bad but became an awful loop hole for me to consider. After all, there was one time that I felt I was 'only' a pot head. Maybe I could drink alcohol?

Regardless of your slip, each fellowship would definitely welcome you 'back' and no one gets mad or scolds you because many people do slip sometimes more than once. That is life on your own (which can suck often) while not working the program with attending meetings, keeping in contact with your sponsor or 'Network', doing the Steps, etc. Coming back to start over is not a requirement but sometimes helps to prove to that individual that it really does not work in the outside world when they leave. It makes them 'hit their bottom' harder and encourages them to work the program better. There really is no failing or being kicked out of any fellowship. Except for me but that is later.

March 1, 2008 was my thirty days of being 'clean' in MA and got my 30 Day Chip. It was also my thirty days of being 'clean' in NA and got my 30 Day key tag stating I was "Clean & Serene" for 30 days. That was a cool, rewarding feeling that when shared with the group makes them feel the program works and makes me feel the program works! There is only a 90 day anniversary in my AA groups and then it is celebrated each year. Both MA and NA had celebrations for 30 days, 60 days, 90 days, 6 months, 9 months, one year, 18 months, and then 'Multiple Years' each year. That was nice extra incentive for the first two years but should not be the only reason to stay for that time period. On March 31, 2008 was my sixty days of being 'clean' in MA and NA and I got my 60 Day Chip and key tag respectively. I had to wait 30 more days to get a 90 Day coin in AA. It was worth the wait when received.

It was important to try different meetings of each fellowship until I found the right combination of meeting or meetings for every day of the week. Each new meeting meant being nervous, scared, and not knowing who will be there and how that meeting is run. There are a lot of people who attend these things and each meeting may have several you have met but also a lot you meet for the first time. Eventually, you can go to another new meeting in the area and already know many people. Usually, a meeting book with a list of all the other meetings in the area (for that fellowship) is given to new comers. The meeting book is typically passed around so people with at least 90 days of continued sobriety and clean time write down their first name, initial of their last name (for anonymity), and phone number. This is voluntary but almost all of them do this to help you because they were in the same exact situation at one point.

The men write down their information for the men that are new in the program. The women write down their information for the women that are new in the program. There have been lots of problems in the past when men and women 'help' each other to recover because of emotional or physical attachment sometimes used to fill in that emptiness of their addiction. Even if your intentions are pure, these things still do occur when time or the other person possibly changes. Then you have something hurting, and not helping, either person's situation and recovery. The men should stick with the men and the women should stick with the women for support in their contact list and especially as a sponsor! This is sometimes difficult to do because some women were never really good around other women. Many times, men were not really good being sincere, honest, open, and willing around other men. Getting over these feelings does allow you to eventually work well in life with people of the same and of the opposite sex.

Every one of them once came in new, scared, and got support from the others already there. This is considered giving back freely of what was freely given to you. Kind of a neat concept since nothing is expected from you and there are no dues, fees, or catches. Calling at least one person on the list each day means you are making contact with someone who identifies with you and you with them. That is especially good to do if you need advice or are thinking about picking up a drug, drink, or doing anything to hurt yourself, others, or your recovery. If everything seems to be going well then there are many other reasons to call someone each day including not isolating or feeling alone while having a sense of belonging. This not only helps you but also helps the other person for the same reasons and also to feel wanted or helpful in life.
April 1

#93 (Day 93) Honest Open Willing 2012 Post
Some people in AA told me about a meeting Saturday mornings that breaks into two groups. One group is for beginnings in a back boiler room of the church. The people under one year get to sit around a long rectangular table with someone over 4 years' sobriety and clean time chairing the meeting. After a brief 5 to 10 minute talk about once being a beginner and some suggestions they ask for a topic from the table. This is then discussed (shared) around the table in order with each person having the opportunity to get up to 2 or 3 minutes to talk if they wish. There is always the option to 'just share the time' if you have

nothing to say or really do not feel like talking. That is totally fine until you are ready and have anything to 'let out' or express.

People with over one year sobriety sit in chairs around the outside perimeter of the table. They too can share their beginning experience and later experience with the topic if there is time after all those with under one year sobriety has had the turn to share their thoughts or just share the time. These 'non-beginner' people are there not just for moral support but to also listen and remember what it was like when they sat at that table. 'Keeping it Green' means to always remember that 'working the program' (the right way) is important to....stay recovered. It was and still is an excellent meeting!

The first time that I attended this Saturday morning meeting was on Saturday, March 1, 2008. I still was not quite sure about many of the phrases, terms, and concepts of things related to the meetings and the program. The collecting money and support idea was grasped but things like why you really need a sponsor and what you do together was foreign. Many of those 12 Steps did not seem like something I would do and some did not sound like they were anything concrete to actually or physically do. There was a lot of talk about a 'power greater than ourselves', 'care of God as we understood Him', 'admitted to God', 'have God remove', 'conscious contact with God as we understood him', and more. All this about 'God talk' sounded a lot like religion and that religious faith was required. I was Jewish and that had always seemed to be more about religion than about God.

Then the term Spirituality was explained to me which has nothing at all to do with religion. Spirituality simply means that we all believe in something greater than ourselves which could be God, could be the group, and could just be something greater than feeling we are God or that we are alone. No one person's idea or understanding of God had to be agreed or shared with anyone else. That is what religion seemed to me where people had to agree together in one way and agree together that other ways were wrong. Spirituality is a way where everyone is able to work together without totally needing to agree. A spiritual awakening is simply starting to understand all this and then life seems to get easier with less conflict and more peace.

A sponsor is someone that has been around the program for a while and knows the ropes. They have worked 'The Steps' and can take you (their sponsee) through these same 12 Steps when you are ready. The topic at that next Saturday, March 8, 2008 morning meeting was sponsorship. By then, I thought and accepted that it was time to get and trust a sponsor so I stated my case to get one when it was my turn to share. My short speech was that I was also an ex-pot head, had mental problems too, and was Jewish. If anyone thought they could sponsor me to see me after the meeting. No one did. They are not supposed to really come and ask you. You are supposed to find someone you relate and can identify with and ask them. Unless they are not qualified or have too many sponsees they almost always are willing to be your temporary sponsor. If you are comfortable with each other then it can become permanent as what happened with my first sponsor.

The following Saturday, March 15, 2008 is when I asked someone to become my first sponsor. He said yes and that he was waiting for me to ask him. This seemed like a good fit and he told me to call him every day even to just say hello and all was good. That was all I had to do in the beginning besides going to AA meetings each day. He knew I also was attending NA meetings and said to try and go to as many AA meetings as possible else NA meetings those other days. Either way, a meeting a day and a phone call a day seemed like nothing too horrible to do. About two weeks had past and I was doing as told.

Most members of AA should own and read often The Big Book. This is also called 'Alcoholics Anonymous'. My sponsor highly recommended that I get a copy and start reading it from the very beginning until the end of the main 11 chapters. I had my $5 (which was all they charged......what a bargain!) and was going to purchase this important book after the very next Saturday morning meeting. The person who was chairing the beginners meeting that Saturday, March 29, 2008 asked if anyone did not have this book and held up The Big Book in his hand. I raised my hand and said that I was going to buy one after the meeting. He immediately slid me the book across the table and said it was his gift to me. That was something that he liked to do on the last Saturday of the month he was chairing each year. That was really nice of him and I did read the book as my sponsor recommended and then again cover to cover.

When things start to become better, the pain at first subsides and life looks brighter. This is when you start to have a feeling of 'being on a pink cloud'. That is a serene, peaceful feeling that comes and goes but feels great while on it. My pink cloud was amazing but I knew it would not last. Everything in my past that was good (or not horrible) always had the roof cave in or the other shoe would drop. My pink cloud was still enjoyable because I knew it was real and also knew realistically that it would end but not necessarily end horribly. That was a nice relief whenever it would end (and would always come back at times and go away and come back, etc.).

Wednesday, April 30, 2008 was my anniversary of celebrating 90 days clean and sober! The last 7 days of each month is typically when groups in AA celebrate every one that has an anniversary that entire month regardless if 90 days, one year, or multiple of years. The Saturday before my actual anniversary is when my sponsor gave me a 90 day AA coin at that meeting which meant so much to my recovery. Of course that date getting the 90 day coin was Saturday, April 26, 2008 and was four days before my actual date. It was nervous knowing that I could not blow it by drinking or using any drug at least until my actual date. That is lame and seems funny to have thought but I did think it. Then I would have to give the coin back! Man, it was still semi-sick thinking to have that mentality. Those four days were just like the previous 86 days which I made it through....One Day at a Time. On my actual 'Day 90', I was able to get my 90 Day Chip and key tag from MA and NA. Then I had 90 Day positive indications from each of my three fellowships!
April 2

#94 (Day 94) Honest Open Willing 2012 Post
Each meeting would end (or sometimes begin) with the Serenity Prayer. It took a while but eventually my confused head was able to start working again. All three fellowships used this Prayer and it was exactly the same in all three! That made it easier to memorize so I could say it with more and more confidence (and sincerity) from my mind, my heart, and eventually my soul. No one else looked at a piece of paper or laminated business size card with this Prayer. It means a lot because of the words and meaning. Every morning I say this Prayer and say it first since it was the First Prayer I learned in the fellowships because it was Spiritual and not 'Religious'.

THE SERENITY PRAYER

God, Grant Me the Serenity to
Accept the Things I Cannot Change,
Courage to Change the Things I Can,
and Wisdom to Know the Difference

Shortly after my 90 day celebration is when I asked my sponsor about these Steps. He said not to think about them too much for now until ready. Of course I still had to dig a little bit more which was alright to him. This was one of the many similarities of the people in the program and one of the more similar traits that he and I both shared (needing to ask and needing to know). Regarding Step One, he asked me why I first came to AA. I told him because I was desperate and did not know what to do anymore. He asked if I had realized my life was unmanageable and that there was nothing I could do about it. Yes, I said. Then he replied how I had come into the program for the same reason as everyone else....because "We Admitted We Were Powerless Over Alcohol – that Our Lives Had Become Unmanageable" and that is Step One. Wow, I had already been working on that first Step the entire time while also admitting that I was one of the many who 'belonged' here as a true member of Alcoholics Anonymous!

That first Step, Step One, is the same with all other Anonymous groups with the exception of the 'problem topic'. Here in Alcoholics Anonymous (AA) it is 'Alcohol', in Narcotics Anonymous (NA) it is 'Our Addiction', in MA (Marijuana Anonymous) it is 'Marijuana', in Overeaters Anonymous (OA) it is 'Food', in Gamblers Anonymous (GA) it is 'Gambling', in Sex Addicts Anonymous (SAA) it is 'Addictive Sexual Behavior', and so forth. This is a Step that must be done and admitted every day to keep moving forward. Now I needed to work Step One thoroughly each day as my sponsor in AA explained. To me, this made sense to say to myself 'Powerless Over Alcohol, Marijuana, and Our Addictions' instead of 'just' alcohol. There was already MA, AA, and NA in my life for my marijuana, alcohol, and other drug problems.

However, I did also have eating, gambling, sex, and many other addiction problems which meant becoming a member of over a dozen different fellowships? Step One eventually came to me as saying 'Alcohol' but understanding it is every single thing that has, could, and most likely would take its place. Today, Step One means "We Admitted We Were Powerless Over 'OURSELVES' - that Our Lives Had Become Unmanageable." Until that was understood, there was a lot of self-confusion and differentiating between every fellowship that I was involved with which became my greatest problem with setbacks. My sponsor was helping me to recover in AA which was sort of going to carry over into my other fellowships which had no real sponsor. A sponsor in each fellowship would seem to get me more confused than I already was and that was very confusing!

When I later asked him about Step Two, he again asked me a question. He wanted to know if I felt that I could get better all by myself now that I realized I was powerless and that my life was unmanageable. My response was very much 'NO'. By then I knew that my powerless, unmanageable life could only get better with the help of the people in these fellowships, my sponsor, my psychiatrist, and other people to help. He then confirmed to me that I "Came to Believe That a Power Greater Than Ourselves Could Restore Us to Sanity" and that is Step Two. Never have I felt that I was ever sane but did feel that I could eventually become less insane. As someone mathematical, it was easy to know than Just Me < Just Me + (All These Other People) which indeed is a power greater than myself.

Now my goal was to work on Step One and Step Two every day while working on Step Three. Without the first three Steps being worked effectively and continuously there would not be any progress. My sponsor explained Step Three which is "Made a Decision to Turn Our Will and Our Lives Over to the Care of God, As We Understood Him." Step Three meant believing strongly and consistently to do something every second of every hour, and One Day At A Time without hesitation or doubts. All that had to be done was to know Step One, Step Two, and everything else involved with our recovery (and new improving lives) was not ours to ever stop and decide not to do anymore. When we take back our will and our lives then the rest of the program eventually does crumble for each person doing so. It was proven time and time again by many people that I have (and had) known.

Taking back my will and my life instead of continuing with the Steps and fellowships have caused problems especially in early recovery that have not made me drink, smoke pot, or do drugs. They have given me the ideas, thoughts, rationalizations, and more that I could start doing or

feeling old ways again that would cause a back slide and hurt me and my world. Then I would start to drink, smoke pot, or do drugs. If I did do one of those things then I know that I would start to do all of these things again. When I go against Step Three (and try to take back my will and my life) to do it 'my way', means that Devil on my shoulder and those voices will come back. Those things will get me into that vicious cycle ending in jail, being institutionalized, or dead. Once you have this determination to work the program, work the Steps, and work at a good life is when you can proceed with the other important Steps. Right then I could not go to Step Four because I was still not entirely ready to do Step Three 100%......yet.
April 3

#95 (Day 95) Honest Open Willing 2012 Post

The Third Step Prayer took longer to eventually memorize than the Serenity Prayer. This is in The Big Book of Alcoholics Anonymous and is almost never said at meetings except sometimes if it is a Big Book meeting. Even then we were told to turn to page 63 in that book right in front of us. My sponsor thought it would be good for me to start saying the Third Step Prayer each day to get the Willingness to work Step Three more until I was ready to actually have the Willingness to move on to Step Four.

Around that time is when another man in Alcoholics Anonymous just handed me a laminated little card that had the Third Step Prayer on one side and the Seventh Step Prayer on the other side (to be used when ready). Now I had a reference in my wallet which was needed because I only had a RAZR Phone and not a Smart Phone to rely on for documents and PDF Files like now. Every morning I now say this Third Step Prayer right after the Serenity Prayer. It reminds me each day not to take back my will and my life to do what Steve wants.

THE THIRD STEP PRAYER

God, I Offer Myself to Thee - to Build With Me and To Do With Me as Thou Wilt. Relieve Me of the Bondage of Self, That I May Better Do Thy Will.

Take Away My Difficulties, That Victory Over Them May Bear Witness To Those I Would Help of Thy Power, Thy Love, and Thy Way of Life.

May I Do Thy Will Always!

There were still a lot of memories, regrets, and things that had been with me and were coming back getting worse and worse as my head was becoming less cloudy. These included feelings that had been numbed, suppressed, and forgotten over the years of my marijuana and other addictions. All this was crap that I did to others and myself, crap that happened to others and me, and things that just kind of sucked in my life. Those reading these daily HOW Posts can probably understand that there were maybe a 'few things' over my almost 40 years that could be a little overwhelming to come rushing back all at once. My sponsor recommended that I maybe start putting these things in my head out on paper but it was not Step Four...yet.

I did not use paper as I stated earlier because I liked word processing programs on the computer which is easier to spell check, edit, and move around. Everything that bothered me was put together in a Microsoft Word .doc Document. That is not the way Bill W. and Dr. Bob (the founders of AA in 1935) would have done it but maybe they would have if computers were better back then.

My 'pre' Step Four was put together, edited, rearranged chronologically in one file called 'Steves_STEP_4.doc' as things were remembered. A lot of that was painful so early in my recovery but it would have continued to eat me up inside unless I put everything down as rough notes. These were not stories (yet) but just an outline or cliff notes of 'things' in my life. That Microsoft Word Document grew and became 10 pages by the time I did finally do my thorough Step Four...with my second sponsor in August 2008.

Meantime, I managed to attend one of the far away MA meetings in Valley Cottage and even one of the further away MA meetings in Nyack. Each one was good in different ways but did not seem to be worth traveling so far when the Sunday night Paramus MA meeting gave me a basis for the entire week. That one MA meeting allowed me to work with AA and NA meetings and people like ... Hamburger Helper?!?! That MA framework was what I tried to take and get out of these other fellowships that were being attended about 4 to 5 times a week each. It does not work if you take one MA meeting, five NA meetings, and about four AA meetings a week and create Steve's Anonymous! I did try to give and take from each fellowship. Step Three divided by three fellowships is a little too spread out and started to not work for me causing some crashing, burning, and worse.

In the middle of May 2008 is when the people at one of my weekly Narcotics Anonymous (NA) meetings on Wednesday nominated and made me the meeting secretary. The duties include asking who was celebrating any of the anniversary levels from 30 Days to Multiple Years near the beginning of the meeting. Then they come up and I would give them the appropriate key tag, the traditional NA hug, and then they give a short talk about HOW It Works! This was a big honor and I was very excited, touched, and proud. When I shared this happy new position with my AA sponsor he said it is not good for me to hug celebrants which include 'young women'. He implied that he had problems with women early in his AA days and so might I. He thought I should not take the position which was very upsetting but I still took the position.

Back at one of the Saturday morning meetings on May 24, 2008 is when I was at my usual beginners table in the back boiler room. My sponsor always stayed in the main room when the meeting broke into two parts. The main room had a speaker from another group sharing his experience, strength, and hope for 10 to 15 minutes and then a group discussion. He had only been going in the back room the first month that I started attending because that was his month to chair the beginner meeting. Now it was not his month and he was in the other room. When they asked if anyone had a topic or a problem related to alcohol or might be affecting their sobriety is when I raised my hand. I shared at that AA meeting how upset I was that my sponsor did not want me to be the secretary at 'another fellowship' because it involved hugging people of both sexes. Pretty much I said something like "Just because he may have had problems with women does not mean I will."

This got back to him after the meeting from other members in that back boiler room. We did not speak later in the day since we spoke before that Saturday meeting started. On Sunday I called him like I was supposed to do each day. He did not answer so I left a message on his phone saying all is OK and that I was checking in. The next day when I called it was Memorial Day. Again he did not answer and again I left a message. That Memorial Day (note the word memorial) on Monday was May 26, 2008. My wife and kids were attending a Memorial Day BBQ at a friend's house with other parents and their kids. About an hour into this party is when my sponsor returned my call......

Every person in AA (and other fellowships) either have or should have a sponsor. These people that sponsor you will usually tell you that they are there for you and will never 'quit'. They say that the only way this sponsorship would stop is if you 'fire' them as your sponsor. Many times it would be a mutual thing that a sponsor and sponsee grow enough to a point where the sponsee needs to move on. The sponsee and his ex-sponsor still remain close friends as do all the people in the fellowships try to do with each other. It is important to always be there for your fellow alcoholic in AA.

On the phone that day is when my 1st sponsor officially dropped me as a sponsee. His reasons were that I opened my mouth too much and he did not feel that he can work with me any longer. Another AA friend then called me a minute or two later from the same sober BBQ that they were attending elsewhere. He asked me to 'lose his number to help his sobriety'. He had about one month less time than me and his sponsor felt that I was not a good influence to have. Needless to say, the rest of that party was not as enjoyable but I still stayed away from the tempting beer, wine, and other tropical drinks.
April 4

#96 (Day 96) Honest Open Willing 2012 Post
Right away my mind kept racing, over analyzing, and thinking too much. I felt lost, rejected, and betrayed but was determined to figure things out. Now without direction is when I would again feel that I was superior and not need this 'stupid program' one minute while feeling inferior the next minute that I did not belong. Either way, my doubts and bad attitude made it was hard to concentrate or listen at meetings. This was only for eight days but seemed like a much longer time.

When I was at my lowest after being kicked out of my Outpatient rehab there was that Tuesday afternoon AA meeting on February 26, 2008 that gave me hope. This became one of my regular Alcoholics Anonymous meetings every Tuesday afternoon since that day. The format of this particular meeting is the speaker meeting type where someone different shares their experience, strength, and hope for 10 to 15 minutes each week and then there is a group discussion. Now it was Tuesday, June 3, 2008 and I was at that same weekly meeting (as usual) feeling extra depressed, extra lost, and feeling great desperation without any more hope.

The chairperson asked if anyone had a topic or problem when the speaker was done. My hand went up quickly and I was picked to share how my sponsor dumped me because of messing up with my stupid mind and mouth. I admitted how I was definitely wrong, was without a sponsor now, and needed advice because I felt confused. The people there knew me well enough by then to know I was 'cross addicted', had mental problems, and always felt confused (because I usually mentioned how I was in other fellowships, had mental problems, and often felt confused). Several people at that meeting gave great advice when it was their turn to share on how they handled similar situations. After the meeting, a man came up to me saying he heard my Saturday morning vent that one day, has heard me share several times before and after, and if he could maybe give me a suggestion.

This man already had a lot of respect from me so I told him to please tell me what I should do. He said not to expect one fellowship or place to help me with every problem. Then I expected too much from everywhere for everything and would be disappointed or confused. Instead concentrate on one fellowship or place to help with one type of problem. The example told to me was something like if I had a problem with my teeth, taxes, marijuana, and alcohol to not expect a dentist, accountant, Marijuana Anonymous, and Alcoholics Anonymous to all help with all those problems. Just let the dentist deal only with the teeth, the accountant deal with only the taxes, Marijuana Anonymous deal only with marijuana issues, and Alcoholics Anonymous for my alcohol problem and recovery. Then I can focus exactly where needed by the right place. He also informed me that Alcoholics Anonymous can help me with all my recovery needs including The Steps for all of my addictive problems.

That is when I believed that one problem was connected to another and that one problem could easily be replaced by another problem. AA did focus on alcohol because that is the main identification and problem. Many people in AA had several other problems including pot and harder drugs but know focusing and directing their underlying problem as alcohol that it is less confusing and more universal for all addictions. If I did smoke pot, suck nitrous oxide, or do any illegal or non-prescribed drugs that it is considered a relapse and is very bad in AA. All this opened my mind and seemed to make everything so clear and no longer as confused! This man became my 2nd sponsor and eventually took me through all the Steps which helped with all my other similar fellowship type problems.

I was still going to MA and NA meetings (although primarily focusing now on AA) as the added support to vent directly about marijuana and other drugs. Now being a full time member of AA made some of that added support, feedback, advice, and feelings from those other fellowships start to feel more foreign. There were soon several problems that would occur in each. Maybe it also had to do with the wrong feelings that AA was the correct fellowship and these other two were doing things wrong (at least for me). Part of me wanted to hold onto my Marijuana Anonymous and Narcotics Anonymous fellowships so I did not put all of my 'Step Three' in only one fellowship. However, the whole idea of Step Three is to turn our will and our lives over to your 'Higher Power'. My decision to continue with three fellowships was indeed 'my' decision and ended up being wrong until 'my' decision was taken away indirectly……by me!

The same day where I was at my lowest after being kicked out of my Outpatient rehab there was also that Tuesday night NA meeting on February 26, 2008 that gave me even more hope. This became one of my regular Narcotics Anonymous meetings every Tuesday night since that day. On Tuesday, June 3, 2008 I was walking from my car up to the church for that night's meeting. One of my many fellowship friends was a young 16 year old female friend from MA and NA who told me that a mutual 19 year old male friend of hers and mine may have gotten her pregnant. She missed her MA meeting that Sunday night two days ago which she was supposed to chair. Instead, I had to nervously run it last minute and get another friend to give a secretary's report. The reason she was not there was to go to a different meeting to see this boy about this possible situation. She claimed he said "If you are pregnant … we are gonna have to rip that sucker out!" which got me very upset. This same boy was with at least 3 other young women in recovery and broke up with them, broke their hearts, or had them relapse. I thought I would try to 'help' her and to 'help' him without looking like a bad guy.

Three days later (Friday, June 6, 2008) I arrived 15 minutes earlier to an NA meeting at Bergen Regional for the afternoon meeting. My reason for getting there earlier was to speak to someone in this same fellowship as this boy who may have gotten this girl pregnant. The thoughts and emotions in my crazy mind still did not quite allow me to think clearly and properly. If I could have someone else get involved or tell me what can be done then this concern and load off my mind would be lessened. The only person who was there was the guy who I had been having on and off personality problems with who chairs that Friday NA meeting. No one else was around and I figured he may be able to give some advice.

Normally, this man is always giving advice to me and others when not asked. Over and over he would tell me AA and NA phrases like I was a little kid with my clean time (technically I was). When he heard that I was writing some 4th step things, he stated that I should not be doing that. He acts like he is my sponsor and he knows everything. Many others seem to also have problems with his cross talking and dictating ways. New people have left because he interrupts them and adds comments. When people leave the meeting, he then says things about those people! For these reasons a part of me felt he could and would give feedback about this situation when actually asked.

He wanted to know why I was getting involved. It was none of my business. Leave it alone and concentrate on myself. This went on for a few minutes and his agitation kept increasing...at me. Two younger boys entered the room for the meeting still a little earlier. These boys were friends with both the other younger girl and good friends with the boy. It took maybe 30 seconds before they figured out the guy was berating me about wanting to get involved about a young girl getting pregnant by a young boy at a Tuesday night meeting and that it was my concern. They even said the names and asked questions which I really tried not to say too much since it was private. Finally I had to quiet this guy down before he says more or additional people entered the room. Our voices and tempers both got louder. He just would not stop. Someone had mentioned that he did something after 8 years of clean and sober time to make it he had only 11 years of recovery instead of 19 years like he always liked to claim. This really pissed him off and he started to get violent and threatened to beat me up in the hospital's parking lot. I left that meeting and never wanted to go back there again.
April 5

#97 (Day 97) Honest Open Willing 2012 Post

The two boys who were at the Friday afternoon NA meeting went back to their male friend about what I had 'been saying'. He then confronted the female who told me he had gotten her pregnant in the first place. Either she lied to me, got over dramatic and denied it, or ended up not being pregnant and said I made this whole thing up having no idea what I was talking about to cover things up. That Tuesday, June 10, 2008 NA meeting had me confronted by a few of these younger people outside before I got in. This was the same place, same meeting, and about the same time that the girl talked to me about her situation last week. All my helpful efforts unfortunately back fired. Many of the young NA people told everyone including older NA people what I had been saying and that I was an asshole or dick head for spreading rumors. The mood and vibes in that meeting sucked as I saw many people looking at me, whispering, and some had disgusted looks or giggles. It was very uncomfortable and embarrassing. I left that meeting and never wanted to go back there again either. Now there were becoming less NA meetings that I could or would want to attend. There was still my Alcoholics Anonymous and the old faithful Marijuana Anonymous if I could no longer feel right about most of my Narcotics Anonymous meetings anymore.

The following Sunday, June 15, 2008 was Father's Day. I had attended a 3 pm AA meeting in Closter with my normal plans to attend my weekly 7 pm Marijuana Anonymous meeting at Bergen Regional Medical Hospital in Paramus. Little did I 'plan' it was going to become my last MA meeting ever. Some younger kids at that Marijuana Anonymous were looking at me funny, whispering, and laughing. Then my paranoia kicked in and asked what was up? They announced knowing about the problems I was having with the Tuesday Night Hillsdale Narcotics Anonymous meeting's 16 year old girl and 19 year old boy. Many of the younger people attending the MA meetings also attended the NA meetings. A lot of them also go together each day to that same Outpatient Rehab center that I was asked to leave three and a half months ago. There is a separate part of that center for the younger people 18 and under. Now both the younger and the older members of both Narcotics Anonymous and Marijuana Anonymous thought I was an evil, old asshole (and/or dick head) spreading rumors, looking to make trouble, and find drama. I really was not trying to do anything maliciously or hurt anyone at all. My real intent was trying to help but I guess my judgment and mannerisms were not correct.

All of a sudden it hit me that this was not a good situation which got me severely panicked, totally freaked, and greatly over dramatic. I felt that members of both NA and MA were making me feel like an outsider and different from all the rest of the other people. Those made me feel dismal and detached because Marijuana Anonymous was the first fellowship that started my recovery. Marijuana Anonymous was the first fellowship to make me feel welcome. Marijuana Anonymous was the first fellowship to give me hope. Now there was no welcome and of course 'poor old me' thought that I was defective with no more precious hope from my first fellowship MA...Marijuana Anonymous.

Now that it is years later, there is one common pattern that I noticed just as I am writing about this incident. There are many different patterns that I had but one stands out so much that I can tell how it dominated a lot of my life. This common pattern is that 'everything crumbles', 'everything becomes dismal', 'all my hope disappears', and 'my life becomes empty' quite often (in my own head). This still happens a lot and ruins parts of my day which I try to quickly turn around and remedy. Every time that I get dumped or feel detached is when my insecurity releases all these feelings of despair and emptiness. At that point on Sunday, June 15, June 2008 I was a little better but still over dramatic to express my emotions.

Right there at that Marijuana Anonymous meeting is when I shared about my desperation and even said "If I could not go to these NA or MA meetings that I might as well go home and slit my wrists and kill myself. Without these meetings I would use drugs and end up dead somewhere anyway so screw it, I will just slit my wrists and end all of this misery!" Then my manic personality went from depressed to despair to anger as I abruptly got up and left the meeting. Someone at the meeting quickly called 262-HELP which is a number to call if you know someone that may hurt themselves or others. If a specific action is expressed then it is a good enough reason to bring them in for evaluation to make sure no one (including themselves) gets hurt. This happens to be done in the Emergency Room at Bergen Regional Medical Center's Behavioral Health Unit (Psych Ward) which is where I was already.

Before I made it half way to my car is when security and hospital staff ran, caught up, and stopped to question me. I explained that I would never try to kill myself now and I was just being highly dramatic tonight. However, because I said 'end my life by slitting my wrists' is what got me a mandatory, involuntarily, overnight stay locked up there in the

Emergency Room at Bergen Regional Medical Center's Behavioral Health Unit (Psych Ward) for observation and psychiatric evaluation. They took my clothes, belt, shoes with laces, and personal items. I was allowed to use their phone so I can call and tell my wife where I was, why I was there, and that I was not coming home for Father's Day. She needed to tell the kids something else because they were really excited waiting for 'daddy' to come from his meeting. The family was going to have a Father's Day celebration and my children wanted to give me the presents and cards they made for me.

The first person to see me was a woman from the 262-HELP department to ask a lot of questions and thoroughly take down all my information. This included my history such as prescribed medications, mental problems, drug addictions, any suicide attempts, and about my psychiatrist. Afterward there was numerous hospital staff coming in and out asking me several questions over and over. The 262-HELP woman was going to try and get me out as soon as they could when I was deemed 'safe'. I kept insisting that I would not kill myself and was being 'over expressive'. My situation was repeatedly explained to these same people coming in and coming out of my room. I told them how my drugs, alcohol, and other recovery depended on this fellowship which I was no longer safely welcome. It was an overreaction of desperation to release my emotions and frustration while being a drama king. The senior staff director of 262-HELP called my Psychiatrist in the middle of the night to ask his opinions. I was brought in around 8 pm on Father's Day and was released about 6:30 am that next morning.

My son got to see me before he went to school and my daughter before she was dropped off at day care. They gave me their presents and love which was greatly needed especially then. My wife was told everything exactly as it happened and that it was me acting like I sometimes still do. It was right then I made her my sincere promise that there was absolutely no plans or real thoughts of committing actual suicide ever again. My sponsor said I should have called him so he could come down to be with me and that was comforting to know. He related and sympathized with me about what I went through. This guy really knew what to say and really knew what I was feeling without giving me any B.S. at all. I then made him my same, sincere promise that there was absolutely no plans or real thoughts of committing actual suicide ever again and if I did to call him first! This was also promised to my psychiatrist because he was called that night by the hospital and was concerned. Then I humbly and sincerely looked up and promised God that there was absolutely no plans or real thoughts of committing actual suicide ever again and if I did to call him first!

From that moment I honestly believed that there is a reason to be here alive on this planet and eventually 'He' would show me the way to go. Without sounding like a fanatic or holy profit, my spirituality that night grew leaps and bounds. The time alone in that Psych Ward gave me plenty of time to think about how I took my will back by saying and doing all that crazy stuff at the meeting. My will and life is NOT mine to take back. They both belong to my Higher Power which from that moment on was the 'God of My Own Understanding' (as allowed in Step Three) whom I just started to call God. Since then I have had many times of quickly thinking 'Life Sucks', 'O Crap', 'Wish the Pain Would End', and maybe 'God take me away!' These are all just venting of frustration which does not last too long. Then I look at the good, look at the reality of things, and get past these negative feelings before they even get to the point of feeling despair. That is the point where going past is not good. However, that is a point not reached again in years and every year this point gets further away.

God (of my own understanding) introduced me to all these people in my new life. They helped me (and still do) as I tried (and still do) to help them. My life will always be powerless and unmanageable which is something I must admit and accept every day. Luckily, there is something that helps overcome that feeling of "What Do I Do, Now That I Can't Do Anything!?" That is knowing all of these professional, fellowship, and other good people God brought into my life have been preventing my insanity from getting worse and has already restored me to a little bit of sanity. Continuing and understanding this is the way I need to live as one of the 'We' and not just as 'Me'. My recovery and life proceeded (and still proceeds) to get better 'One Day at a Time'. Now becoming 'teachable', I was taught (and learned) to follow that same path so the rest of my recovery and life will continue to get better each day.

Finding the Spirituality of the program (which was my program) was not really that difficult afterward. The Big Book of Alcoholics Anonymous has a two page section in the back entitled 'Spiritual Experience'. Those two pages were looked at again as I wrote this paragraph and I found the last few lines interesting. It states "Willingness, Honesty and Open-mindedness are the essentials of recovery. But these are indispensable." Move those three essentials required for recovery slightly around, take the first initial, and you can see...HOW It Works!

April 6

#98 (Day 98) Honest Open Willing 2012 Post

The decision not to return to (the now uncomfortable) Marijuana Anonymous was made for me. The chairperson of that meeting called me to say my presence there was not good for anybody else. Until further notice, I was not welcomed back there and told if I do that there would be a problem. Maybe in seven months they would 'let me' come there to get my One Year Clean Chip. But there was no way that I could show up at the end of the following month for my Six Month Chip. The stipulation is that I must call her in advance so she can alert the other members of that meeting. What a wonderful welcome, open feeling that was! That was when I did just stop going to those meetings because these wild, young Narcotic Anonymous addicts were making Marijuana Anonymous too different than it was when smaller five months ago.

If I wanted this B.S. from these 'kids' then I might as well still stick to the Narcotics Anonymous meetings that I felt safe. At those NA meetings the older, wiser addicts would tell the young, new addicts to shut up if they were acting or doing stupid things especially toward someone else including me. At the Marijuana Anonymous meeting no one would tell the young, new addicts / pot heads to shut up if they were acting that way because they were all too mellow. Besides, each day was making Alcoholics Anonymous appear to be the one fellowship for me. The slight flavor of NA added to AA was cool without needing MA. Now if all these AA, NA, MA, NA, AA, MA, AA, NA sounds confusing and hard to follow for those hearing about my triple fellowships and triple recoveries then image me doing this in the 'still fragile', 'uncontrollable emotional', 'tragic life' state I was in (in my head).

My sharing was less trying to be funny or sounding good and became more sincere and honest. I felt like I was doing good still as the secretary of my NA Wednesday afternoon meeting. There I was still making announcements and handing out "Clean and Sober" key tags for people 'New', 30 Days, 60 Days, and all the way up to One Year and

Multiple Years. Hugging all these different men and women was not ill affecting me the way my first sponsor was afraid. I do understand his concern because there were people becoming attractive and friendlier to me over time. That is normal in situations with recovery where you can feel empty or lonely and need something or someone to fill that void. That was something which I kept in check extremely good.

My heart was with my wife, my mind was with my recovery, and my soul was with my Higher Power whom I had already started to call 'God'. He may not be your God, my families' God, or the God of my youth but He was there waiting for me when I walked away many years ago. Now just He and I could work together so I no longer felt like 'It' or 'Shit'. He is 'The Man' in charge and I am NOT that man. Also, if He made me then how can I be crap? It was good to have someone else responsible for my good and to care for me in my bad. That is enough about my 'God' because this whole program and my recovery is just based on Spirituality and not forcing my definition of my Higher Power or to turn any of this into religion. With all this being said it is more important to continue with HOW this new, free feeling helped me to proceed further.

Thursday, June 19, 2008 was just four days after my Father's Day overnight stay in the Psych Ward at Bergen Regional. That afternoon was one of two NA meetings that I still attended (besides my Wednesday afternoon NA commitment as secretary). That Thursday night my newest (second) sponsor picked me up at my house and we drove together for a speaking engagement about 25 minutes away to a town and meeting unfamiliar to me. The format was three speakers in front of a large group to share their experience, strength, and hope for about 20 minutes each. There was no discussion afterward, all eyes are focused on you in front of a podium with amplified microphone, and 48 of the 50 people in that room were men with a lot of sobriety.

My first time 'up there' was nervous but with my 'speech' in my hands I was willing to give it a try. Having papers in front of you was not speaking from the heart. I was told to put them away and just go up and tell my story the best I could. No one would judge, boo, or throw things at me (I hoped). It was scary right away but got easier after a few minutes when I saw the looks from their eyes and felt the release from inside of me. Afterward many came up and said it was good, my story helped them, and/or they were able to relate to me! This did not inflate my ego, give me a big head, or make me feel like I was better than any of them. This did give my self-esteem, self-worth, and sense of belonging the boost needed.

The reason for my realization and admission of powerlessness finally arrived on Saturday, June 28, 2008 which would last until Thursday, July 3, 2008. This is the cruise that my parents were taking all their kids and grandkids on for their 50th Wedding Anniversary. We would all be on this big ship with each other to Bermuda and back over five days. There was no way to bring marijuana and my wife's helpful recommendation to 'just drink heavy' alerted me of a need and trapped existence to many things such as pot, drugs, and alcohol (and more). Then I went with the beginning of Marijuana Anonymous, Outpatient Rehab Center, and soon to Alcoholics Anonymous and Narcotics Anonymous. Now it was five months later and had enough recovery, support from other people who were told about this cruise in meetings, and my sponsor telling me it would be fine. His advice, words of assurance, and telling me to email or call him when possible (and cheapest) made me a lot less nervous than if this was a few months ago or even prior to January 31 of that year.

There were no NA meetings on this ship and usually are none. There were 'Friends of Bill W.' meetings on this ship and usually on almost all others. That is the code word for being a 'friend' of Bill W. who was one of the two founders of Alcoholics Anonymous. Saying there was an AA meeting in one of the board rooms would not be very anonymous. Day One was Saturday, June 28, 2008, the first day at sea, and there were really no meetings being scheduled for any 'specialty' groups, clubs, or...fellowships. That night I put up a card on the ship bulletin board for a 'Friends of Bill W.' meeting that next day scheduled at 5 pm in one of the available meeting rooms.

At 4:45 pm that following Day Two (Sunday, June 29, 2008) I was already in that room finding one or two Big Books of Alcoholics Anonymous and even a binder to run a meeting. The ship had a few different types of binders there because meetings of different types do normally occur in there for each cruise. They did have the foresight and convenience to keep one binder and books for those who don't bring their own AA materials with them. Never have I 'run' an AA meeting so I hoped someone with years of sobriety would attend. At 5:00 pm there was still no one there but me. Then a friendly, face popped in the door asking if this was the 'Friends of Bill W.' meeting. There is a saying that even when two alcoholics or more get together that it can be an AA meeting. Now it was!

The younger woman had a little less sobriety than me. With only one other new person who was from the other side of the USA (and just cute enough for me to notice) we had to start a meeting even if no one else came in during that hour. We 'winged it' by basically telling our two stories of experience, strength, and hope. Then we discussed our feelings of the program and ended with the Serenity Prayer. This was a very good meeting to have especially on a cruise ship with many wonderful, pretty looking, eye catching, tropical and other alcoholic drinks going past you every second.

Day three was when we reached Bermuda. That Monday, June 30, 2008 there was an Alcoholics Anonymous meeting from 1:00 PM to 2:00 PM in a church there in Hamilton, Bermuda. That was a great, welcomed experience and rejuvenation. Later that night my wife and kids retired to our cabin. There was music, contests, and dancing on the main deck with drinks all around. That was not a good place to stay. Then I saw this fellow Bill W. friend having 'fun' with two of her shipmates. She looked like you can really have fun with all this alcohol and mostly drunk people all around. That amazed me as the four of us acted silly and had fun until midnight. That was the beginning of a new day which happened to be her birthday! We cheered, had a Red Bull, and said goodnight until our Friends of Bill W. meeting later that next day at 5 pm.

Tuesday, July 1, 2008 was Day Four and the second Friends of Bill W. meeting on that cruise ship. This woman (my friend and fellowship member) attended at 5 pm. There were also two more people that joined this time. Now we had a four person meeting. They asked me to share my experience, strength, and hope and then we all shared about a topic. This meeting was special like my first speaking commitment almost two weeks ago and the meeting there on the ship two days ago.

The next day was Day Five of the cruise on Wednesday, July 2, 2008. This was the last full day at sea and the third, final Friends of Bill W. meeting for that cruise. My first female friend could not make that meeting but the people from the day before showed up with two more family members. This last cruise ship AA meeting of five people was a good way to know things seem to build and grow with Alcoholics Anonymous. No matter where you are there are people just like you.

This female fellowship friend really was and still is special because we needed and found each other there when support was needed. She and I are still friends keeping track of each other's progress and positive (sometimes for me) lives on Facebook. Occasionally, one of us will 'like' or comment on the other's posts as a way of saying hello and acknowledging we are in all of this together because this IS indeed one of the many ways HOW the program works! This made my next recommended advice from my sponsor easy to decide.
April 7

#99 (Day 99) Honest Open Willing 2012 Post

It was inevitable (and for the better) to now focus everything on the one place that did the most for me. The other places were great and are probably better for some people. Having this one place was less confusing and still had every single thing I needed to control my problems with marijuana, alcohol, many other drugs, addictive problems, and negative traits. Wednesday, July 16, 2008 was the day I resigned as secretary of my Wednesday 12:15 pm NA meeting in Paramus. That was the last day of my recovery involving Narcotics Anonymous and the first day of my recovery sticking entirely to the program of Alcoholics Anonymous. Having one fellowship to concentrate all my efforts, with less confusion, really started to make a difference for my life. Many people can (and do) have more than one fellowship for their problems which works their program best for them. Some people cannot (and do not) have more than one fellowship for all their problems and that actually works best for them. I found out after much time, difficulties, plus trial and error which one fellowship was best (for me) to work my program with all my problems......Alcoholics Anonymous!

Our company was having financial problems and decided (on our own) to vacate the upstairs office we had been renting and move everything to the downstairs repair department area we had been renting in the same building. We were very comfortable there after over 20 years and did not want to move entirely out. All we wanted was to pay less money and also happened to need less space. The letter my parents and I sent our new landlord indicated our plan and that the new monthly rent was approximately half of what we were currently paying. This was sent even before the family went on our cruise to give much more than 30 days' notice.

We all thought everything was fine, my parents had everything arranged wonderfully, and the phone and cable companies came on Thursday, July 31, 2008 when we moved out of the upstairs to everything downstairs. That same day is when we received our notice that this was a breach of our lease. The landlord never officially agreed to all of this and found this loophole to evict us. Of course this notice was given very late in the day after everything was already moved into the right spots and after the phones and cable was moved entirely there too. Now we were told to totally vacate the building in 30 days.

It may not have been my tact and disposition with her maintenance and other people always in the building doing construction. It may not have been because I was too demanding and not handled things correctly getting our new landlord upset. However, we do think she had wanted us entirely out to renovate our office spaces which was already being done to the rest of the building. Then the offices could be rented out to other companies for much more money than what we and other tenants were paying. There was 30 days to find new business space, move everything, and do all the stuff needed for changing locations. Phones, Internet, movers, insurance, new address on literature, and much more needed to be done immediately.

Recovery suggests not making any major decisions or doing anything major within the first year. This includes getting into new romantic relationships, changing jobs, or moving (even your office and especially if it is yours and need to do 90% of the work). This really was a huge change in my life especially to me. The stress, pressure, and aggravation trying to move my entire office by the end of August helped make that month the most difficult and challenging times of the year. Soon something else happened that made it one of the saddest months too.

It was only Tuesday, August 5, 2008 and I had already been expressing my feelings at meetings about finding a new location for my business since that Friday, August 1. A woman who had wanted me to speak at her Sunday night 7:30 pm AA beginners' meeting was there at my usual Tuesday afternoon Westwood AA speaker meeting. She saw I was upset and asked if I could come that upcoming Sunday, August 10, 2008 to qualify (which also means to speak about my experience, strength, and hope). My sponsor thought it would be a good idea in order to get out of myself while giving back to help others.

One of my Alcoholics Anonymous friends that I got along and connected great with since my first meeting was a slightly older woman. She was originally from the South with an accent that gave it away and had been living in the West with a rather pampered lifestyle. Eventually she had come back home to receive help from her family a few months before I started my recovery. She was always so sweet, nice, and supportive of me as I tried to be with her. We always said that we were each other's 'biggest fans' with a genuine concern for one another. It really was like she was my older 'Southern Belle' sister and we both seemed to always know when the other one was a little down or out of it.

There are many different meetings each week in my area but a lot of the same people attend a lot of the same meetings. This woman and I attended about 8 of the same meetings each week like most of my other AA friends. That Sunday, August 10, 2008 we were at our Sunday afternoon 3 pm AA discussion meeting sitting next to each other. She seemed a little distant and upset but told me everything was alright. When I was almost done with the Big Gulp that I brought to the meeting she asked if she could have it. There was nothing really too strange hitting me about that request and gave her my cup. Then she popped off the drink top and started to chew on the ice which was all of a sudden a little odd. Some mutual friends noticed with a questioning look and mouthing to me if she was OK? I thought she maybe had things on her mind, it was hot wanting ice, and felt close enough to me that my germs did not gross her out. Then after the meeting she again said all was fine and went home. That Sunday night was normally a 7 pm meeting that my sponsor, she, I, and a lot of other people go to each week. However, that exact Sunday night was my speaking commitment at this other 7:30 pm meeting across town. I was not at our usual Sunday night meeting that exact night.

She was not there the next day on Monday, August 11, 2008 at the usual Monday afternoon Westwood Step meeting? It was a little strange because that meeting was almost never missed and her sponsor was always there. A few people said she seemed a little out of it the night before but had said she was just very tired and wanted to get home. Maybe she was under the weather and not feeling so good is what I thought and hoped she would feel better soon.

Later that Monday, August 11, 2008 night was the Closter Big Book meeting. My sponsor came into the room just about when it was going to start looking very bleak. The meeting chairperson at the time (ironically my first sponsor) begins at 8 pm with the usual greetings, introductions, reports, and announcements before we all recited the Third Step Prayer and begin reading from the Big Book of Alcoholics Anonymous. After the secretary, booker (of speaking commitments), and treasurer reports the chairperson asked if there were any announcements. My sponsor raised his hand to tell us all about our mutual 'Southern Belle' friend.

Her mom and sisters found her dead earlier that morning swinging from a noose. She was only a month or two away from celebrating one year of sobriety but could not handle being financially insecure or the pressures of life itself. That is what she gave as the reasons in her note for hanging and killing herself along with apologizing to her family and all her friends. It took all of us by surprise that a minute or two was needed for the reality to set in and comprehend what my sponsor had just said.

The meeting became a topic discussion instead of a Big Book meeting so we could all share our feelings of sorrow and loss. I had to go outside and breathe after a few minutes when the shock wore off to cry like a little kid for 5 to 10 minutes before I could go back inside. My sponsor knew we were close and that I was in pain just like everyone else plus a little more. Everyone cares about each other very much in Alcoholics Anonymous like they normally do in all the fellowships. She was the type of nice, thoughtful person that almost no one had any problems or arguments with her. Never would she think about herself and always thought about everyone else. If she thought about everyone else then why would she do this and leave all of us with this pain? It felt like a part of my heart was ripped out.
April 8

#100 (Day 100) Honest Open Willing 2012 Post
The mental turmoil was worse and now a little too intense to handle especially at this point in my recovery not dealing with such emotions while being clean and sober. There was a few times where I was sobbing

uncontrollably. This included at Alcoholic Anonymous meetings the next day and meetings over the next week. All of this was because of several things including the company moves, friend's suicide (and viewing), and still living with all of the crap in my head from the past 39 years. That had to come out soon or I really felt like I was going to have a nervous breakdown. My sponsor knew how I felt and where I was in my program. He confirmed that I have made a solid enough base of Step Three over the last few months. Now that I "Made a Decision to Turn Our Will and Our Lives Over to the Care of God, As We Understood Him" he knew exactly what to do.

He recommended that I come to his house a couple of days later so we can spend a few hours together. There I would start from the beginning of my life chronologically discussing all the good, bad, and horrible things that 'I felt' happened to me and my loved ones. However, the major emphasize would be all the bad, cruel, horrible (and sometimes unspeakable) things that 'I felt' was done wrong by me to anyone and everyone in my life. Finally it was officially time that I "Made a Searching and Fearless Moral Inventory of Ourselves" which is Step Four!

But wait...I already had everything needed for this particular Step pretty much all done. My 'pre' Step Four was put together, edited, and rearranged chronologically in one file called 'Steves_STEP_4.doc' over the past few months. Then things were researched deeper as I found, read, and added things that brought back more memories and events I forgot or blocked out. There were yearly planners from the entire 1990's, school documents, letters from many people including psychologists, psychiatrists, social workers, therapists, lawyers, court, and anything else to make my Step Four an extremely searching and fearless moral inventory of everything possible regarding me. That was fine. However, he wanted to do a combined Step Four while I "Admitted to God, to Ourselves, and to Another Human Being the Exact Nature of Our Wrongs" which is Step Five.

The words on my many pages needed to stay in my pocket during this session and the next session a few days later. Until then he wanted me to tell him all this Step Four stuff to the best of my ability without notes or outlines. Afterward, I can show and discuss with him the many pages in my pocket which I worked intensely on doing for what I thought was a different way of doing Step Four. No 'way' is bad if done with the same effectiveness. Actually, I did do both 'ways' because we went over this list on the pages to go over everything I missed telling him. Most things were not as bad as I thought in my reality. Many things were not different from those many others have done in life or the fellowships. A lot of things done to me or that I had done were because of situations where either I and/or others were sick, confused, too young, or not responsible. Regardless of how my sponsor reacted to everything there was a great sense of relief, this huge burden was lifted off my shoulder, and all that crap was flushed down the toilet.

These many pages were also read clearly and thoroughly four other times before I thought I would be 'reading' these pages to my sponsor. Nothing was omitted even if the exact nature of my wrongs included very embarrassing, regretful things. First, this was read on my knees before God. Second, I read this closely and slowly to myself in a quiet place. Third, this was read to a very close friend who knew at least 50% of my stuff but not all. Fourth, this was read to my weekly Therapist for his professional feedback. The after effect of each of these four admissions gave me a very similar sense of relief like with the different but amazing way done with my sponsor! I really did admit everything to God, to myself, and to three unique human beings.

Step Four never stopped even after it was told as Step Five. You do not work the Steps and graduate. Every day you think about them, try to work them more into your life, and never forget each one. Then over the next few years it was continually updated until it seemed like I truly did my Step Four even better than the first time. When it was ready to do again....my Step Five was done 'privately' for over 200 friends who knew me or could relate to me in a group called 'HOW Posts'. That started on January 1, 2012 and continued chronologically even more in depth than I thought could ever be done. This included the same and newer added things that were just as embarrassing and regretful (and sometimes more) as the last time with nothing at all omitted. Admitting every single exact nature of every single one of my wrongs to this wonderful mixture of people cannot make a new Step Five any better!

Our office vacated our old building by August 31, 2008 and we were successfully moved into our new location by September 1, 2008. Technically, our office moved twice in almost one month. First we moved everything from the second floor down two flights of stairs to the repair department and shipping area in the warehouse. Then one month later we moved everything down there to the second floor of a building in the next town over. In between, the hardship of losing a close, special friend did make August a very difficult, challenging, sad month. Yet......I did not drink, smoke pot, or do any drugs although the thought entered my mind briefly a few times. Even better was that the thought of suicide never entered my mind once for even a second. I still don't know exactly how all of this was accomplished. The last six to seven months of my recovery is what many told me 'might' have helped.

Immediately after my Step Five was done with my sponsor is when Step Six was introduced to me before I even left his house! He gave me one sheet of lined paper and a 'homework assignment'. There is another book in Alcoholics Anonymous that has 104 pages discussing the Twelve Steps with a small chapter on each of the Steps from One to Twelve. Chapter Four was about Step Four (which sounds like that would make sense) and is the second largest Chapter with 13 pages which is not very large at all in reality to a normal person. On the bottom of the 7th page in that Chapter they list and then discuss the Seven Deadly Sins.

My 'homework assignment' was to write a one sentence easy definition of each sin (in the same order as on that page) followed with a one sentence way it was part of my Step Four and Five. A two sentence limit for each of Seven Deadly Sins meant there could only be 14 sentences total and had to fit on one side of that one page. That seemed like an easy, quick thing to do but to simplify a word's meaning and how it was part of your entire life in that little sentences and space took a long time. This way my sponsor would review what I wrote so together we can identify every one of my personality and lifestyle flaws if I "Were entirely ready to have God remove all these defects of character" which is Step Six.

Here are the Seven Deadly Sins in the order told to go by followed by the dictionary's simplest definition.

PRIDE – An unduly high opinion of oneself
GREED – Excessive desire for wealth
LUST – Excessive sexual desire
ANGER – Hostile feelings because of opposition
GLUTTONY – The habit or act of eating too much
ENVY – Desire for something that another has
SLOTH – Laziness or idleness

The next sentence after each stated how this was (slightly or majorly) related to my problems as it was part of my Step Four and Five. At this point in my recovery and life I cannot remember exactly what I wrote. My Sponsor eventually took that original sheet of lined paper when we were through, ripped it up into little tiny pieces, and then threw them out (like my defects should be). However, I did have the name and definition on my computer of each deadly sin that I had found which are exactly as what I wrote.

Now I was alerted to my actual character defects and personality flaws. These were not told to me by my sponsor. These were admitted by me in my definition and reference in my life. He helped me see and realize the ones that were bad or very bad without self assuming they were not. The opposite was also done which was extremely helpful. He helped me see and realize the ones that were not that bad or bad at all without self assuming they were. Concentrating on the things where I needed to work gave me that focus and willingness to have these removed. They could not (realistically) entirely be removed. They could (realistically) be something that I wanted to have entirely removed. That is the willingness to now work on "Humbly asked Him to remove our shortcomings" which is Step Seven!
April 9

#101 (Day 101) Honest Open Willing 2012 Post
Being willingly to get rid of my worst defects gave me a new prayer to add to my repertoire. That laminated card previously given to me had The Third Step Prayer on one side which was said at least once a day until finally memorized. The other side of that laminated card had The Seventh Step Prayer to be used when ready...now I was ready! Here is that prayer which I now say every morning after the Serenity Prayer and Third Step Prayer.

THE SEVENTH STEP PRAYER

My Creator, I Am Now Willing That You Should Have All of Me, Good and Bad.

I Pray That You Now Remove From Me Every Single Defect of Character Which Stands In The Way Of My Usefulness to You and My Fellows.

Grant Me Strength, As I Go Out From Here To Do Your Bidding.

Amen!

There were still other things that happened before I was able to make my Eighth Step List and make my Ninth Step Amends. Until then it was important to keep working the first seven Steps each day. I needed to wake up every morning and remind myself that I was powerless in an unmanageable life, something more than just me can help, that I will live and work at my program to the best of my abilities, get over the pain of my past, know my defects, and be willing to control them as much as possible.

It is not easy to do all this every day and there were still a few times my emotions (and my will) got the best of me and got me into trouble. During those times is when my sponsor thought it was best for me to go back and concentrate on Step Three for the time being. This meant reading that chapter in the Step book, reciting the Third Step Prayer, and thinking about how my will and my life is better when I allow my higher power to...drive the bus.

The thing to always remember is that no one will ever achieve 100% perfection. That is practically impossible! However, constant progress is very obtainable and possible (with occasional back sliding). Nothing new that happened to me felt like it did back in my 20s and 30s. Nothing new that I did to anyone (or myself) was even close to the way things were then too. The quantity and intensity of these things were now a small fraction of how it was. Today it is even a fraction of that from over three years ago. My hope is that it continues each week, each month, and each year until the day I die which is hopefully a very long time from now.

At a later Monday night Big Book meeting (Monday, September 8, 2008) was when I made fun of someone who uses their hands very expressively when he talks. It was only my intention to be a clown or comedian as I was sometimes known to be. It was not my intention to degrade or make fun of him. My back was to him as I too made expressive use of my hands. Then I felt his eyes burning a hole into me because I was not hiding my humor very well. He looked pissed when I turned around so I got up and left the meeting but he followed me outside. This guy had a year more time than me but still had anger issues and was very big into the martial arts. In other words, he could have easily beaten the hell out of me and maybe killed me if he wanted to. There were words said about me being immature and he being self-centered, conceited, and not humble. Luckily there were three mutual friends in the parking lot to keep him separated.

He left and I felt like 'O crap' why did I make fun of him to make myself look better? That is not a good trait and quickly I felt bad about what happened more because it was wrong, embarrassed him, and made him lose him temper. None of this was his fault and I am the one that hurt his feelings and made him feel this way. Still I was a little scared and asked my sponsor to mediate so I can speak to this guy civilly man to man. He agreed and we spoke to each other about one week later before a different meeting started. I told him that I was wrong and did not mean to do him any type of harm. He understood, accepted my sincere apologizes, and asked if I would do him a favor to make this up to him. This favor would also benefit me and others needing recovery.

One of his commitments was to 'bring an AA meeting' into the Inpatient Rehab part at Bergen Regional Medical Hospital Saturday early in the evening. This is where I used to attend my Sunday Marijuana Anonymous meeting and most of my Narcotics Anonymous meetings. On Saturday, September 27, 2008 is officially when I made my peace and closure with this guy by speaking at 6:30 pm inside the locked up confines of F1. This was also the first time back to Bergen Regional since Wednesday, July 16, 2008 when I stepped down as secretary and attended my very last Narcotics Anonymous meeting. This was the 'place' where I had difficulties including being involuntarily incarcerated on Fathers' Day. That and everything else was my doing so I made my peace and had closure with Bergen Regional 'Mental Health' Hospital.

Saturday, January 31, 2009......was my One Year celebration of being sober (and of course clean from marijuana and all other mind and mood altering things)! Over all I had attended 514 meetings in those 366 days (because it was a leap year in 2008). Instead of '90 meetings in 90 days' and then continuously repeating '90 in 90' to average 1 meeting a day, I 'impressed' myself with averaging (about) 1.4 meetings per day...ummm wow (sarcastically). I also thought it would help better to cram in a lot of meetings. This used my Obsessive Compulsive Disorder (OCD) to what I thought was my advantage. It definitely did not hurt and that is for sure! The feeling of knowing I went an entire year without substances or 'crutches' to get through life, and that life had gotten even a little better, was amazing! Now...my sponsor felt it was time that I "Made a list of all persons we had harmed, and became willing to make amends to them all" which is Step Eight.

It was a good thing that I had my Step Four on the computer. What I did is take all of the proper names and people on those many pages and listed them by name. Then I arranged them by importance. Those were the people (or things) that I had harmed and actually a few that had harmed me or had resentments against. It was important to list them. Once I could forgive those that 'harmed' me (whether real or imaginary) is when I could ask for forgiveness for those I 'harmed' (whether real or imaginary). My sponsor went over this list with me in his car for over an hour. Many people and things were crossed off the list or rearranged for one good reason or another. There were people and things on my list that really were bigger in my head and imagination than they really were. Then came the official list so I was able to have "Made direct amends to such people wherever possible, except when to do so would injure them or others" which is Step Nine and I was most certainly ready and willing to do this...now.

The list was divided into different parts. They were almost all proper names with ONE STAR AMENDS, TWO STAR AMENDS, NORMAL AMENDS, or PRAY FOR FORGIVENESS. The 'One Star Amends' were the first to be done whenever possible. The 'Normal Amends' were to be done after the One Star Amends and/or whenever possible. Soon after a few person to person amends were made then I could go to the 'Pray For Forgiveness' list and mentally, emotionally, spiritually, and sincerely pray to be forgiven if I harmed them. Also on that 'Pray For Forgiveness' list was people or things that I needed to forgive. Like I said earlier, you cannot expect to be forgiven if you cannot forgive others yourself. There were people on my list that I could not see because they lived very far away or were dead. There were also people on my list that should not and would not be contacted as directed from my sponsor. These are the "except when to do so would injure them or others."

Injuring someone does not mean only physically and could be mental or emotional injuring. It could also be if it ends up hurting another person that is innocent. If I told someone (or someplace) that I stole money from them, and they did not handle things too well, that they may press charges or insist on having the money returned. That money is long gone. Any money that I had then and still now was very limited. Taking money away from my family that actually pays the mortgage, food, heat, power, water, medical and other necessities does injure my wife and children. The same is true if I go to jail and they are without a husband or father. In these cases then either an indirect amends or praying to my Higher Power for sincere forgiveness could be made. However, if it meant that this injury would only affect me then it might still be done no matter what the reaction or consequences. The Promises of Step Nine told me (and still very much do) to expect even more wonderful things to happen and look forward to at this particular point on my journey.

THE PROMISES

"If we are painstaking about this phase of our development, we will be amazed before we are half way through. We are going to know a new freedom and a new happiness. We will not regret the past nor wish to shut the door on it. We will comprehend the word serenity and we will know peace. No matter how far down the scale we have gone, we will see how our experience can benefit others. That feeling of uselessness and self-pity will disappear. We will lose interest in selfish things and gain interest in our fellows. Self-seeking will slip away. Our whole attitude and outlook upon life will change. Fear of people and of economic insecurity will leave us. We will intuitively know how to handle situations which used to baffle us. We will suddenly realize that God is doing for us what we could not do for ourselves.

Are these extravagant promises? We think not. They are being fulfilled among us —sometimes quickly, sometimes slowly. They will always materialize if we work for them."
April 10

#102 (Day 102) Honest Open Willing 2012 Post
Somewhere in January is when my wife had noticed (and told me) that there were more and more times she would wake up in the middle of the night and notice my breathing would stop for several seconds. Then I would gasp for air and breathe naturally again but that it happened often. After going to my primary physician, he thought that I should see a Sleep Disorders doctor who was one of his partners. My appointment was made with him where he then explained that I should get a Sleep Study. On a Thursday night in February 2009 is when I spent the night at Englewood Hospital. They put me in a very comfortable, hotel-looking

private room with a big comfortable bed and 50 comfortable electrodes with wires all over me hooked up to a big machine. There were several people in that wing having a Sleep Study performed. In a separate room are Sleep Study Technicians that monitor our readings while watching and listening to us. It was pitch dark but I guess their cameras were able to see without any light. They wanted to also investigate if we kicked our legs, sat up in bed, or if any parts of our face or body looked like they were moving.

After two weeks the results came back. There was an average of 60 times per hour that I stopped breathing and needed to slightly get out of a deep sleep to take a breathe and go back to sleep. It was not that I woke up entirely but that I would just barely get out of proper sleep. The inside of my throat was flabby and got too relaxed blocking my breathing tube when I slept. That was the very simple and not really correct thing to say but is funny and kinda true. In other word......my diagnosis was Sleep Apnea and now I needed to start using a CPAP Machine to breathe correctly and continuously at night. A CPAP uses a face mask, nasal mask, or nasal pillows to force air into your mouth and/or nose but still allowing you to easily exhale. It is a fun thing to have strapped to your face when you sleep and the machine makes its slight 'white noise' humming sound. That was less poor me and more O crap......a CPAP but hey I can sleep better......yeah!

Now I could sleep better and could be more sincere and ready to make amends with the people and places that needed to be done. This started (I think) in March 2009 with a scheduled breakfast meeting with someone important on my One Star Amends List that I was able to track down thanks to Facebook. I sent a message and a few days later got a response. Then I sent back a message saying that I was in Alcoholics Anonymous, feel great remorse for things I did, and needed to meet for a much needed Ninth Step Amends. It was such a sense of relief to have the meeting accepted but very nervous not knowing exactly what I would say word for word and how things would be received or accepted. Saturday after my morning AA meeting is when I went to the diner to sit down and talk with......my first wife!

We met on the (ironically enough) 'steps' of the diner and saw each other for the first time in over 16 and 1/2 years. I told her how grateful I was to have her give me a chance to talk to her (also for the first time in 16 and 1/2 years). She was skeptical but had researched about AA and the Ninth Step. She was willing to hear me out with an open mind understanding this Step was important to me and my recovery. First, she told me how badly I had hurt her, what she felt then, and what she thought now. Her life since our divorce did have some good things happen as a result of our experience together.

She said that it may have also been some small things that added to our situation. This included her wanting to change me into the man she wanted, have been blinded by things in her life, and that maybe we were both immature. This was not necessary and that I told her. However, my sponsor had said that some people might express things to me while I was making amends. It is sometimes important to provide validation of their feelings without immediately telling them or treating them like they are wrong.

Very graciously I thanked her saying I understood and greatly appreciated this. However, I still told her a majority of this was entirely my fault and that I needed to accept responsibility for any and all wrongs done to her. None of this was B.S. like she was used to from me in the past. I really meant every word that I said sincerely, honestly, and humbly. She accepted my apology and said she still cannot forget but can forgive. We hugged each other and wished each other well.

Later that week she friended me on Facebook. We have been very civil since. She no longer hates my guts, wishes my wife would hurt me like I hurt her, and does not wish me harm. She thanked me for teaching her things than made her life, her second marriage, and outlook for the better. My first wife even said that I had now become the man she tried to change me into. Her respect towards my second wife was expressed for standing by me, being patient, and working with me in my recovery. To have my first wife tell me she forgave me, that I was now a good or better person, and that my current wife was probably the one meant for me was......I cannot describe.

By chance (and coincidence) there were two others that I was able to make amends. These two were done before I met my first wife that Saturday morning. It was not planned as I wanted the first amends to be with the one I felt was owed the most. However, they were in the right place at the right time with the right motives, willingness, and sincerity. One was done that Friday evening right before I was going to meet with my first wife the next day after my Saturday morning AA meeting. I saw this person at my son's basketball practice and politely asked if we could talk for a minute. This individual was on my list as a Normal Amends which did mean a direct amends was eventually due. This was the state policeman that chased me, threatened to have me arrested or house searched, and thought that I was ultra-crazy.

We had a very nice conversation where I admitted my wrongs done to him. Before I gave my first sincere and honest amends it felt like the right thing by quickly explaining my previous alcohol problems, recovery, and the steps. Nothing was mentioned about any marijuana or drug aspects since he was and still is a state policeman. It would not be good for my family to be arrested. We only spoke for 5 minutes but it seemed like longer and that was not bad. Then I asked him to please accept my apology and to tell his wife how very sorry I was for any annoyances or wrongs done to her. He thanked me very much, wished me well with my recovery, told me he respected what I just did, and shook my hand. Now there is no awkwardness or hostility and only friendly greetings when I see him or his wife at places, events, or even when I pass their house.

The other person that I was able to make direct amends with was on my One Star Amends list. My sponsor was there with me at the Saturday morning AA meeting. He knew I made my first amends the night before with the state policeman and was scheduled to meet with my first wife after the meeting. Because things seemed to have gone very well with the first amends is why I asked if I should make this second amends before the meeting started. This person attended always attended this meeting each week along with me, my current sponsor, and sometimes 100 other people. This second person for me to make a Step Nine amends was my first AA sponsor.

This man had become my initial sponsor who worked with me in the way needed during the beginning of my recovery giving advice and recommendations that he felt was best for me. He took me though Step One and Step Two getting me up to and working on Step Three. It did greatly bother and upset me when he later told me that being a secretary for NA was not a good thing because it meant hugging people celebrating clean time and some are attractive, young ladies. Then my venting and accusations at a different meeting in another room got back to him. This did not tarnish his reputation even a little bit but got him mad and also must have thought that I was ultra-crazy.

He had dropped me as a sponsee and it was my actions that warranted it. I went up to him and asked for a moment of his time. He agreed but said it needed to be quick because the meeting would be starting in a few minutes. There was a lot of sincerity in my voice and mannerism as I told him how truly sorry I was for doing what I did back then. Then I apologized for that wrong and any other wrongs done to him by me humbly asking to please be forgiven. He did forgive me, thought my current sponsor was the correct one for me now, and shook my hand.

At least these first two amends gave me a little needed practice. When it was my first wife's turn for her much needed direct amends I was a little less nervous and even more ready. However, after my first wife, the state police officer, and my first sponsor it was time to continue with as little hesitation as possible. Next came many more important people in my current life that were owed an amends big time! There was a lot done over the entire course of my life to several people. A few had seemed to have harmed or done me wrong at various times but all that I forgave. Now I was really hoping these and all the other people would allow me to apologize with all my heart and soul. My mom and dad definitely needed to be next!
April 11

#103 (Day 103) Honest Open Willing 2012 Post

My parents had to deal with me my entire life. They are my real parents so I would hope they would have had to deal with me my entire life. Always have they been there no matter what I did or how many times I did it. Never did I enjoy this type of negative attention nor the time, money, embarrassment, sadness, and aggravation it caused them. There must have been at least 100+ major things (plus countless minor things) over the past 35+ years which hurt them in more than one way. Everything that they went through was known and realized by me over all that time and especially more as I grew older. That caused me guilt, regret, and embarrassment too. I always loved and liked my parents and never meant any harm. All I wanted was to be 'normal' like my sisters, brothers, and all other kids (that I thought were all normal). The greatest harm to another person was done to both of them.

Of course they tried to be as understanding, supportive, patient, tolerant, and all the other things great parents strive to be while their kids are growing up. All the stuff they said, did, and acted towards me 'negatively' were things I did not like or feel was necessary at the time. Most of the things 'I went through' were blamed on them as a kid and then again as an adult thinking what they 'did to me' to make me the way I am. Anything and everything they did was to help to the absolute best of their abilities considering what they had to work with...me. There is not a single thing either of them did which demanded an amends to me. I understood, accepted, and saw the reality of anything that I twisted in my head to forgive both of them unconditionally. Every part of me hoped that they knew exactly how very much I appreciated everything they did, how much they put up with, and that I loved them so very much. This change of my life was being done because I wanted to be a better me but I felt they also deserved a better me.

March 21, 2009 I went to my parents place for their Step Nine amends. This was not a surprise to them because I had been keeping my parents 'in the loop' with what was happening, what was next, and what was yet to come in my recovery. They felt an amends was not needed because they too had unconditional forgiveness to me being the amazing parents they were, are, and will always be. However, I needed to express my sincere, humble, honest, love, regret, and appreciation for everything in order for my program to proceed further. The goal was not to rehash anything, get them upset, or even dwell on any one specific thing. It would harm them now to open up old wounds or cause pain for things they forgot or did not know about.

They first needed to know how there was nothing at all I needed to get from them such as an apology or any excuses. Many times in the past I had brought up stuff because I was the one hurt. My dad and mom must have heard me say things like "He used to yell and hit me!", "You held me out the window saying you should drop me!", "I am this way because of you!", "You were horrible parents!", and so much more hurtful things hundreds of time. Those things were neither their fault nor mine but I had to blame someone else other than myself. It is even more twisted when you want to say these mean things because you are the one that is hurting while knowing perfectly well they did everything to help with their love and best intentions. What do you do with this? You continually turn around and smack them in the face. Now they knew I had no bad memories, thoughts, grudges, or regrets towards them.

After an hour or two of their undivided attention (but for good reasons this time) the amends was very beautifully expressed, felt, and accepted. They were very understanding (as usual) and wanted me to know that all of this is behind me, they love me so very much, and are very proud. My mom said all she wants is for me to be happy, to continue getting better, to keep being a good husband to my wonderful wife, and best possible father to their precious grandchildren. My dad hugged me and said to keep being good which I know is the best thing I could do for him. Having that 'other shoe drop', like he waited for but hoped would not happen (but did), always disappointed him. It was not that he never had faith in me. He had a lot of faith in me but after a few hundred times of being let down it may have been better to expect the inevitable. Then my mom hugged me tight, gave me a kiss on my cheek, and said how happy she was to have her little boy back.

Every Step Nine amends on my Step Eight list was very important to me if not for the other person. Some people told me they never really felt I harmed them, forgot I harmed them, or forgave me long ago. Several people who have known me a long time through the old, the bad, and the new said it was not necessary. Luckily all these people were at least willing to let me do my amends because they knew what it involved and how important it is for my recovery. A few amends lasted one to two hours like my first wife and my parents. Most amends lasted 5 to 10 minutes like the state police officer and my first sponsor. Some lasted only a minute or two because these were people that did not really understand the whole thing, could never really give me more time, or expressed that actions would speak louder than words. Those people were semi skeptical and just wanted me to show all of them I'm different today (in the present) and from now on (in the future).

March 27, 2009 was one of those occasions where the longer type of amends was important. This was for someone who was not as unconditionally forgiving like my parents, chose to become part of my life like my wife, or had to deal with me for the rest of my life like my kids. This person knew me their entire life and went through a lot of their own crap including horrors and great tragedies that were all real just like a lot of mine. I always loved this person just like they loved me. Their amazing, strong, and loving disposition made them one of the more tolerant and patient people in my life until I just kept going and eventually went way too far.

Metaphorically, hitting someone when they are down by saying the cruelest things possible is a lot more than just teasing someone. Being directly and personally affected by many things that I have mentioned in my life is long term harm. Two of the most horrible things that happened to my family were not done by me. However, using strong, hurtful words years later to point the blame and responsibility back to them is worse than 'just' horrible and cruel. It was one of the most despicable things that I ever said to anyone in my life. Forget about 'Sticks and Stones Will Break My Bones But Words Will Never Hurt Me'. Bones heal while words can cause a lot more damage than physical things. Probably one of the worst things anyone ever said and probably one of the worst feelings anyone ever gave this person was by me......her brother Steve. Now it was time to make my sincere, honest, humble, and most heartfelt Step Nine amends to my second oldest sister.

Both of my sisters and my brother received the e-mail I sent back in February 2008. This admitted my problems to them including being in recovery and now finally getting the help I needed. They definitely knew I had problems but did not know all of them and that the type of help I now required involved recovery. It was important to let them know where I was in my life. The e-mail did not ask for immediate forgiveness, pity, or anything else. I did acknowledge how apologizes alone could not be enough for some of the things I had said or done. The major thing that I wanted to express was my hope to recover enough to be a positive part of their lives. All I did ask was for a little patience, understanding, prayers, and love.

There was a need to give a very early apology to some people when I was just solid enough in my recovery and program even though I was far from Step Nine. One of these people was my second oldest sister who I knew was going to be at a family gathering a few months into my sobriety. My sponsor knew this was something important to do for many reasons and had given me some advice prior to that day. My sister and I did get a chance to sit down and talk together for about 10 to 15 minutes. There was a decent amount of closure after I expressed my love for her and remorse for my actions which she knew was from my heart. Then I told her a proper amends would be done when it was that time in my Step work.

All was good between us since that family gathering. More than half a year had gone by without her bringing up the past or waiting for her 'official' Step Nine. She knew what it was about when I called her that day (March 27, 2009) to ask if I could come over to her house and talk. That Step Nine amends was so much better and even more meaningful than my initial apology. There were tears and her encouraging questions wanting to know how things were going with me. We ended with a huge hug, her telling me she loved me very much, and me saying "I love you...you're my sister!" We have remained close without any fighting and almost no teasing ever since. And for many brothers and sisters......that incredible!

The people on my "to forgive" list are ones that you would not confront or contact. The only exception is if you need to make an amends to them asking for forgiveness of something you did to harm them. Even if you must contact them then you cannot express your resentment, anger, or request any apology. If they give one while you are making your amends then it is something added to make the two of you feel better. Then always be humble, gracious, and show gratitude with a "Thank you!" instead of feeling or saying it was deserved. Forgiving someone by accepting their live apologizes or amends does not mean you will ever forget. It just means you are willing to let it go and move on. They may not even acknowledge anything they 'did' to you, offer one little apology back, or even take your amends as good as you wish. If it ends with either person being mad or bitter then it does not end well and there really is no closure which is required to proceed further.

There are also those people you will not or cannot confront or contact. You might not need to make an amends or ask for forgiveness if there was nothing you actually did to harm them. They may also be far away or no longer alive. Praying for total forgiveness of each person, each group, each place, and each act must be done. If it is not sincerely felt then it will never be let go. The bad, hostile feelings will always stay with you unless you forgive everything from everyone that harmed you real, enhanced, or imagined. Then you honestly can continue making proper Step Nine amends by asking for forgiveness from everyone for everything that you 'did' to harm them real, enhanced, or imagined. Most of these people were on my 'Pray For Forgiveness' list.
April 12

#104 (Day 104) Honest Open Willing 2012 Post
I had to be totally willing to forgive anyone even those that harmed my entire immediate and a lot of my extended family. This also meant that I

could have the courage and determination to continue making amends with everyone that I 'felt' was 'harmed' by me. My thoughts were they may not want to meet, talk, or have any contact with me yet alone be receptive of receiving an amends and then accepting it.

My sponsor told me that it was done well enough even if rejected in any way. This was as long as I had 100% of the willingness, sincerity, and made the best effort possible. Then I should just pray and meditate to my Higher Power for the harm I 'felt' was done for that particular person or thing. No matter what, if you try your best and need forgiveness, then there is one that will always forgive you whenever it is not possible or no one else is willing.

However, I was in motion and needed to continue as best and often as possible. My motives really were very well intended but I was afraid that if I slowed down that it may be hard to start up again. I needed to at least plan who to approach next. It was not an obsession or anything to be taken lightly like it was a conquest or scavenger hunt. This was something that had to be done correctly, personally, until done even if it took a year or longer to complete. Luckily, the remaining Step Ten, Step Eleven, and final Step Twelve were something that could and must be done once Step Nine has begun before it was half way done. Those remaining three Steps are known as the 'Maintenance Steps' which I was soon able to do. In the meantime, I continued on my list......

One person who I felt was harmed was a little surprised to hear from me. They never really thought I did them any major harm but was willing to meet with me. This person understood what a Step Nine amends means to someone. It is important to the person making the amends even if the recipient does not think so. In those cases the amends is easier when you have a very cooperative person willing to work with you that does not just brush it away like it is silly or stupid. I was so glad my friend from over 20 years ago met me at a diner so my reality with this amends was settled quickly on Tuesday, May 5, 2009. Now we are friends again but this time I wanted to be a real friend that is honest with my only motive to be supportive and appreciative in our new lives.

There were a lot of people that felt the way she did who accepted my amends easily saying I did not harm them but appreciated the sentiment. This includes some of my wives best friends who sometimes made me feel resentful that she seemed to like being around them more than her husband. There were times when I was rude, distant, and just did things I knew would piss them off or not like. That gave me a sick, smug feeling like I was getting back at them when the reality was they did nothing but try to make me feel welcome and I was just blinded and insecure. Even my best friends were sometimes treated badly or not given the equal respect that I would want. All of these people said I owed them no amends and had no grudges, resentments, or any ill feelings toward me. Basically they felt like I was the same as many people out there. Those many times I was the one with a twisted outlook making it seem worse than it was and 'lashing out in retaliation'. That was sense a relief with each person or people telling me these things that took a load off my mind and opened the door to a better understanding with them!

The very last day of that same month was Sunday, May 31, 2009. My wife, me, my kids, and my in-laws flew down together to Orlando, Florida for a five day (and five night) Disney World adventure. There were many times that I was rude, nasty, or negligent towards my wife's parents. There were many times that I was that way to their daughter...my wife. An amends was necessary to them although they are always so nice and forgiving anyway. I knew there would still be times where I would back slide and get upset at them and again act like an asshole with my attitude. That is something I still have a problem with certain people because I cannot handle the difference in personalities but it is my problem with each person and not their fault.

The flight down was a partial 'bonus' amends because I used my own personal upgrades so the two of them could be in First Class while the rest of us (including me) sat in coach. Then when we were down there and got to the hotel all of us went to the pool. My wife knew I wanted to have a talk with her parents and I got my chance that same day we arrived. They knew what was going on with my recovery and being in AA but were not familiar with any details. I was sincere saying I am trying to be a better person including to their daughter and grandkids. I told them I was not perfect and would try my best not to cope an attitude as much with them but did appreciate everything they have done including raising the woman I love with all my heart. They accepted and then asked some questions because they cared and genuinely wanted to know more about what was going on with my program and Steps. That was appreciated. There are still times where the old me goes back against them but I try hard to quickly or eventually remedy my wrong.

A few days later on Wednesday, June 3, 2009 is when I got to officially tell this woman I love with all my heart, my biggest supporter, my sweetheart, and my best friend how much she meant, means, and will always mean to me. It was appreciated for all she has done to be patient, tolerant, and understanding during my life and through my recovery. That everything in the past hurts me now because I had hurt her. I promised to try my hardest to make the future better each new day. This was my special, planned amends to her that evening alone as her parents watched our kids back at the hotel. We got to be together just the two of us out on a much needed, mature, husband/wife romantic date. She knew I was going to make an amends to her which was not needed (by her). The way I felt made it a very important, crucial amends to make (for me). Then on Friday, June 5 we all flew home together. Life was not perfect and I was not an ideal son-in-law, husband, and dad 'magically' from the trip to the Magic Kingdom. However, the understanding and communication was out there making it easier to express myself when needed many times later on.

It was important to reflect on all the good and all of the bad of each day. The goal is to try and see why and where things were bad to try and avoid them again. Seeing the good of the day also helps with trying to do more of that again. If there was a conflict or problem with someone then there is a need to make amends right away. This avoids nasty, resentful, worried crap from staying, festering, and soon causing more rotting in my brain. Whenever I reverted to my 'old ways' then I would make sure to quickly do something that is called "Continued To Take Personal Inventory and When We Were Wrong Promptly Admitted It" which is Step Ten.

Saturday, August 29, 2009 was the first official return 'performance' of me as 'DJ Flash' at a charity fund raiser. Then there was a second 'performance' on December 19, 2009 for my two kids' joint birthday party at an Elks club. My third (and last) 'comeback performance' was a surprise birthday party for someone's boyfriend. After these three parties (of my comeback) I discovered something. My motive during the height of my previous 10 year DJ career was the glamor, the spotlight as center of attention, the pride, the ego, and the money.

Now the money did not buy as much happiness like it did back in the 80's and 90's. The money and the other 'positive' (back then) aspects of being a party DJ included a lot of stuff and a lot of negative traits I no longer desired. I gave it a try, thought it would be rewarding, but instead it taught me a lesson. These three parties allowed me to know that I tried it again and it was no longer for me. Instead, I could have wondered for years if I still 'had it' and should try to DJ again. That was answered and now I knew and could move on but not as cocky DJ Flash. I was just me Steve and no alter ego personalities were needed in my life and in my head...anymore.

My brother first got married back before my wife and I got married in 1993. He and his wife had three wonderful children. Then the sometimes drifting apart of a couple occurred with them. Now my brother had been dating a new wonderful woman with two of her own kids and they wanted to join together as husband and wife. Sunday, February 21, 2010 was my brother's 2nd wedding in central NJ. This was an added positive, person experience for a few reasons. There was someone at the wedding that knew I was in the program because I do not hide that fact too much. They asked me to be a temporary sponsor that day because of a similarity. I was proud to try and be a good influence for someone at my brother's wedding instead of a bad influence or neglecting everyone.

My brother and oldest sister were not really as easy to make amends because they are usually busy and did not quite understand the concept. They did feel the 'proof was in the pudding' and were very willing to see how things developed together in the future. However, I was able to get a few minutes with each to express my feelings and at least resolve my peace of mind. My extreme willingness allowed me to make amends of one type or another to everyone in my family. After hearing how each of these went, my sponsor said 'It was all good!' Now let it go and take it from this point here in the present into the future with all of them.

That was great to clear away the wreckage of my past with all the major people on my list including everyone in my family. My Step Ten allowed me to make sure not to cause any new wreckage with them or anyone else so that just each "One Day At a Time" could try to be made good. Now I had to incorporate something to allow even more growth. The more that I allowed myself to feel and do the right things would help each day. It was time to look more at my perfect Higher Power (who I called God) as a role model instead of other human beings (who were people like me that can be fallible with faults). Thus I began to "Sought

through prayer and meditation to improve our conscious contact with God as we understood Him, praying only for knowledge of His will for us and the power to carry that out" which is Step Eleven!
April 13

#105 (Day 105) Honest Open Willing 2012 Post

Now with Step Eleven came The Eleventh Step Prayer which I had always loved and looked forward to the day I can strive to be like this. It was the last one added to my repertoire of morning prayers for the correct guidance of the day. It was (and still is) too long to memorize so I am glad it is a PDF file in my Smartphone. Now I look and recite it after my last memorized prayer and before I start looking at my Smartphone for Email and catching up on Facebook. This is the bridge of technology between prayer and the 'real world'....so to speak.

THE ELEVENTH STEP PRAYER

Lord, make me a channel of thy peace--that where there is hatred, I may bring love--that where there is wrong, I may bring the spirit of forgiveness--that where there is discord, I may bring harmony--that where there is error, I may bring truth--that where there is doubt, I may bring faith--that where there is despair, I may bring hope--that where there are shadows, I may bring light--that where there is sadness, I may bring joy. Lord, grant that I may seek rather to comfort than to be comforted--to understand, than to be understood--to love, than to be loved. For it is by self-forgetting that one finds. It is by forgiving that one is forgiven. It is by dying that one awakens to eternal life. Amen.

After a short while with the Willingness to try and become even more spiritual made it time to make a few more of the special types of amends. It is one thing to look at someone in the face, eye to eye, and with body language tell them you apologize. You can feel it in your heart and soul with the proper words to express yourself. The other person was always able to know I was sincere and could acknowledge back acceptance (or doubt) afterward. Some people were no longer around where my chance to make direct amends was impossible. This meant that it was time to Pray For Forgiveness to those it was too late to physically see.

An indirect amends could also be done to the loved ones left behind or something that honors their memories. The first ten Steps and now Step Eleven (especially with the words and meaning of The Eleventh Step Prayer) helped me get to the point of being ready for this type of special amends. Sometimes this was not planned and seems to just...come about. Then you know it was meant to be and that individual, specific, departed soul would appreciate that particular indirect amends...directly.

Giving back to other alcoholics is what makes Alcoholics Anonymous function. All I needed to try and do is freely give back to others what was freely given to me. The more I started to recover, learn the program, work the Steps, and become willing to 'join society' made the giving back increasingly better and more often. Sharing for even a minute from the heart during a meeting helps others like you. Volunteering to make coffee, set up, greet people before, or clean up after a meeting helps others like you. When your sponsor feels you are ready then you can be a speaker at certain meetings to share your story of experience, strength, and hope for about 10 to 15 minutes. This helps others like you.

Every time you do these and other helpful things then you are making the program (and any other program) function and continue to work. It helps yourself to do what others did for you with a sense of purpose, gratitude, and good instead of bad. Eventually, you can take these feelings, qualities, attitudes, and other good things learned into the 'real world'. Slowly more and more was I "Having had a spiritual awakening as the result of these steps, we tried to carry this message to alcoholics, and to practice these principles in all our affairs" which is Step Twelve!

Step Twelve is the final Step which you essentially do a little more and more from that first time you 'helped others like you'. At least the first part gets better and even more effective with each of the first Eleven Steps but it does take learning and working all the Steps to technically 'reach' Step Twelve. Although it happens more and more each day, week, and month it is when you reach Step Twelve that you notice the most how life seems to be better! You feel a little less crazy, insecure, isolated, depressed, and more like a 'normal' human being. Now reaching Step Twelve you still remember, work, and incorporate all of the first eleven Steps together with this one.

The Twelve Steps is ongoing and you never 'graduate'. If you do not make these Steps part of every day of your life then you are doomed to eventually forget these important things learned. Almost every person that stops working the Steps, attending meetings regularly, and 'takes their will back' will return to their old ways. This has been shown true with pretty much no exception. It is not just a statistic because I have personally seen it happen 9 out of every 10 times. These old ways are usually slow at first and then speed up ridiculously right back to where they were. This could take weeks, months, and sometimes years instead of days. If they can make it back to the rooms of Alcoholics Anonymous (or whatever fellowship they were affiliated with) then they are always welcome back with much support and without guilt.

There are many times that they cannot just walk back into a meeting because things had gotten much worse than before. These people may end up in jail, institutions, or dead. Those facts scare the crap out of me (and keeps the crap out of my head) making it so much better, easier, and happier to stay where I am and keep it going. I have been in jail and institutions for short periods of time and do not recommend it especially long term to anyone. I have never been dead but have tried to get there and would now be afraid to get there even without trying.

A real life was something I always thought I had but did not. My old world and the real world were two different places. Now my new world was better, clearer, and real so I wanted to join the two worlds together effectively. I could not stay confined nor abandon my new world. Neither could I let myself go back out in the old world and forget everything learned and how far I have come. I wanted my new real world and the old real world to incorporate into one good real world. That was my new goal with over two years in recovery and working my program. I slowly wanted to begin having a real life...so I started.

The first 'social event' that I arranged was a get together type reunion with old friends on Saturday, May 22, 2010 at a county park. It had been at least 20 years since we would all get together, go to parties, and be crazy kids. Now we were adults and got reacquainted thanks to the Internet. While there, I explained my recovery and things that occurred so they knew where I was now. I was always known as the nut job, womanizer, get-into-trouble person, and being irresponsible. Now they needed to know my act was getting together for a better, brighter future. It was important to me that they now knew I could be an equal friend. Previously I felt like I would only want them around at certain times and for my own selfish reasons.

One of my first real female friends and I had some closure over misunderstandings which I did not expect to happen. This was very good for her and also for me. There were some deep wounds healed that day which were not caused by me. These wounds could have been healed long ago if I were more open, willing, and giving many years ago instead of being egocentric. That type of unexpected amends made the entire get together even that much more rewarding. This first 'test' of beginning to try and have a new, real life worked out pretty well!
April 14

#106 (Day 106) Honest Open Willing 2012 Post

After that day in the park, the day at the cemetery, and finally my amends with the last two of my siblings there were still other amends. The Praying for forgiveness amends was done for my friend who died on 9/11 and my co-worker who had hung himself the year before 9/11. There were reasons to make amends on different levels. I prayed and talked to them and felt like they and my Higher Power knew I was sincere.

There was even an amends to the 9/11 terrorists because they were sick and led wrong by their leader and friends. I cannot say that I forgave them for what they did. That I did not do. However, I can say that I let go some of the resentment and personal anger towards each one of them individually. They were sick, twisted, and not in their 'right mind' (so to speak) but in the past neither was I. Thankfully I never did great physical harm or killed anyone like they did. But there were times in my life where my actions could have......

One of my biggest, stupidest, impulsive, insensitive things (which meant it was not a good thing) was said at a meeting of my fellowship on a Friday in June possibly the last Friday, June 25, 2010. There was a woman chairing (leading) the meeting that I was rather close, good friends with. She is smart, personable, attractive, and a very nice person who does not seem to ever harm anyone with words....unlike me. While she was up in front of everyone, I made a bad, sexist joke while honestly trying to just be funny and not thinking it was wrong at that time. It really did get her upset as well as a lot of the other women and several of her male friends.

There was emotional, embarrassing, and self-esteem harm done in a place with people that should make you feel safe. We are all the same getting together to help each other and not make others feel bad. I majorly goofed. She totally stopped trying to be my friend and now basically ignores me like I were just someone in the fellowship that she does know. There were other joking comments in the past which never 'seemed' (to me) to get her angry except one other time. Then I had apologized and said I will try not to do something like that again......but I did.

Even my 2nd sponsor was extremely upset with me. He was close friends with her, knew she was self-conscious and sensitive (like most of us), and that my words greatly harmed her. Because of this, my other manic behavior, and restraint of pen and tongue is why my 2nd sponsor felt we could no longer work together and quit. My sponsor did eventually forgive me and is a friend whom I greatly appreciate and respect for many reasons. He had first helped me with my first 'open mouth insert foot' comment about my first sponsor (who also got appropriately mad and also quit). Since then he became my 2nd sponsor, spent time working with me, got me to focus, took me through the Steps, and is still willing to give me advice whenever I ask.

With his help and guidance I was almost done with every one of my Step Nine amends. We had just been working and discussing the last three 'Maintenance Steps' which helps to 'maintain' my clean and sober program towards a better life. This was good because I was able to eventually make a sincere Step Nine amends (or Step Ten's When We Were Wrong Promptly Admitted It) for my actions and behaviors. He thought my newest medications, recent health problems, or things occurring now in my life attributed a lot of this and ever offered to be my temporary sponsor till I found someone new.

The 'funny' thing is that I got my original 1st sponsor about a month into the fellowship of Alcoholic Anonymous. My big fat mouth opened which embarrassed him greatly just a few months later prompting him to quit. Then I got my 2nd sponsor (who knew how I was) that asked I do not do the same to him as I did to my first sponsor. Two years later, I again opened my big fat mouth but did something worse than embarrass (and harm) him. This time I embarrassed and greatly harmed another person in the fellowship especially one he is friends with prompting him to quit...I had gone full circle.

My newest and current 3rd sponsor is great for support and advice. This 3rd sponsor was obtained on the advice of a very special female person from within AA. He knew about both (and others) of my different 'open mouth insert foot' comments and how it affected both of my previous sponsors. I was the one more hesitant this third time around to ask anyone to be my sponsor. My fear was embarrassing or hurting another sponsor or not being able to work with him like my last sponsor. All my current short comings and personal defects were expressed to him and yet he offered to become my temporary sponsor. This would be until I found someone 'better suited' for me or I asked him to be my permanent sponsor. A few weeks later I popped the question and wanted to make this commitment. He said yes and then we were 'pronounced sponsor and sponsee!'

All of a sudden there were numerous events, health issues, and other problems going on at once that started to make life rather miserable. These put my recovery, steps, and 'maintenance preparation' to the test. I was sooooooo glad to have the fellowship, my family, God, and a new attitude to deal with these things. My self-pity, anger, and other negative traits and outlooks were under control or somewhat dormant. My humor, support, and things I learned from January 31, 2008 until Friday, June 25, 2010 was unbelievably helpful indeed!

These things will just be summarized as simply as possible. There is no need to elaborate on every sucky thing that mysteriously started from June 2010 up to May 2011. They are not fun or funny but are almost 'humorous' when you put them all together in less than one year (11 months) and think about it. At least (warning...spoiler alert) May 2011 to the present kept getting increasingly better and better! This sort of means you need to sometimes must go through Hell to reach Heaven.

After my temporary setback on Friday, June 25, 2010 with the very inappropriate comment my self-assurance was rather low. Then I had been feeling exceptionally tired both mentally and physically even with my Sleep Apnea CPAP nighttime breathing aid machine. It did not seem to be working and even after 7 to 8 hours of sleep I was practically falling on my face all the next day needed a nap which still did not help too much. Almost all of my different body parts were in pain ranging from bad to intense agony. Some of the worst parts were my toes, feet, legs, chest, stomach and remaining digestive system (aka 'tummy').

That Tuesday, August 24, 2010 a few of the answers were revealed. My specialty Neurologist doctor determined that I had Polysensory Neuropathy. This is damaged nerves that really cannot get better and need to be dealt with by certain medications...and learning to live and cope with this constant pain especially in my toes, feet, and legs but moves all around the body often. Sure but why the %^@&# was I freakin' exhausted, getting chest and other muscle (not nerve) pains, and have such 'tummy' problems? I found out one by one over the next few months.
April 15

#107 (Day 107) Honest Open Willing 2012 Post

My doctor recommended and started to prescribe Provigil for me to take in the morning. Then he later changed it to Nuvigil because it was longer lasting through the day. These prescription medicines are typically used to improve wakefulness in adults who experience excessive sleepiness (ES) usually due to one of three diagnosed sleep disorders. These are Narcolepsy, Shift Work Disorder (SWD), or Obstructive Sleep Apnea (OSA) which was one of my problems. The CPAP machine was not really allowing me to wake up with that fresh, happy, well rested feeling. Like it says at the website..."Nuvigil may help with the sleepiness caused by these conditions, but it may not stop all of your sleepiness. Sleepiness can be a symptom of other medical conditions that need to be treated. Nuvigil will not treat Obstructive Sleep Apnea and does not take the place of getting enough sleep."

Pretty much it only gave me a few hours of alertness so I can get through the day without falling down and walking into walls. My doctor (and all my many other doctors) were told in advance that I was in Alcoholics Anonymous and have had addictive problems with pot and other drugs. Provigil and Nuvigil are non-Narcotic so it was fine especially when they wore off about late afternoon or early evening resulting in the inevitable crashing on the couch for 1 to 2 hours. These 'naps' helped but then I had difficulty falling asleep later that night.

However, it was almost impossible to stay awake all day until 10 or 11 pm without a nap. At least I could get through enough of work to be productive before I was totally useless at home for the rest of the day.

The doctor thought it would be good to get looked at by a Gastroenterology medical group for my intestinal and 'tummy' pains and problems. I was so excited to finally have my first Colonoscopy which included starving, taking laxatives, and drinking a gallon of that crap in clear Gatorade continuously for like two hours. However, the after effects did make me feel empty inside. The procedure itself on Tuesday, September 7, 2010 was not too bad considering it really is considered a pain in the ass. My results showed that all was good except for having Diverticulitis.

Diverticulitis is small, bulging sacs or pouches of the inner lining of the intestine (diverticulosis) that become inflamed or infected. Most often, these pouches are in the large intestine (colon). No one knows exactly what causes the sacs, or pouches of diverticulosis to form. Eating a low-fiber diet is one of the most likely causes. As a result, constipation and hard stools are more likely to occur - causing people to strain when passing stools. This increases the pressure in the colon or intestines and may cause these pouches to form. Diverticulosis is very common. It is found in more than half of Americans over age 60. Diverticulitis is caused by small pieces of stool (feces) that become trapped in these pouches, causing infection or inflammation.

Symptoms of diverticulitis are more severe and often start suddenly, but they may become worse over a few days. They include tenderness (usually in the left lower side of the abdomen), bloating or gas, fever and chills, nausea and vomiting, and not feeling hungry. It was recommended to avoid beans and peas, coarse grains, coconut, corn or popcorn, dried fruits, skins on vegetables and fruits, tomatoes, strawberries, pickles, and cucumbers. I was also told to not eat other nuts or things with seeds because they can become trapped in those pouches and cause pain. Drinking too much coffee, tea, or alcohol can make constipation worse. I did not drink tea but was a teetotaler (which is someone who abstains from alcoholic beverages). However, I had started drinking a lot of coffee since attending AA meetings. That answered some more of my problems with the solution to be careful of what I ate, did not eat, and to eat a lot more fiber so I could poop better and more often!

Sunday, September 26, 2010 was a town police open house like each year. There are inflatable rides, face painters, food, drinks (non-alcoholic), and separate tables about different things like bike safety, drugs, and weapons. The different types of weapons are out on display but are not for handling by the public and not loaded (usually). The different types of drugs and drug paraphernalia are out on display at the D.A.R.E. table but they are not for handling, smoking, inhaling, snorting, ingesting, or injecting by the public. My wife was home and I took my two kids this year by myself. It was not too bad considering that I really had not been a good friend, neighbor, son, brother, uncle, husband, and especially father during my many years of marijuana, alcohol, drug, and other untreated addictions and problems. It is not pleasant to admit that I felt like I was 13 and just starting to learn dealing with pressures including fatherhood.

One of the inflatable obstacle courses allowed someone even my age, height, and weight to go through it. There was two halves of this big thing so people can race at the same time to see who can reach the finish line first. My son (age 9) and my daughter (age 5) wanted to race and each took one side of the start line. After a minute, another kid said my daughter was stuck in between the second and third obstacle, could not get out, and we all heard her crying hysterically. The ride attendant said I could go in and get her which I did.

Crawling through the little tunnel and then jumping onto the huge inflatable barrel is when I looked down and saw her between the barrel and two inflatable parts that are pushed against each other and are meant to squeeze through. She did not realize she could squeeze between the two butt cheeks looking things and also could not get back up on the barrel looking thing. That is why she had freaked out. Immediately I jumped down (only 6 feet or so) onto the canvass to rescue my daughter. Because she was sitting down in the middle is why I jumped down to the left side on a part which had no give.

The way I landed gave me an immense pain that was excruciating on the left side of my left foot. I yelled really loud but wanted to get my daughter and myself out of that thing. With all the pain, I was able to push her through the cheek looking thing, over a bridge, through an inflatable hallway, up a 10 foot rock wall, and slide down to the finish line. Now I just wanted to get home soon to put heat or ice or something on my foot. Until then we stayed so my daughter could get her face painted, my kids could go on another inflatable huge slide (by themselves), and have some more food before we walked the two blocks back home. When I finally took off my left sneaker I saw the huge, discolored, bump which hurt even worse now that the sneaker was not holding everything together and in place. All I could take for the pain was Advil. It was not a good time to be an addict in recovery and could not take any unprescribed drugs or painkillers.

The next day one of my doctor's associates was able to see me right away. He looked and felt my foot (which hurt). Then he had me get X-rays of my foot to determine exactly what was going on. There was a fracture just below the little toe on the long, thin bone that goes all the way down the foot. The muscle attached pulled and cracked it when I jumped down and landed on it the wrong way. Then the next day was Tuesday, September 28, 2010 and I visited my Podiatrist who looked at my foot and saw the x-rays in his office. Another inch or two higher and I would need a hard cast. Instead, he showed and told me how to tightly bandage my foot the right way, direction, and wrapping style. Then he gave me 'The Boot' which is like a removable cast that keeps everything in place.

Crutches along with the boot were needed the first two weeks. Walking slowly on the boot without crutches was done the next two weeks. Then the amount of time wearing the boot each day was reduced for about another four weeks until it was a total of about eight weeks later. The entire foot (especially the left side) continuously hurt for weeks and weeks without a great reduction in pain. Having the Polysensory Neuropathy making it tingle and in extra pain made it a nightmare in my fractured foot...which did eventually heal but still hurts quite often almost two years later. My doctor says the bump might never go away and the pain may still flair up at times. He was right.

This added mortality and more humility into my life. Now I was made aware that although I may think, feel, and act like someone much younger that my body was not. These extra boosts of reality made me want to honestly try and make amends with the one woman I humiliated. I did try to make my most willing and sincere last Step Nine amends apology on October 2, 2010 taking full responsibility for what I did to her about four months ago. The response was not too receptive. She still did not want to be friends again but understood my remorse and appreciated the sentiment. It was expressed that she wanted to always keep this emotional distance from now on since she was afraid I may do this again which is understandable.

It makes me a little more vigilant to realize what harm I can still do this much into my own recovery. It is like a reminder whenever I see her and know I blew a perfectly good relationship with a friend who now wants nothing to do with me. Part of me is still not sure if she hates me or what she thinks of me. I am told not to worry what people think, not everyone will like you, and that I tried my most willing, sincere way to make a Step Nine amends apologize. Still......I wish I knew that the harm caused her was fading or will fade away so eventually there can be a time that I know for certain she does not hate me, resent me, or fear my mouth using the wrong words again but that is not a reality...and that I need to accept.

This last amends was added to my existing Step Eight list shortly after it happened. My 2nd sponsor was also added to that list. He forgave me a short time later and was crossed off the list. She did not quite forgive me but......it really was done sincerely, willingly, honestly, and to the best of my ability. All the other names of the list were completed in one way or another. There were many I had direct amends with and many that I prayed to be forgiven by who were dead, could not be found, or who would result in harm to them, my family, or others if contacted directly. Even co-workers that I was rude to and relatives that would not want to get a direct Step Nine amends got an e-mail from me expressing my regret for my actions, hope all is well now, and that they had my prayers and wishes for a great future.
April 16

#108 (Day 108) Honest Open Willing 2012 Post

Now the list was completed and it was time to stop beating myself up and being so hard on myself. There were the One Star Amends, Normal Amends, and Pray For Forgiveness Amends but there was one last type of amends that I did not mention. This was a Two Star Amends which was to be the last amends when all the other amends were attempted. That Two Star Amends was made on October 3, 2010 and it was for Steve because I was told it was about time to forgive myself and move on.

Here I was already practicing all of The Twelve Steps. The first seven Steps were the beginning so I could proceed with the next two Steps to make the amends. Now I 'simply' needed to focus on all of The Twelve Steps with emphasize to always remember the last three Steps which were the maintenance steps. This would keep me where I was and has helped to keep me going forward without eventually forgetting, failing, and falling back into hell.

Two days after all of my Step Nine amends were completed it was Tuesday, October 5, 2010. I had to go back to the Gastroenterology medical group to take another test. This was just a test that meant drinking a special liquid and breathing into a special device. Then I would go back into the waiting room and come back into the lab room every 15 minutes to breath into the special device again. This was done for over two and a half hours to see how much Hydrogen was in my breath and in my system.

This was known as a Lactose Intolerant Test to see how my body absorbed Lactose. My body did not absorb Lactose and was causing the other types of 'tummy' pains that were sometimes very severe, inconvenient, and even debilitating. I was officially Lactose Intolerant and now had to be even more careful of what I ate or drank. No more regular pizza, cheese, ice cream, butter, or anything that had Lactose including foods or drinks that had any form of normal milk. If it was not Lactose Free and made with any milk products then these major 'tummy' problems and pains would and have occurred again.

The boot for the fracture on my left foot was soon not going to be necessary at all. It was about seven weeks later from the time I got the fracture until my 42nd birthday on Tuesday, November 16, 2010. The boot only had to be worn when I was out of the house and could be off for several hours at home and all night. That was good because the next day had something major happen that would have gotten my boot and foot very damp if I could not occasionally wear sneakers...or rain boots.

That next night was Wednesday, November 17, 2010. My typical Wednesday night meeting in Closter was one that I was beginning to chair and would remain the chairperson for the next few months. The honor and privilege to give back while proving (to me) that I could do good things was exciting. The meeting starts at 8 pm but I wanted to get there around 7:30 pm to get settled, see people when they arrived, and nervously arrange everything needed so I did not panic when it was actually time to begin.

My son was in his bedroom alone but playing his Xbox online with his school friends while talking to them on his headset. He needed a bath which was already filled and the water was turned off. Every few minutes my wife would yell from the kitchen (where she, my daughter, and I were) for him to get into the tub. He would always yell back "In a few minutes!" This ongoing 'conversation' had been lasting well over 30 minutes. All of us (except my son) had been in the kitchen the entire time which is on the other side of the house. Now it was just about time for me to leave to the meeting. That was when my son finally decided to take a break from Xbox to get into his bath. He was going to take his bath earlier but it was not hot enough for him then. That is why he had turned on the hot water and returned to his game...for half an hour while the water was running!

We were alerted that there was a lot of water pouring out of the tub (which had an overflow but was clogged). It was all over the bathroom floor, running out the door, and into the hallway. It only looked like a few gallons which was still quite a lot. Luckily, water did not reach either of our kids' bedrooms or even much past the hallway closet. In there was my wife's huge scrapbook carrying bag with all her supplies. It got a little wet but not majorly damaged. Other things in the closet were not too bad and all the water was eventually sucked up by a bunch of bath towels. It was a bad experience but got under control in 10 minutes or so.

I was now going to get to the meeting only 15 minutes before it started and ran downstairs to throw the wet towels into the washer before I left. The laundry door and room is on the immediate right side of the basement by the stairs. Straight ahead is my wife's desk for work (as the bookkeeper / office manager) with the accounting computer and important company files. Behind her desk were big folding doors that divided part of the basement where all my DJ equipment including speakers and numerous CDs were kept safe. Lastly, to the left side of the entire basement is a wall that was put up a few years ago with double doors.

Behind those doors was my personal 'lair' or 'fortress of solitude' for the many years when I 'required' privacy to do important things without my kids seeing or bugging me. This was smoking marijuana, drinking, watching TV, playing on the computer, and other things. My office and desk was also in there in case I 'had' to work or take phone calls that really was business related. In other words, this was where I had isolated, gotten worse with my addictions, and become more of a resentful, angry, nasty monster until January 31, 2008. Now this side of my basement (behind those doors) were really more about working for my business with two computers, copy machine, facsimile (fax), office supplies, and all the files cabinets. The couch, entertainment center with TV, VCR, Cable Box, Stereo, and other non-office things were still down there but actually used a lot less often than pre-recovery! It was still memories of what it once really was down there. This part of the basement was underneath the bathroom hallway.

When I first reached the bottom of the basement steps is when I heard a weird type of noise from my side of the basement. With the wet towels from upstairs in my hands I looked into the doorway. The upstairs hallway floor is wooden and not sealed 100%. The reason it did not look like a lot of water was in the hallway is because it was all dripping down between the cracks and pouring down into this place that had once been my trapped addiction hell. Now this more inviting, lovely place to do serious work was filled with many small waterfalls coming down from several spots in the ceiling past the tiles. Many of these ceiling tiles had already exploded from the weight of the water and many more were about ready to burst.

Now I was the one yelling upstairs in a major panic. My wife and the kids ran downstairs and it was a major shock to everyone for a minute. I was watching everything get washed in a way not intended. The panic that hit me for the first minute or two now stayed a little more with my wife who was like Oh my God, Oh my God, Oh my God. That was still my sentiments but I knew things needed to be done immediately. Quickly I moved fast and was rather collective (not calm but collective) as I ran in and out of the rooms to save what could be and in the right priority. I was the director telling my wife what to clean and move and where my kids to go and move to. They were hugging each other on the stairs like it was the end of the world. My daughter was probably hugging her brother as a way of saying goodbye to him. He was probably hugging her back thinking soon he would be dead. None of this was the case although reactions, moods, and the tension in the house were not light and fluffy right then!

Luckily I was able to call and reach my last sponsor (who also attended that meeting) to ask if he could fill in as chairperson that night with short notice. Each part of the basement that was then reviewed kept making things even worse. The back room behind my office is where the office supplies and files cabinets were getting wet. The main, middle part of the basement was not too bad because it was not directly under the bathroom hallway. My wife's desk with main office computer and important company files was not damaged or getting wet. There was dripping sounds on the other side of those big folding doors behind her desk. This was where all my DJ equipment was kept but no longer safe because the water had spread into that part of the ceiling and was damaging all those things.

The amount of destruction, loss, and hardship was crushing especially to me with my memories and equally being as particularly OCD as I was with my things. There was a lot of work, a lot of tears, and a lot of rebuilding required. We did get insurance money to reimburse things we needed to replace. There were a lot of things that could not be replaced. My long time entertainment center and many electronic items that I had even before my first marriage could not be saved. The wetness, odor, disruption, and everything to get past this 'tragedy' took a long time. We got new carpeting installed and both my wife and I repainted the basement.

In the past, I would have just let her do everything or be a wet rag and just pout, mope, and stay depressed. This was not the same as if it happed two years ago or even before then. Now there was a determination to move on and even get new ceiling tiles myself and install them...correctly! This seemed to be yet another test of my sobriety, program, and recovery. This flooded basement made it necessary to change everything and it majorly sucked until it was all done. Now it seems like it was worth all the trouble because it is now improved for a better, new life in the future...sort of like me.

Just as my fractured foot and flooded basement were almost as totally healed as they would get, it was now Xmas eve December 24, 2010. The family including my parents, the wife's parents, my sister, and several friends were all over the house. These were people I had difficulties with in the past and many that I made amends with. It felt good to have a lot of things settled even though I still had many moments (and still do) with loss of patience and mood. What did not feel good several times that day before guests arrived where my chest pains. This was something I kept having at various times in the last year which once included an Emergency Room visit to the local hospital. They ran many tests but saw nothing wrong with my heart and said it was probably stress or something else.

Now everyone was at our house for a happy, joyous holiday gathering and the pain was back again really, really bad! My wife saw the expression on my face as I quickly put down my buffet dinner plate and sat at the kitchen table. No one else saw this because they were in the living room and I was going to wait for it to pass again. There was no need to worry anyone else and damper the Christmas spirit. The pain got so much worse and eventually my family came into the kitchen. All of them saw me looking so bad that they were concerned including my poor kids. My face became very pale and I was fading in and out of consciousness almost totally passing out. Even though I was insistent this would pass everyone told my wife to call 911 which she did.
April 17

#109 (Day 109) Honest Open Willing 2012 Post
This got a 'rescue' from the 'female police lady' and also the 'new, young police officer' from my town that I had problems with in my past. They responded first to the 911 call and were there to help me! What a turn of events to have the same two police officers that I harmed the most (or was an asshole towards the most) respond first to the 911 call and were there to help me! It had now been almost three years since I behaved, gave the proper respect, or made a type of amends with them. The sense of relief, lack of tension, and proper appreciation to have these exact two town police officers in my house was the ironic humor in all of this to me and to my wife. The ambulance arrived in the front of my house as the EMT and police officers helped me to the stretcher slowly so the episodes of pain were not that bad.

Everyone felt it was my Gall Bladder that would probably need to be removed as these seemed to be all the symptoms. The main EMT thought it would be best to go directly to the hospital a few towns over. The one near me was only for emergencies and would transfer me to this other full time hospital anyway. My wife went with my father-in-law as he drove behind us to the hospital. After we were there for a short while it appeared all this was only due to a pulled chest muscle and not Gall Bladder like everyone was telling me. I was not as worried and had less fear because many things were good and I was with God on Xmas eve along with my wife and her dad. However, there was still a lot of wonder why I was experiencing severe muscle spasms and pain all over my body and sometimes my chest. That was sort of answered later on the next year to fill in (almost) all of the remaining blanks about my fatigue and other health problems.

Sharing at my usual Saturday morning meeting was the irony of my pre and post recovery. I briefly explained about the types of bad stuff that I did before recovery with the bad things and bad difficulties that I then experienced. Now I was practically doing no bad stuff in my current recovery but yet all these totally different types of bad things and bad difficulties were now being experienced. It all 'seemed' like a 'test' which somehow I was getting past without failing (but also not getting straight A's).

After that meeting someone said they related a lot to me and what I said. They asked if I could become their sponsor. This was both a surprise and shock to me that someone would want me as a sponsor. My reply was that I would be honored to be their temporary sponsor until they felt sure to have me as their permanent sponsor. The short, simply instructions that I gave him was to call me each day, do not drink or pick up any drugs, and go to meetings. That is what was told to me in the beginning when I first asked someone to be my sponsor. This was now my first time being asked and becoming what would be a permanent sponsor.

The year 2010 was finally over! It was a messed up year with medical procedures that provided non-positive diagnoses, a painful long lasting injury, a disastrous house flood, Christmas ambulance trip, and more (Oh my)! Things like this are not uncommon and even worse happen to a lot of people that I know. When 'stuff' happens to you then it could be a broken shoelace that ruins your day because everyone reacts to everything differently. I was not used to reacting to anything so it was a lot more than a broken shoelace at least to me.

My positive outlook in 2011 was that the past was behind me and the present was determined to be rather blessed for a brighter future. This was due to a lot of special people who were active in my life again especially my family. Hundreds of previous friends and people from my past were back who I now considered all to be my friends. Many people in the fellowship had been with me since the start and were all my friends to help and support each other. Several were really close friends that cared, comforted, and joked with me which gave a great sense of belonging to my life. This third sponsor that had me as a sponsee since last summer was working out well with little complaints from either one of us. This first sponsee that had me as a sponsor since the end of last year was also working out well with little complaints from either one of us.

January 31, 2011 was my actual three year anniversary. The Saturday morning meeting announces the celebrants of the entire month on the last Saturday of the month. Saturday, January 29, 2011 is when I received my Alcoholics Anonymous coin with the Roman numeral III. As I have said many times, this is more than just about not having any liquor for three years. It was about total abstinence from alcohol, marijuana, drugs, and anything else that was addictive while also working a program at a better life. The Alcoholics Anonymous coin that I am given in front of everyone each year is special because of all of these things. The brief presentation and brief speech show everyone that the program and recovery do work.

This year was extra special because not only was my first sponsee there to share in this occasion but so were my wife and son. I never insisted that they come to the meeting that day. They both wanted to be there for me and that made me very happy and proud. When it was my time to receive my coin I thanked my wife and said that my son was one of the main reasons that I wanted to become changed. Most of my negative ways were behind me and these recent bad things from last year were over. Considering this and considering my friends all around to help and be in my life then what else could possibly go wrong......

Monday, March 7, 2011 was my typical Monday night Big Book meeting in Closter. One of my closest friends was there as almost every Monday night. When I first started to attend more and more nighttime meetings is when I got to know and be around him more and more. From the beginning he was always there outside the meetings before the starting times to say hello and wanting to know how I was sincerely doing. The more he wanted and got to know me, the more I wanted and got to know him. We were very similar people that both had troubles in our lives, always seemed to be aware of everything in our surroundings, and loved to crack jokes trying to make others a little less stressed or depressed. He had a few years more time in the program than me and was only a few years older. It was not long before we were major supporters of each other and great friends.

Another thing we both had in common was a great love for Facebook. Each of us would always post things many, many, many times a day. It seemed like we had no life outside of this but we did. This was part of our lives as it brought us both closer together and closer to all our friends. We had many mutual friends and over the months and years those mutual friends increased. He and I would also comment on (or at least 'Like') each other's posts back and forth. We also liked to 'Poke' mutual friends, our other friends, and sometimes each other. This may sound a bit 'odd' but it is a funny Facebook thingy that lets you know the other one is there to kind of say "What's Up?" and now "Tag you are it!"

The only real time that I started to get upset with him is when it 'seemed' he was getting too personal with people in my life that he did not know such as my sister and my first wife. It was soon that I apologized to him about how I was feeling and knew it was not anything he did with ill intent. Whenever he commented on something that was too personal is when he would quickly remove that comment from my post or my wall. This was the same with me and there were a few times where I had (and still do) the disease of non-repent-of-tongue-and-pen-and-typing or foot-in-mouth. We always made up and I thought he would always be there for me as I would be there for him in our recovery, lives together, and Facebook. He was there that Monday night in Closter for the Big Book meeting and I got to meet another woman that same night that was friends with him on Facebook. That night she friended me and I think my friend and I both gave her a 'Poke' shortly afterward.

Tuesday, March 8, 2011 there was a very funny post that he put up that morning saying "NO. You can't be Charlie Sheen for Halloween Son." We had a few comments back on forth on that post and one or two others. Then it must have been the first, very rare occasion that I was not on my PC or Smart Phone checking Facebook until later that evening. When I did check my phone to see what was up in the Cyber world there was two things. The first was a personal message from this woman I met the night before saying how sorry she was because she knew he and I were best friends and that it must be devastating. I was baffled and had no idea what she meant? Then I replied back something like "What do you mean?" or "Huh?" but it was more like e-mail and not real time chatting or texting.

Then I checked the News Feed where he and I had about 80 mutual friends. Almost every one of these friends had posted things just as bizarre as that personal message but on this News Feed for the last several hours. He was found at work later that day dead from a heart attack. Apparently, heart disease ran in his family as it took the life of his dad also at an early age. Wednesday, March 9, 2011 was my typical Wednesday night Discussion meeting in Closter. One of my closest friends was usually there as almost every Wednesday night. That night he wasn't......

It was beyond sad and it was beyond real. The mourning, emptiness, and emotional damage lasted longer than a year and will never totally end. These are things that I know he would NOT want from his family and friends which got me past the devastation period. He made a huge impact on me, my life, and the lives of many people in the fellowship and just as many people outside the fellowship. We did all find each other becoming part of a memorial group on Facebook to remember and honor him for a long time. Through this I did get to meet and become close with much of his other family and friends. An extended way to keep his memory ongoing is by trying to be the type of person and friend that at least he was especially to me......caring, humble, sensitive, and to make me smile whenever possible. Life had to go on for the world, for his family, for his friends, for me, and for him. This is something that I know he WOULD want!

Then I had another sleep study on Easter eve and should have known better than to have another hospital holiday 'vacation' adventure after my Christmas Eve Emergency Room adventure. However, that was not intentional while this visit on Saturday, April 23, 2011 was planned overnight from 9:30 pm Easter Eve until 6:00 am Easter Day. The doctor wanted me to get an updated sleep study test with a different CPAP nasal mask now that it was about two years after the first one. This hospital annex was not too bad and was even more like a hotel room than the previous one.

Before the results were even back to my doctor it was necessary for me to get back to my doctor again. Apparently the combination of the bed, pillow, wires, tubes, and other medical stuff around me that night gave me (and of course would only happen to me) a pinched nerve that was unbelievable painful. Starting Tuesday, April 26, 2011 you had me now in a neck brace for several weeks. During that time my neck had to remain stationary with as little movement as possible. That way it could heal enough for my doctor to crack it better into place which also hurt each time too. How funny was all this getting? Well it was not really funny but finding at least a little bit of humor in this and other things helped the pain be...less serious.
April 18

#110 (Day 110) Honest Open Willing 2012 Post
Eventually, I stopped seeing the same psychiatrist that started with me when first kicked out of my Outpatient Rehab center in February 2008. There was another psychiatrist who worked in the same office as my neurologist and primary medical doctor. It was better to have all three doctors and all of my medications being prescribed and supervised under one roof. There had been yet another doctor that I had seen who started me back with taking Ambien before bedtime.

The Nuvigil was helping me stay awake and be alert during the day for my Sleep Apnea but it was thought to keep me from falling asleep and resting enough at night. One pill to make you sleep and one pill to wake you up just don't make sense? This new psychiatrist who first started to see me on April 27, 2011 was very good. She noticed I seemed a little hyper and diagnosed that I was ADHD like when I was a young kid. Medicine to treat the ADHD was now prescribed and both the Nuvigil and Ambien were stopped by June 2011.

Sunday, June 5, 2011 was a father / daughter Girl Scout bowling event. This would have been overwhelming and bothersome to attend in the past. Instead it was actually very sweet, fun, and special to go with my precious daughter that day. Little things like that were slowing changing. Life was beginning to commence and become much more rewarding. It was not a bowl of cherries but I was growing and things from that point on kept getting better and better!

That summer of 2011 began my quest to seek out and find family from my dad's side. There was a name change at one point and maybe a grudge or resentment at another point over one or two generations ago. This tension and awkwardness was something I really wanted to end. Now I knew a lot more about my grandfather's side of the family besides one of his sisters who had no children. My great grandparents not only had him and this one sister but seven other children. These children had children who had children and now I had a few dozen cousins.

Most of my 'newly found' cousins are like me in many ways (and I am like them in many ways) and live all over the USA plus countries like Israel and England. Two different family tree group sites were started so I can get everyone to know each other and put the pieces of this puzzle together. Now there is a group on a heritage, ancestral type website and a group on Facebook. We are all learning about each other and I love the fact that I am now friends with many new relatives!

Thursday, November 3, 2011 continued my other quest to find out why I was always so fricking tired and in pain. My Rheumatologist told me why. I had *Chronic Fatigue Syndrome (CFS)* which is a debilitating condition that involves ongoing fatigue and tiredness. In CFS, fatigue symptoms may not improve with bed rest, and may worsen with physical or mental activity. There is no cure for CFS. There are no medications developed specifically for the condition. Fortunately, there is treatment for the symptoms that come with CFS. Symptoms affect several body systems and may include weakness, muscle pain, impaired memory and/or mental concentration, and insomnia, which can result in reduced participation in daily activities. In other words, this was another 'illness' that could not be cured but could be learned to live with better when understood (and found to be......funny).

Because I was not crazy (or at least not as crazy) and the tiredness, pain, and health issues were not in my head (well some of them were but they were not imaginary) is why I pushed myself to do a little more in life but at a gentler pace. Besides chairing Alcoholic Anonymous meetings like one on Thursday afternoons (since that same Thursday, November 3, 2011 day) I figured there must be more that I could do.

There needed to be several other things for me both in and out of the fellowship with equal importance.

Sunday, November 6, 2011 was my decision to wake up and do something I never would normally do all at once. After showering, shaving, and putting on nice clothes is when I got in my car and drove into New York City and over to Brooklyn for a newly found family member's Engagement party. My invitation was there but there was a lot of anxiety even though I really wanted to attend. I used to go into New York City quite often but this was the first time in over 10 years ever since 9/11. It also took more than twice as long since the New York City Marathon was going on and the directions I figured out took me directly into and not up and around the route. But still I eventually got there even though I kept getting lost, kept going around in circles, and kept getting frustrated. Never did I get insanely angry or even cry with deep despair which I cannot say would have been the same over 5 years ago.

There were a few real live people that I met for the very first time who were family. This was so worth overcoming the obstacles both real and imaginary. Coming home was another adventure in a good, cool way. I got lost again and ended up taking the wrong highway and wrong route which brought me through the Brooklyn-Battery Tunnel directly into (instead of up and around) lower Manhattan. Straight ahead of me soaring into the air was the newly built Freedom Tower. Somehow there was a calm peace looking up to where the World Trade Center once stood. Then I got onto the West Side Highway up past many old familiar sights and over the George Washington Bridge back home. To not being in NYC since before 9/11, and regretfully not going into NYC the ten years in between, this huge accidental 'push' to where I needed to be that day (in many ways) was appreciated from some unseen force!

The forward ongoing movement continued on Tuesday, November 22, 2011 to finally have my teeth taken care. They were grinded down to less than half their original size and were super sensitive. Getting there when I did was good timing because it was just in time to prevent a lot of major damage and root canal. Had five later visits within two weeks to get all of the bad drilled out and patched up plus two teeth were re-crowned. Then there was a few dozens more visits before I received temporary full teeth and being fitted for the permanent ones. As of April 18, 2012 the completed date for everything to be done is probably still several months away but it is already worth it to have full teeth that look good, feel good, help restore jaw structure, and do not hurt from years of abuse and damage.

December 14, 2011 is when I finally got around to getting a new car for the first time in 11 years. This was also something that I did myself for the first time in my life. The whole thing took six hours at the car dealership which to me was a long ordeal considering the salesman said this would only take two hours at the most. Work was waiting for me back at my office but I was able to go home the same day with a very nice, affordable, leased car. This was a new clean car that never was smoked cigarettes, marijuana, or had anything immoral done now with me in a new clean life.

The next year was 2012. I thought a new year after all of these new things deserved something new with more growth. Sunday, January 1, 2012 began the year on day 1 and it was decided to go through my life like a huge Step Four and Step Five the way my second sponsor took me. The "HOW Posts Group" was started on Facebook to go on a chronological, brutally honest, thorough, account of the good, the bad, and the entirely real things that happened in my life.

Coincidentally, that same Sunday and the next four Sundays in January was the start of my speaker / chairman commitment at a beginner's meeting to share my experience, strength, and hope. Over five weeks my life was divided up and told with little held back although some things were scary to admit. Each week there was a lot of people who said they related and went through very similar things. That made them feel good, and it made me feel good, not to be alone or feel different. On Saturday, January 28, 2012 is when I got my four year Alcoholics Anonymous coin with the Roman numeral IV for 4 years of recovery.

Another fear and advancement was going out into the scary world on a Saturday, March 3, 2012 night to a Comedy Club over 30 minutes away to see a friend. This was not in a bad area and not several hours away in the middle of the night but was more than I typically would ever do in many years unless there was something more than a funny time involved. There was some weirdness with a memorable adventure of a table of drunk, wild, weird people including one smashed, neck licking woman. That is another innocent but messed up strange story that would not have been so funny if it was not witnessed by several people that became my friend or better friend that same night. Again, it was worth the 'Steve effort' for the outcome to be part of my new life.

My feelings of regret for not seeming part of my high school class in the past (like it was now in the present) made me want to add something to now be shared with everyone. Pictures were put up on Facebook and everyone was tagged and got together which also included me. This was not an ego or pride thing. This was something I wanted to be a part of for over 25 years. In fact, the reaction of everyone getting together with posts and comments threads got people interested in having a 25 year class reunion.

On Wednesday, March 14, 2012 it was suggested, arranged, and agreed for me to be the chairperson for this reunion! Arrange a reunion of my classmates...the classmates that did not seem to be classmates to my reality back then? Yes, it was cool and an honor by starting yet another group on Facebook for this reunion in September 2012. Doing something for friends because you want to be there and they actually want you to be there is the best feeling of belonging that I never had in the past.

I was in several different fellowships since January 2008 and have stuck with Alcoholics Anonymous exclusively since about August 2008. Knowing that I had a lot of different problems, I felt that AA has and can eventually help them all. There was never any reason (in my mind) to ever return to any of the other fellowships. However, I did come back to a Narcotics Anonymous morning meeting at 10 am on Sunday, April 1, 2012.

The reason for this return was for a sponsee of mine in Alcoholics Anonymous. He is also cross addicted (just like me) but does prefer to attend that one particular NA meeting each week. His two year anniversary of being clean and sober was that exact date and he was going to be celebrating. He made me proud and the feelings were special and rewarding that I wanted to be there for him (and for me). The unexpected, funny thing was that I still related to all these people too. We are Anonymous people in the fellowship we need but are all together!

Scary is trying new things. Trying new things does mean change. Change means to grow and to grow with the world as part of your life means you

live and help as part of the world! The past is history, the present is a gift, and the future is a mystery with one exception......tomorrow will conclude my Honest Open Willing 2012 Posts.
April 19

#111 (Day 111) Honest Open Willing 2012 Post

The date of this post used to be a yearly 'Holiday' to me. It is April 20 which is 4/20. The term '420' has many meanings and myths in relation to marijuana. The last few '420 Holidays' were so much better without using it as an excuse to get stoned, isolate, and basically say screw you to life like every single day. The '420' of 2012 is extra special because my H.O.W. Posts started at #1 on January 1 and (due to a leap year) got to #111 on April 20. This is the last H.O.W. Post since it is today and I am caught up.

Where am I right now in my life? I think that I am right where I am supposed to be. Do I have a better, brighter outlook for my future? Yes, much more than I ever thought there could possibly be. What do I do each day to maintain my specific program and be prepared for life? There are a few simple things besides attending meetings regularly and keeping in touch with many different positive people.

First I get out of bed in the morning which is usually never easy with Sleep Apnea affecting my...sleep and Chronic Fatigue Syndrome making me...fatigued. If I do not make the bed before almost anything else then my concentration is only on making the bed. That obsession is due to my OCD which also takes making the bed now only 3 to 4 minutes to make perfect (it used to take longer and get me much more frustrated). Then I do something that at first seemed 'un-Jewish' and not something I ever thought I would do.

On my side of that bed I go down on my knees for about 5 minutes to pray and meditate. It makes me feel good to acknowledge my Higher Power, God. Knowing He is there and I am not alone is a great feeling. My thoughts, image, or religious aspects regarding Him is not something I need to push, persuade, and preach to anyone about. This daily commune allows me to know something else that was always my problem. That He is in charge, and NOT I, which takes a burden off of me.

There is a little black book called 'Twenty-Four Hours a Day'. Each day of the year has a one page thought, meditation and prayer just for that day. Many people find it a simple, yet effective way to help relate the Twelve Steps to everyday life. It helps many to find the power not to take that first drink or do that first anything that presents a problem in our specific recovery. For me this also includes taking that first smoke of marijuana (or cigarettes) or doing that first other drug of any type. It also gives me strength to protect against other things that may want to take place of these specific problems now that I may feel a little empty inside. My life has had issues also with gambling, shopping, eating, lusting, and other addictions that will affect my body, mind, emotions, spirit, and life as it is now if my guard is down.

After my daily reading in the Twenty-Four Hours a Day book is when I do all those other prayers which slowly accumulated throughout my recovery. It started with The Serenity Prayer and later had The Third Step Prayer, The Seventh Step Prayer, The Eleventh Step Prayer, and then even the Lord's Prayer added. When I recite the Lord's Prayer there is nothing religious in it that I hear which would go against even my most religious Jewish family members. The words have a very broad, deep, Spiritual meaning to me.

Once I am done with these prayers at my bed side then I stay right there a little longer. The Twelve Steps do not need to be memorized but I have read, studied, and done them so many times that I do know and feel them by heart. The Steps are said in order one by one and I make sure to acknowledge them plus know where I was before and after each. Then I agree to try my best to continue working and living them in my life even just for those 24 hours. Even though I may veer off that path for part of the day (or the entire day) the next day will be a brand new one.

The future needs to be anticipated and not feared. Even if things are planned they should not be dreaded or projected. If it sucks, then it sucks. If I plan it to suck, then it will suck at least from now till then. If it does not suck when it eventually happens then I worried about it sucking all that time for no reason...which would have sucked. What is planned in the future without negative projecting? Well there a few things......scheduled.

Thursday, May 10, 2012 is the wedding for that relative who I visited in Brooklyn for her engagement party. My wife, me, and our kids (but no dogs) are driving together in the car for five hours each way to the D.C. area from that Wednesday before until that Sunday afterward. I look forward to seeing my family members for the first or second time in my life. This should be a fun adventure no matter what happens.

Saturday, September 29, 2012 is the 25th Year Senior Class of 1987 High School Reunion. Right now I am technically honored to be the main chairperson working with six of my other classmates. Hopefully all works out smoothly and everyone will have as great of a time as they possibly can. If one person does not, and it is me, then it is meant to be. Either way I know that I will have a rewarding, friendly time with my own personal closure that I am part of my class. This is after feeling for well over 25 years that I was part of nothing but myself.

Saturday, January 26, 2013 is when I hope to get my five year Alcoholics Anonymous coin with the Roman numeral V for 5 years of recovery. God willing may I reach that date and get to many more anniversaries while helping others grow and be happy which doing so helps me to grow and be happy with them.

Chapter Five of the Big Book of Alcoholics Anonymous is called HOW IT WORKS. The first paragraph is often read at meetings right before the Twelve Steps. This paragraph had always fascinated me in the beginning. Eventually, I understood what it meant more and more. Now it means a lot to me because in many ways I can strongly relate. This is the first paragraph of Chapter Five.

"RARELY HAVE we seen a person fail who has thoroughly followed our path. Those who do not recover are people who cannot or will not completely give themselves to this simple program, usually men and women who are constitutionally incapable of being honest with themselves. There are such unfortunates. They are not at fault; they seem to have been born that way. They are naturally incapable of grasping and developing a manner of living which demands rigorous honesty. Their chances are less than average. There are those, too, who suffer from grave emotional and mental disorders, but many of them do recover if they have the capacity to be honest." Rigorous honesty is the greatest place to start and has helped millions of hopeless people over the years...even me.

Recovery, Fellowship, Program, and the Twelve Steps are different for everyone and there is no exact right way for each person. Everything that I was taught and the way I followed and continue to work my program was right for me. Some people have asked very curiously what I did to get from where I was to where I am now. Today I would simply show them these posts and explain that 'One Day at a Time'...this was H.O.W.
April 20

Epilogue

April 21 Honest Open Willing 2012 Post
Did H.O.W. What NOW?
April 21

April 22 Honest Open Willing 2012 Post
'Did H.O.W. What NOW?' was the question asked yesterday on Saturday, April 21, 2012. The answer today (Sunday, April 22, 2012) came to me after person to person as well as chatting and messaging with several people from this group.

Several people in my fellowship say that they are grateful to be a recovering alcoholic. Others have said that they are lucky to be an alcoholic to have the program of Alcoholics Anonymous and the Twelve Steps. Yet others have said that there are people outside the rooms who could benefit from a program like this and the Twelve Steps. As I have repeatedly said, I am in AA but is much, much more an alcoholic. There are many different fellowships for someone like me with an addictive nature or personality that presents one or more problems like marijuana (especially to me) or any type of drug, gambling, eating, cigarettes, seeking love, sex, and more.

There are many different fellowships besides AA. Almost every single one of them is the same type program and steps. I just use AA as my basis because it helps with every single one of my problems. It helps manage my OCD, Bipolar, and ADHD as well as life itself with economical, family, work, health, death, and every other powerless thing. Honestly admitting you can't do it alone, Openly believing others can help, and Willingly making a decision to permanently accept others to help change things in your life to help without taking back your personal will can make a 12 Step program benefit you.

No one has to identify themselves as anything to use this program for themselves to deal with just about any problem, show compassion for any or all loved ones within a fellowship, and especially to understand and be vigilant watching signs, traits, and things with loved ones before they get bad. In other words, the stuff I went through, learned, and now finished sharing can benefit others which is my way of spreading the message to alcoholics, other people with problems similar to alcoholics, and to practice these principles in ALL my affairs. Several people with many years of recovery, great sobriety, and numerous sponsees have given me 100% blessing to continue doing all of this if the people in my life and stories continue to remain anonymous.

Therefore, I continue here each day. However, input of any type is needed and appreciated. You can help me, I can help you, and we all can help each other. Please let me know HOW it can work for you!
April 22

DO I POSSIBLY HAVE A PROBLEM?

All twelve of these below questions were answered 'Yes' by myself when they were directed in regard to marijuana. This is where I first learned that 'I' had a big problem which was not harmless...'to me!'

Just now, I changed these to be more general that I would still have answered 'Yes' to many in regards to several other things in my life years ago. If you think there may be a problem with anything in your life then you may want to answer these same questions that I did. Just insert the word and correct verb usage.

1. Has _____ stopped being fun?

2. Do you ever _____ alone?

3. Is it hard for you to imagine a life without _____?

4. Do you find that your friends are determined by your levels of _____?

5. Do you _____ to avoid dealing with your problems?

6. Do you _____ to cope with your feelings?

7. Does your _____ let you live in a privately defined world?

8. Have you ever failed to keep promises you made about cutting down or controlling your _____?

9. Has your _____ caused problems with memory, concentration, or motivation?

10. When _____ is not available, do you feel anxious or worried?

11. Do you plan your life around your _____?

12. Have friends or relatives ever complained that your _____ is damaging your relationship with them?

Count the number of times you answered 'YES':

1 to 3 --- You may begin to develop a problem.

4 to 7 --- You may already have a growing problem.

8 to 11 -- You almost definitely have a problem that will get worse.

All 12 --- Stop thinking and do something now because that was me!

However, only you can say or decide if you have any problem with some sort of addiction or dependency. People told me that I did. People may have told you that you did. If you (and only you) admit this about yourself then you are already facing the right direction. Many people then feel totally powerless and realize there is nothing they can do to manage these types of problems alone. This is exactly how I felt.

Our specific problem or problems, what we are powerless over (alcohol or anything else), and who we carry this message to (alcoholics or anyone else) is not as important as doing it together for the same purpose. Here are the steps we took, which are suggested as a program of recovery:

THE TWELVE STEPS OF ALCOHOLICS ANONYMOUS

1. We admitted we were powerless over alcohol - that our lives had become unmanageable.

2. Came to believe that a Power greater than ourselves could restore us to sanity.

3. Made a decision to turn our will and our lives over to the care of God *as we understood Him.*

4. Made a searching and fearless moral inventory of ourselves.

5. Admitted to God, to ourselves, and to another human being the exact nature of our wrongs.

6. Were entirely ready to have God remove all these defects of character.

7. Humbly asked Him to remove our shortcomings.

8. Made a list of all persons we had harmed, and became willing to make amends to them all.

9. Made direct amends to such people wherever possible, except when to do so would injure them or others.

10. Continued to take personal inventory and when we were wrong promptly admitted it.

11. Sought through prayer and meditation to improve our conscious contact with God as we understood Him, praying only for knowledge of His will for us and the power to carry that out.

12. Having had a spiritual awakening as the result of these steps, we tried to carry this message to alcoholics, and to practice these principles in all our affairs.

Made in United States
Orlando, FL
18 October 2022

23571416R00124